MW00653489

JUST PLAIN DOROTHY

The Life of Dorothy Hunt Finley
Cowgirl, Teacher, Tycoon
Philanthropist

Dorothy H. Finley

with

Allen R. Kates, MFAW
Author of *CopShock*

HOLBROOK
Street Press

Published by
Holbrook Street Press, Tucson, Arizona USA
(520) 616-7643 (888) 436-1402 www.writingpublishing.com

Printing History
First printing: October, 2009
Printed in the United States of America

Copyright © 2009 by Dorothy H. Finley

Publisher's Note
This book is sold with the understanding that the publisher and author are not engaged in rendering psychological, financial, legal, or other professional services.

All Rights Reserved
No part of this book may be reproduced, stored or transmitted in any form or by any means, without written permission from the publisher, except for brief quotations for review purposes.

Cover design and photo insert by *1106 Design* www.1106Design.com
Color cover photograph by Ray Manley, 1990

Writing and editing by Allen R. Kates, MFAW
www.writingpublishing.com

Publisher's Cataloguing-In-Publication

Finley, Dorothy H. (Dorothy Hunt)
Just plain Dorothy : the life of Dorothy Hunt Finley : cowgirl, teacher, tycoon, philanthropist /Dorothy H. Finley ; with Allen R. Kates.
p. cm. Includes bibliographical references, notes, and index.
LCCN: 2009932244
ISBN-13: 978-0-9668501-3-0 ISBN-10: 0-9668501-3-0

1. Finley, Dorothy H. (Dorothy Hunt). 2. Philanthropists—Arizona—Biography. 3. School principals—Arizona—Tucson—Biography. 4. Businesswomen—Arizona—Biography. 5. Finley, Dorothy H. (Dorothy Hunt)—Family. 6. Arizona—History, Local.
I. Kates, Allen R. II. Title.

HV28.F48A3 2009 361.92 QBI09-600114

"The life of the individual has meaning only insofar as it aids in making the life of every living thing nobler and more beautiful."

—Albert Einstein

Contents

Foreword

Dorothy makes you feel like you have known her all your life. The first time I met her, I was President and CEO of the Tucson Urban League and she was on the Board of Directors. She listened to everyone, analyzed the situation, and then spoke her mind. And she was never wrong.

I liked her from the start. You can count on her for her honesty, for keeping things focused where they need to be. She is the kind of person that when she believes in you, she makes you feel even better about what you are doing, even though your job may be tremendously challenging.

Dorothy is also without prejudice. She doesn't care if you are white, black, brown, Hispanic, Native American, Asian, Republican or Democrat. She only wants to know what you will do for Tucson, the state of Arizona, the country and, most emphatically, for children.

What I admire most about Dorothy is her courage. As a child, she grew up in hard times on a ranch in the wilderness without electricity, water and the usual comforts we take for granted like indoor plumbing, heat in the winter and air conditioning in the scorching desert summer. She lived through *the troubles*, a time when her father and uncles were indicted for killing a man during a range war shootout.

She endured severe droughts, treacherous terrain, and severe monsoon storms. From the age of four, she was on horseback herding cattle. At ten, she learned to drive a ranch truck, loaded 100-pound bales of hay in the back, and fed the cows. She attended a one-room schoolhouse in the middle of a cow pasture with Yaqui Indians and was taught by some of the finest teachers. Through it all, she persevered, persisted and thrived.

She read everything she could get her hands on, books, magazines, newspapers, and discussed the issues of the day with her family. She dreamed big dreams of visiting far off lands and making a place for herself in the world. And she did it all, traveling to countries around the globe and becoming one of the most important people in the state of Arizona.

I loved reading this book and I think you will, too. It takes the reader on a voyage through the Old West with gunfights and western justice; through the terrible times of the Great Depression; it takes you to cattle roundups where cows are branded, dehorned and doctored; it shows folk medicine at its best and at its worst, using turpentine on wounds and odd concoctions that often worked; it exposes Dorothy's terror when she nearly dies from a scorpion sting. The reader will sympathize with Dorothy's fear that she is an uneducated hayseed when she leaves the ranch as a teenager and goes to a California high school. What's most impressive is that she becomes sophisticated, yet never loses her common touch. She always knows who she is and why.

The book leads the reader through the first and second World Wars, shows us Dorothy's years at the

University of Arizona and reveals her loves and disappointments, her struggles and successes. We see Dorothy as a school teacher and as a principal. We follow her when she meets and marries her husband Harold, and we see the tough times they share starting their beer distribution business. We see what makes her laugh and cry, and pick herself up again.

What's really great about this book is that Dorothy doesn't hesitate to give the reader a good laugh, sometimes at her own expense. And in the book, we see through her eyes what it was like to operate on the boards of more than fifty nonprofit organizations, helping them raise funds and succeed; and we see her love for our military and their families, and how she helped save Davis-Monthan Air Force Base.

This book will inspire and encourage everyone: teachers, principals and school administrators; community organizers; parents and their children; military personnel; ranchers; nonprofit organizations; and it will satisfy anybody who wants a real good read. And at the end of the book, Dorothy's *60 Rules for Success* will motivate you to reach beyond what you think you are capable of. I predict that this list will be pinned to bulletin boards across the country.

Dorothy is a treasure, a model of true community caring. She is a rare individual, someone who belongs to all of us. When you look at great leaders in terms of what they have achieved, they have a certain quality, her quality. Call it insight, elegance or grace, but whatever it is, she instinctively knows how to help in the moment, to make sense out of chaos, to put you on the right track.

Dorothy is a teacher in every sense of the word, but is not limited to the traditional classroom. She uses her ability to communicate on a grand scale. And when we sit back and read her words, we are in awe. She is the queen on horseback, the mother of all children, the purveyor of good common sense.

She is on the "A List" of movers and shakers. I have had the privilege of knowing many influential individuals who helped me raise millions of dollars on an annual basis for the less fortunate. The best of those individuals not only contributed money, but they also gave their precious time. Few individuals have given more of themselves than Dorothy.

I never dreamed that as a former inner-city kid from the industrialized city of Cincinnati, Ohio, that one day I would discover I have so much in common with a former rural kid from the Grand Canyon State of Arizona. That little girl who grew up on remote southern ranches became a powerful agent for change in our community.

We are fortunate that instead of the national stage, she focused on her own local community, the organizations, nonprofits, businesses and people. She makes you feel that, *Yes*, all things are possible.

To all of the readers, enjoy the book. It is a wonderful American story about overcoming adversity, building bridges to people, with the passion and perseverance of a unique lady and proud grandmother by the name of Dorothy H. Finley. Like a bright shining star in the beautiful Sonoran desert night, she is a beacon for everyone seeking excellence, truth and darn good fun.

—Ray Clarke, former President and CEO
Tucson Urban League, Inc.

1. Good Times, Hard Times

I was brought up in tough times in tough places, and I learned survival. From the age of four, I was on the back of a horse herding cattle. I grew up a cowgirl, fence rider, ranch hand and snake shooter.

I drove a truck when I was ten, learned to shoot straight and talk even straighter. My father and uncles were arrested for killing a man. By all accounts, he had it coming, but the law charged them with first-degree murder. And the first years of my life were unsettled, with fears of fleeing the country and losing everything.

I learned to persevere, muddle through and never stop. Winters were cold, summers were scorching. We didn't have electricity, water, air conditioning, refrigeration or indoor plumbing. My schoolhouse was one room in a cow pasture. My friends were Yaqui Indians and a few ranch kids. After I got married, I taught school in the worst neighborhoods. We started a beer distribution company, and when my husband got injured, I drove our truck, lifted 50-pound cases of beer into the back, drove around the county, fixed my own flats, visited bars, and didn't come home until all the beer was sold or drunk.

After a few years of teaching, I became a principal and, in time, the CEO of our beer company. I've been on the boards of more than fifty nonprofit organizations and have no plans for sitting home.

I've learned something from every stage of my life, but the biggest lesson was to tough it out, don't whine, and reach for the stars. I did things my way and earned both friends and foes. People have called me a lot of names, both good and bad, but, even though I descend from royalty, I prefer to be known as just plain ol' Dorothy.

2. Roots and Cowboy Boots

My strong-minded spirit was formed way before I was born and handed down through generations. Why I am the person I've become was forged in my family's history of ups and downs, good times and hard times, failure and success. We were rich and we were poor, we fought and died for what we believed in, and, for the most part, prospered.

I'm related to Mary Boleyn, mistress to King Henry VIII, who soon turned his attentions on her sister Ann and made her Queen of England. Ann was a bit too outspoken for the time and received the ultimate punishment from the axe man. I wouldn't call this the good part of the family.

Mary had five children and I am descended from countless generations of the Boleyn, Carey, Knollys, West, Dandridge, and Ruffin families.[1]

Many of my ancestors left Ireland, Scotland and England on leaky wooden ships for the Americas. They lived in Virginia (mostly), North Carolina, Tennessee, Georgia, Mississippi and Texas. Apart from their ties to royalty, they were primarily farmers, yet highly educated attorneys, doctors, engineers and other professional people. They were rich when they arrived and their plantations in the south made them richer. They grew cotton, raised cattle, and owned slaves.

To round out my surprising family connections, I am related to William Candler, an Englishman who fought with Cromwell's Army in 1650. His great grandson, also named William, born in 1736 Ireland, landed in Virginia, met and fell in love with Elizabeth Anthony and married her in 1760. In 1776 as a Colonel in either the militia or in the Continental Army, he fought in the Revolutionary War, survived, and died nine years later.[2]

His son Daniel married Sarah Slaughter, and they gave birth to William Love Candler, who married Martha Moore, and they gave birth to Caroline Candler, who married Captain Sampson Leroy Harris.[3]

Captain Harris and Caroline begot Susan Mary Harris. And the point to all this begetting will become apparent. Susan Mary Harris was soon to join the Hunt family.

Here's a quick sketch of the *Huntts*—

Born in 1623, Englishman William Huntt (the original spelling) married a Virginian. Six generations later, in 1806, my great grandfather, Charles Wilkins Hunt (CW) was born while Thomas Jefferson was president of the United States.[5]

Twenty-eight years later, CW married Lucy Ruffin, daughter of James Ruffin and Agnes Dandridge, sister of Martha Dandridge. Martha Dandridge is better known to us all as Martha Washington, wife of George Washington.[6]

That makes Martha and George Washington distant relatives. I'm still waiting for an invitation to spend the summer at the White House.

The Hunts were wealthy. CW owned a large Mississippi plantation and seventy slaves.[7] The real estate was valued at $20,000 and his personal estate at $100,000. Today that amount would be valued at nearly $3 million dollars,[8] and we would consider him a multi-millionaire.

After the Civil War erupted in 1861, everything changed, and he learned that a good lineage did not mean much anymore.

Three of his sons went off to war, he lost his slaves and the plantation deteriorated. He suffered his greatest loss in 1864. The war still raging, Lucy died of consumption, and was buried on the plantation.

> "The Mississippi River was at flood state and she couldn't be buried in the family cemetery. Her grave was dug up by Union soldiers looking for hidden silver and other family items of value. The family was able to reinterred (sic) her before the wild hogs found her remains."[9]

By war's end in 1865, CW's plantation lay in ruins, and for the next five years his fortunes continued to worsen. The 1870 Census states that CW's real estate was valued at $3,000, his personal estate at $500. In just a few years, his net worth dropped from $120,000 to $3,500, or from about $3 million to about $47,000 in today's money. As a further insult, his occupation was listed as "farm laborer," not even a farmer, as before.[10]

Miraculously, CW's sons returned from the war uninjured. One of those sons was Charles Phillip Hunt, also called CP (we were fond of acronyms).

And on April 14, 1870, in Como, Mississippi, despite their poverty, CP married Susan Mary Harris, and the joining of the Candler-Harris-Hunt clans was accomplished.[4]

If CP had been killed in the war, my father would not have been born, I would not be writing this book and my son and grandchildren would not exist today. How we owe our lives to arbitrary turns of fate.

The war took my family's wealth, their status, and they were living almost hand-to-mouth. Disheartened, CP decided that the family should move to Texas and they settled down in Kendall County to farm and run some small businesses.

For CP and my grandmother, one of those businesses seemed to be having lots of children. They had ten: five girls (Lucy, Caroline, Valerie Dorothy, Bessie Mary and Nellie Sue), and five boys (Jim, Joe, Sam, Charles, and my dad, Jack). However, I focus only on the Hunt boys—because of their influence on my father and ultimately my destiny and values.

My cousin Betty Hunt Kaye says that CP was a tobacco-chewing old grump with a goatee. My grandfather was morally straight-laced, a religious fanatic. He wasn't a minister, but he loved to preach. The kids loved music, played musical instruments and enjoyed dancing, especially my father. They belonged to a big Baptist Church and on occasion the church had dances. One night CP and his brood made such a ruckus that the preacher told my grandfather that he and has family were no longer welcome. He'd have to find some other church.

That didn't sit well with grandpa. He liked going to church. But he didn't pine for long. When the church got short of money, the preacher told grandpa he had suffered enough and to come back to church. CP was very devout when the collection plate was passed around.

Despite the church and frivolity, these were tough times for the Hunts. The soil was poor for farming, but they were getting by. CP saw the answer to their hardships in education. My Uncle Charles went to medical school. Uncle Sam went to engineering school. The other boys had the option of going to college, but Jim, Joe and my dad wanted to strike out on their own and seek their fortunes.[11]

Wet behind the ears, Uncle Jim and my dad needed help, and that's where my cousin Stewart Hunt, CP's nephew, came in. He was the most important player and motivator in the lives of the Hunt brothers. He was idolized by my father and his brothers, and if it hadn't been for Stewart, my parents might never have met.

Cousin Ken Hunt says that Stewart was born in Mississippi on July 10, 1872, which makes him about four years older than Uncle Charlie, five years older than Uncle Jim, and nine years older than my father. He arrived in Southeastern Arizona in the late 1890s and then went down to Mexico to trap, sell furs, and round up unbranded wild cows and mustangs. He used the free livestock to start his own ranch and to trade for equipment and foodstuffs.[12]

Where did the wild cattle come from? The state of Sonora, Mexico, was effectively lawless and you could do and get away with anything. The ranges were unfenced and mostly unpopulated. Revolutionaries, banditos, Mexican Army soldiers and wild Indian tribes, especially Apaches, wandered around stealing, rustling, and killing. Over the years, they ran off or killed ranchers in the northern Sierra Madres and the ranchers' cattle became wild and bred.[13]

Stewart had no money, but lots of ambition, and living off the land and accumulating wealth without restriction suited his untamed nature. He was a free spirit and entrepreneur. Think of him as the Donald Trump of his time.

During his cattle business years, Stewart owned as many as three large ranches in Mexico and several in Arizona. Ken describes him as "a remarkably bright, energetic and enterprising man," and his fortunes, for a time, were tied inexorably to the *mis*fortunes of the Hunt brothers.[14]

Uncle Jim was itching to leave the farm. He was inspired by letters he received from Cousin Stewart describing opportunities in the southwest and in Mexico. In 1898, at the age of twenty-two, Uncle Jim headed not to Mexico to join Cousin Stewart, as you might expect, but to Bisbee, a buzzing Arizona mining metropolis. Maybe he wasn't sure if cattle ranching was for him.

Before long, Uncle Jim was the one writing the letters, this time to my dad about the wide-open spaces and prospects in the untamed west. He told his brother Jack to turn in his plow and leave the farm behind. Having dropped out of high school at sixteen, my dad thought that was a good idea.

In 1900, which my dad called "nineteen aught aught," my grandparents took the eighteen-year-old to San Antonio, and there he hopped on a train to Benson, the closest place to Bisbee. Upon Jack's arrival, Uncle Jim had a man with a horse waiting to pick him up and take him down to Bisbee.

Dad got a job right away with mining company Phelps Dodge, but he was too young to work underground. Instead, he was assigned to the OK Livery Stable that Uncle Jim managed.

The kindest thing you could say about his job is that it was entry level. First he cleaned out the stalls by shoveling manure, and then he hauled it from the stable down to Lowell, a "bustling little offshoot" of Bisbee, on the other side of the Lavender Pit Mine.[15]

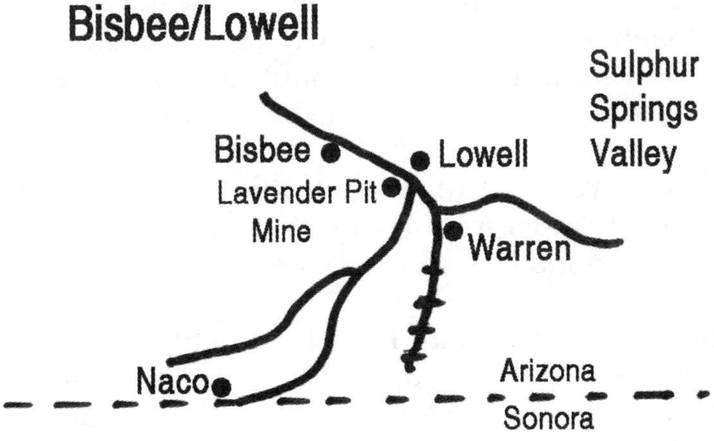

Bisbee was an industrious place. In its heyday, the town, including Lowell, had a population of about 35,000 compared to today's population of about 8,500. The big moneymaker was copper, followed by hotels, ladies-of-the-night, and hootch.[16]

Mucking out horse stalls was not my dad's only job. Driving a horse and buggy, he also delivered groceries and barrels of wine for Phelps Dodge's big store to the bawdy houses. He did such a good job that the bosses often gave him cigars, even though he didn't smoke, nor did any of the Hunt brothers.

Not content with just two jobs, and being young and ambitious, my dad got a third job. At night he drove hacks, the Wild West's version of a taxi, and earned a few cents hauling drunks up and down Brewery Gulch, which was the red light district. OK Livery was at the mouth of the Gulch, and the bordellos were up the hill.

Unlike my dad, Uncle Jim had only two jobs. He managed the stable, and drove the stagecoach down to Naco, a tiny, dusty border town on both sides of the line. After he got back from Naco, he drove another stagecoach to the mining town of Cananea, Sonora, every week, and it was a big haul, a two-day trip each way shuttling the miners to Bisbee and back.

When he reached the age of nineteen or twenty, my father went underground into the mines. This was his goal, for reasons I cannot fathom.

From what I was told, he got into fights down there. He was always a scrapper. The bosses liked him because he was a good worker, and they looked in the other direction.

After a couple of years in the mines, my dad had had enough of the dust and the dark, and realized this was not a way to earn his fortune. Stewart kept writing Uncle Jim and my dad describing his exploits and asked them to join him in his enterprise.

They didn't need further convincing. Dad and Uncle Jim set out for Mexico and joined Cousin Stewart in the horse and cattle business at El Tapila, a ranch in the rugged Sierra las Espuelas mountains, just south of the border, 40 miles east of Agua Prieta. Eventually, another brother, my Uncle Sam, joined them. After a while, because of the Hunt brothers' help, Stewart acquired another ranch, El Alamito, about 20 miles closer to Agua Prieta, and yet another nearby ranch, El Rancho la Lobo, the biggest of all the ranches.[17]

The Hunt brothers liked working with Stewart, but at some point they became homesick and disenchanted with Mexico. Around 1902, my father, Jim and Sam headed back to the United States to work another of Stewart's ranches, Rancho Sacatal, in the Sulphur Springs Valley of Southeastern Arizona.

And it was not for the weak or for the meek.

3. Rancho Sacatal

Rancho Sacatal wasn't a big ranch, but more of a homestead. It took a strong back, a strong will, and a person who didn't scare easily.

Homesteading meant that you got raw land. No wells full of cool water, no buildings to shelter you from the storms, no roads through the wilderness. There were none of the modern conveniences we take for granted. There was no electricity, no refrigeration, no ice, no air conditioning, no bathtubs of warm water to bathe in, no bathrooms, not even an outhouse.[1]

When my dad and his brothers arrived at Rancho Sacatal, they rode into rough terrain. They had to clear the land of mesquite, greasewood brush, cactuses and oak trees. They cut the timbers, laid out the house, and built it one stick at a time.

Everything they needed they brought in from town by horseback and wagon or made it themselves. They carted in water, food, tools, sleeping gear, tents, and hay for the horses.

Nevertheless, they built on a large scale from what they had seen in Mississippi, with big porches and big pillars, and you could bring your horse and buggy around the front and tie it to the rails while you loaded your passengers. As Sam was an engineer, the structures they built were sound.

They dug wells, grew their own vegetables and sometimes hunted. They drove cattle onto their land and set up a thriving business.

The temperatures ranged from 25 degrees Fahrenheit in December to 94 in July. Being up over 4,000 feet, it was cooler than the flatlands. With an annual rainfall of only a little over 12 inches, it was considered a semi-arid area. Summer and winter were the best months for rain, with often heavy rains and flooding in early fall. Nevertheless, droughts were frequent, and there were no lakes or rivers, just the occasional draw with water. The summers were not outrageously hot like Phoenix, but tell that to a cowboy out on the range in the broiling sun.[2]

Besides the heat and infrequent rains, they had to contend with mountain lions, wolves, coyotes, javalina, scorpions, rattlesnakes, fire ants, mosquitoes and noseeums, tiny black bugs that could chew a chunk of flesh off your arm before you knew you'd been bitten.

Then there was cholla cactus, also known as jumping cholla, that hooked you and attached its barbs to your skin if you merely brushed by, and when you tried to pull out the barbs, they'd break off and reattach themselves. And the brothers endured monsoon rains that could sweep you away even when it wasn't raining. A torrent could rush down a mountain from a storm miles away.

Despite the hardships, they loved it. Rancho Sacatal was on 480 acres of deeded land and about 30 square miles of open, unoccupied government land, which the

Hunts used as open range to graze their cattle.[3] They were surrounded by wildlife and waterfoul, shorebirds and songbirds. Thousands of Sandhill Cranes and hundreds of ducks, geese and raptors wintered in the area.[4]

The Homestead Act of 1862 offered plots of up to 160 acres cheaply or sometimes free to the heads of families or to citizens 21 and over. In return, the homesteaders promised to stay on the plot for five years and to cultivate and improve the land and build a house.[5] Stewart was able to get three homesteads next to each other.

The ranch was located at Paul Spur between Douglas and Bisbee about a half mile north of the Mexican border. It had a huge lime plant and a railroad spur or siding that branched off from the main line.

Rancho Sacatal/Paul Spur

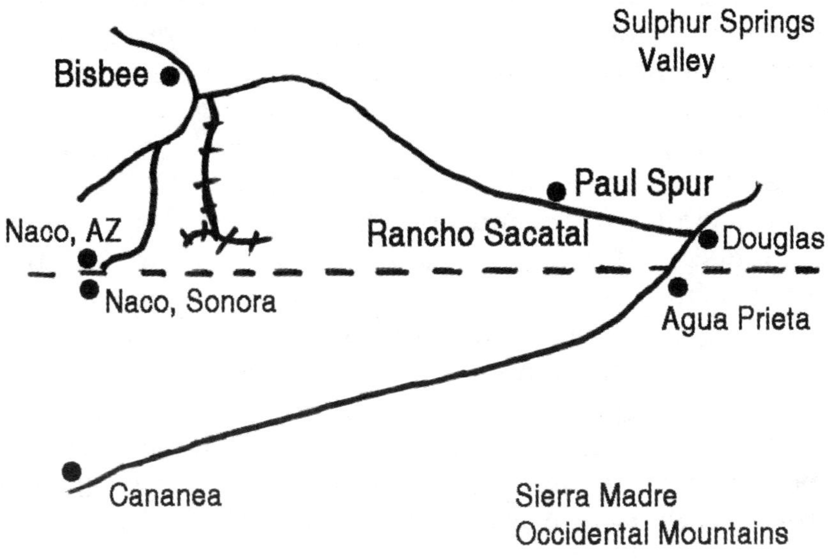

The ranch was originally purchased from frontier cattleman Charles Slaughter. As is typical in the west, this ranch has been referred to variously over the years as Rancho Sacatal, Paul Spur, Sulphur Springs, the Charlie Slaughter Ranch, and the Stewart Hunt Ranch, depending on who you were talking to.

And it gets more complicated than that. Most ranches were known by the new purchaser's name, the name they chose to give it, by the previous owner's name, by its location, and even by the brand they put on the cows.

When the Hunts arrived at Rancho Sacatal, the whole valley was unfenced. The invention of barbed wire in 1874 was both a boon and a curse, for it meant that ranchers and farmers could seal off land where cattle used to wander freely. By 1911, nine years after the Hunt brothers had arrived, many small farmers had homesteaded the Sulphur Springs Valley, and that 30 square miles of unfenced government land the brothers used to graze their cattle? Mostly gone. The newcomers had reduced the rangeland available to the Hunts and my family felt squeezed. They couldn't make a decent living anymore, so they knew it was time to leave the Sacatal.[6]

However, Stewart did not sell the property. He hung onto it while Uncle Jim and dad decided to try something else to earn a living, farming. It seems that the family's first experience digging up Texas dirt did not sufficiently convince them that farming was not a profitable occupation for a cattleman.

They moved to Yuma in 1911, the year before Arizona became a state, and each family member bought 40 acres of raw land in what they believed was a booming farm area.[7] They thought Texas was bad? This was much worse. As my brother Tom says, they couldn't make "enough to scratch a poor man's behind." It was too hot, the soil was poor, and the neighbors too close.

Uncle Jim and my dad slugged it out for two years, but finally abandoned the farm.

The Sacatal, despite the overcrowding of the range, was suddenly looking better, and back they went to cattle ranching. Well, Uncle Jim went back. My dad had other business he wanted to look into.

Around 1913, my dad was employed by two mining engineers to search for the lost Tayopa Mine. In case you thought my dad was a stolid realist, he was also, at times, a dreamer, one who fantasized about buried treasure and huge nuggets of gold sitting on the ground, and although he believed in working for a living, wouldn't it be nice if he didn't have to.[8]

One of the mining engineers had searched church archives in Spain and believed he had the directions for the mine, actually several mines, and their riches.

Apparently, in the 1600s, black-robed, ascetic Jesuits acquired many mines in the Sierra Madre Mountains in Sonora, Mexico. The King of Spain had sent them there to convert people to Christianity, not to enrich themselves, and he declared mine ownership by priests illegal. Consequently, the Jesuits decided to keep the locations of the mines secret.

According to church documents, the Tayopa Mine was seventeen separate mines containing veins of gold and silver. They also held items of great value.

An inventory, written and sealed in 1646 by a Jesuit priest, stated that, among other riches, the mines contained: a 15-pound cross of carved silver, a crucifix of hammered gold, 6 bars of hammered silver, 12 solid gold cups, 6 gold plates, 65 cowhide bags of silver, 11 loads of gold, each wrapped in cloth and cowhide, with a weight of 2,512 pounds.[9]

You can see why my father was interested. Along with the engineers, he left Bisbee or Douglas on horseback with pack mules and proceeded west through Opoto, Sonora. The country was covered with grass for the horses, and there was lots of game, especially wild turkeys, for food.

Three days before they reached the area where they thought the mines were located, they noticed unusual bird calls. They realized right away they were being made by Indians who were following them. Spooked, my dad and the engineers stopped and cooked dinner (turkey, again) while it was still light. After dark they sneaked away to set up camp elsewhere.

Next morning when they returned to the cook site, they found Indian tracks over their own. They were aware that expeditions such as theirs had never been heard from again. This was Apache territory and the Indians didn't like whites treading on their lands. Nevertheless, the determined group continued on.

The documents from Spain told them to watch for a church at a certain spot, and they found its stone foundation. The mines were about one mile east.

Fearing an Indian attack, my dad pulled the horses and pack mules next to a cliff to defend them better. He guarded the animals while the engineers hastily searched for the mines. They found nothing.

They didn't hang around to do a more thorough search because the Indians were still dogging them and my dad headed back to the safety of the Sacatal, empty-handed, but with hair on his head.[10]

4. War and Prosperity

For several more years, the brothers continued to ranch. They opened a slaughter house in Douglas to make it easier to process their cattle and to dip the cows coming over from Mexico in insecticide to kill the ticks and other insects that sometimes infested them.

Around August 1914, demand for their product suddenly took off. World War I had begun in Europe and overseas shipments for beef cattle and its products like leather surged from 500 million pounds to 1.5 billion pounds, a 300 percent increase. At the same time, the U.S. began expanding the Army and Navy in anticipation of joining the conflict, and was ordering tons of beef for their burgeoning military.

Because of the huge demand and depletion of beef stock, beef prices were sky high.[1] The Hunt family was engaged in the right business at the right time, and they thrived. In case you think my family was rolling in dough, it wasn't like that. There were price controls on beef, but the feed that cows ate such as cottonseed cake had nearly doubled.[2] All the same, the brothers were doing well.

Although business was good for the Hunt enterprises, the grazing problem got worse. Many more small farmers and nesters took up residence wanting in on the war action. As a result, in 1916, Stewart bought two homesteads near the western side of the Animas Valley, which is east of the New Mexico border, with a small piece in Arizona. The Animas also runs down toward Douglas into Mexico. His plan was to send cattle to the larger grazing areas in the Animas and have the brothers manage the new ranch while he continued to run the Sacatal.

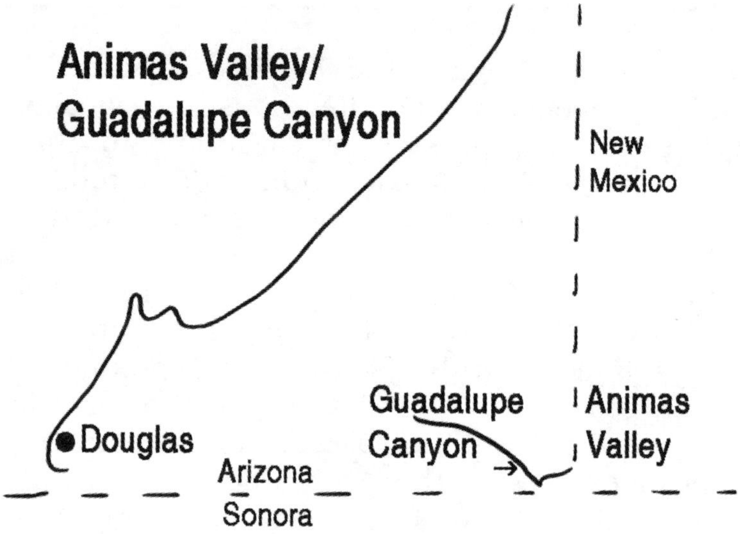

To begin their new venture, the Hunt brothers drove about 1,000 head of cattle from their operations in the Sulphur Springs Valley about 50 miles east to their new home in the Animas Valley and the herd was turned loose to graze.[3]

Around the same time, Cousin Stewart acquired a ranch in the nearby Guadalupe Canyon, at the southern end of the Arizona-New Mexico border, and plunked a large herd of livestock on that land.[4] Stewart and the Hunts lived in Guadalupe Canyon on the Arizona side of the border, but ranched mostly on the New Mexico side.

In February, 1917, Germany announced it was resuming unrestricted submarine warfare on neutral or Allied shipping and the United States broke diplomatic relations with Germany.[5] Then the U.S. government intercepted a telegram from the German Foreign Secretary of the German Empire to the German ambassador in Mexico offering an alliance with Mexico if they agreed to invade America.

To reward Mexico for its support after the Mexicans and Germans had conquered the United States, Mexico would receive the former Mexican provinces of Texas, Oklahoma, California, Nevada, Utah, Colorado, New Mexico and *Arizona.*

The Germans told the Mexican president that he better make up his mind because the Japanese were also joining the alliance and expected territory in the southwestern United States.

The Mexican-American War, only sixty-nine years before, which cost Mexico many lives and much land, was still fresh in the hearts of every Mexican. Having a way to get those lands back was a magnificent dream. Eventually, Mexico's president decided that war with the United States was not a good idea. Mexico did not have the weapons to supply a big war and he declined the tempting offer.[6]

After these shenanigans were published in U.S. newspapers, Americans were cheesed off, but the public felt that the German telegram was a hoax, designed to trick them into joining the war burning in Europe. They didn't think anybody would be stupid enough to write such a document.

Then the German Foreign Secretary did something unimaginable. He admitted he wrote it, and in response the United States on April 6, 1917, declared war on Germany.

Consequently, Arizona contributed more soldiers, sailors, and marines per capita to the military than any other state to fight the aggressors. We were not giving Arizona to anybody.[7]

The country quickly expanded its armed forces from a few hundred thousand men before the war to 5 million men. What this meant for the Hunt brothers was a greater demand for beef.[8]

However, not everybody cared that we were at war. In June, 1917, a couple of months after the U.S. declared war on Germany, unionized copper miners who were members of the Industrial Workers of the World (IWW) or *Wobblies* decided to strike against Bisbee copper mining companies for better safety and working conditions and higher wages tied to the market price of copper. Arizona's economy was based on the three *Cs*: cattle, cotton, and copper. Like cattle prices, copper prices were way up, and all of these products were desperately needed for the war effort.

The copper mining companies' bosses refused the demands, not just because there was a war on, but also because they didn't want to be told what to do. That is *so* Arizona.

By the end of June, 1917, about half the Bisbee workforce was out on strike. The Wobblies were against the war, and, if conscripted, requested an exemption from serving based on their opposition to the war.[9] I can imagine how this sat with my father and uncles. They believed in doing your duty and Uncle Joe was getting ready to sign up to fight. The others would stay behind and look after the family and raise cattle to support the troops.

Uncle Jim was dead set against unions. He was "very much management. He didn't want to be told he couldn't do this or that or he had to do this or that," says his daughter Betty. "That was just against his way of thinking."

He was in good company. Most of the country was against the union and there was a lot of pressure to oppose them for the sake of the war effort.

Uncle Jim belonged to an organization formed to deal with the strikers, most likely the *Workman's Loyalty League*, a posse of miners loyal to the mining companies.

As Cousin Betty tells the story... On July 12, 1917, Uncle Jim was walking on a street in Douglas and somebody came up to him and told him that they were rounding up the union people and running them out of town. He went to his room, got his gun, jumped in his car and went to Bisbee to join the other 2,000 armed vigilante *deputies.* He put on a white armband to distinguish himself from strikers. Then they marched more than 1,000 strikers the 2 miles to the Warren Ballpark.

This was not a peaceful event. A Wobblie shot and killed a Loyalty Leaguer and the men with him shot the Wobblie dead.

This event was referred to as "The Deportation," not a pleasant symbol for American justice. But those were different, uncomplicated times. Things seemed clearer then they do now. Outside forces wanted to attack the

United States, steal its land and resources, and enslave its population. Uncle Jim was one of those fearless people who stood up for what he believed in. He was not a bad person; he was a man of his time.

At 11 AM, a train arrived and nearly 1,200 union men were forced aboard cattle cars heaped with manure several inches high. About 200 armed guards accompanied them and a machine gun was mounted on the top of the train. They were not fooling around.

The train eventually dropped the men off in the hot sun without shelter or water in Columbus, New Mexico. Later another train brought them food and water. Many were held in New Mexico for several months for questioning, a shameful act, but I'm not so sure we would have seen it that way then.[10]

Arizonans couldn't focus on The Deportation. They were getting on with the enormous tasks at hand, especially cattle ranchers who had to expand their operations. The government needed them to raise food for the troops, and that suited many entrepreneurs just fine. There were riches to be made, and everybody in the cattle business was flourishing.

However, with the Hunts' large herds and the rangeland already crowded by other cattle enterprises, the brothers were not made welcome in the Animas Valley. In particular, the Kern County Land Company, a wealthy group of California investors that owned the Gray Ranch, didn't want the family's cattle grazing on land they felt belonged to them.

A deadly conflict was inevitable.

5. The Shooting

According to Cousin Ken, the Gray Ranch, also known by their brand, the Diamond A, was the largest and most powerful cattle operator in the valley.

In 1917, the Diamond A's foreman was William Benjamin (Ben) Robertson, known as a devious man who allegedly acquired other ranch properties by hiring armed thugs to drive off small landholders like the Hunts.

The Hunt brothers were not easily intimidated. They were known as being tough and fair, but hotheaded when it came to protecting their own. They never backed down from a fight, and the conflict could only end tragically. Somebody was going to die and somebody was going to pay.

Robertson was not the only nasty piece of work who wanted the Hunts gone. Rancher W. H. (Hut) Taylor, "the patriarch of an extended family of reputed low-lifes," and his cronies conspired to drive the Hunts out of the valley. Word was that Ben Robertson and the Kern County Land Company collaborated with Taylor to make life miserable for the Hunts.[1]

To encourage other ranchers to hound the Hunts into leaving, a reward was offered, it's not clear by whom, but I think it's obvious who had the big money.[2] One of the Gray Ranch's henchmen, a man named Chester Bartell, must have wanted the reward money real bad, bad enough to kill.

Among verbal threats, were several violent provocations. The details may be slightly exaggerated, as they have been handed down in my family by word of mouth, but their basic truth was established in a court of law.

My dad and his brothers Sam and Joe, sister Bess, and my grandparents lived in the Animas Valley on the Eldridge Place, a 160-acre homestead on which Sam had filed for ownership. Uncle Jim lived in Douglas and looked after the ranch's business. Uncle Charlie, the doctor, lived in Bisbee, and provided financial support to the ranches and medical care when necessary.[3]

Uncle Joe had been shot at on at least two occasions while riding around the ranch, and a horse he had saddled and was about to mount was shot and killed. Joe said he saw Chester Bartell running away.

One day Uncle Jim and my dad came upon some cowboys driving a bunch of Hunt cattle toward the line with Mexico. If they succeeded, banditos or the Mexican Army would snatch the cows. My dad and Uncle Jim pursued them and managed to drive the cowboys off. But my dad recognized one of the cowboys, a relative of Hut Taylor.[4] I'm sure you've heard that stealing a man's horse was a hangin' offence in the Old West. So was stealing cattle, maybe not officially.

On the morning of September 13, 1917, my dad and uncles Sam and Joe were on horseback driving cattle toward a better grazing section. It was hilly terrain at the eastern edge of the Peloncillo Mountains in the far southwest corner of New Mexico. My dad and his brothers didn't usually carry guns, but after all that had happened, they thought it necessary to arm themselves. The details of this story come from Cousin Ken Hunt's book about what happened next.

Several cows had strayed away from the trail and my dad rode after them to turn them back. Sam and Joe continued up the trail. They came upon a heavy clump of chaparral, and as they rounded it, they saw Chester Bartell hiding behind it. Bartell reached for a rifle that was in a scabbard on the side of his horse, but Sam and Joe drew their pistols and shot Bartell multiple times until he fell from his horse. They examined him, and he was dead, by some later accounts several times over.

After my dad rejoined his brothers, they headed back to the ranch, and my dad drove a car to the justice of the peace for a nearby community to report what had happened. The justice of the peace and my dad set out for the ranch, and when they met Joe and Sam on horseback along the way, the magistrate told them they were under arrest and to go on home.

The coroner's inquest, consisting of the justice of the peace and four other men, was held after dark on the same day at the site where Bartell's body still lay on the ground. They examined the body and determined that it had two bullet holes in it.

The Hunt brothers were placed under arrest, again, this time by the constable for Cloverdale, a nearby town, and they were sent home again. Justice was kind of informal in those days.

The body was then taken in one of the Hunts' wagons to the nearby ranch of Hut Taylor, one of the men determined to get rid of the Hunts. Around 4 AM the next day, it was placed on a cot outside the Taylor home.

On the morning of September 14, Hut Taylor said he noticed blood oozing from Bartell's body. He summoned his sons and several neighbors, all who wanted the Hunts gone, and they stripped and examined the body. They later testified that they found ten or more bullet holes in Bartell.[5]

That was the official version of the killing, but I would like to relate another version of the story that Cousin Ken talks about. Uncle Joe was his father and that's who he heard this from.

According to Ken, Uncle Joe was saddling a horse, a shot rang out and the horse fell dead. Joe didn't have a gun to defend himself, so he ran through the corral and into brushy horse pasture. He caught a horse, made a halter out of his belt and a piece of wire, and set out for where he knew his brothers were bringing in cattle. Joe went as fast as his old cow pony could go as he knew his attacker was in pursuit.

He soon found his brothers, told them what had happened, and the brothers drew their 30-30 rifles and .38 caliber pistols.

They spread out to intercept the would-be assassin, Uncle Jim and my dad with their rifles, uncles Sam and Joe with pistols. Jim and dad thought they could get high on the sides of the canyon to see him coming, but it was too late and the hired gun was already upon them.

Fortunately, Bartell didn't see the brothers, who quickly hid behind a clump of mesquite until he was within pistol range. They charged him, firing until he was down and very dead.[6]

This makes for a more exciting story, but I think we have to go with the official version and leave my Uncle Jim out of it. Sam, Joe, and my dad were arrested, but not Uncle Jim.

Yet I do wonder what really happened. How many holes did my uncles put in Chester Bartell? How many may have been added to his already dead body by Hut Taylor and his pals to make it look like a slaughter?

6. Mom Meets Dad

This was the beginning of what my family still refers to as *the troubles*, an understatement for sure.

Then things took another turn, this one good. It was October, a month after the killing, and Cousin Stewart Hunt asked Sallie Stewart, my soon-to-be mother, to come all the way from Texas to help care for their Uncle Denton, who was in poor health.

Sallie worked at the Mineral Wells Health Clinic where people visited from all over the state to take the baths. Having worked at the clinic made Sallie the next best thing to a nurse and Cousin Stewart was desperate. Sallie and her mother made their way by train to Douglas, Arizona, and Stewart picked them up and brought them to his ranch in Guadalupe Canyon near the Mexican border.[1]

Born in Clayton, New Mexico, in 1885, Sallie was a slim, five foot two twenty-two-year-old raven-haired beauty with curly long black hair down to her waist.[2] My dad, Jack, met her at Stewart's and was instantly smitten.

She was attracted to him from the start. At thirty-six years old, he was nearly 6 feet with dark black hair.

Born John Partridge Hunt in Texas on October 29, 1881, he was a handsome man with a long straight nose.[3] He was strong, honest, some say painfully honest, and believed in the power of the truth. He was a great dancer and would sweep a woman off her feet. Actually pick her up and swing her around the room. He loved to dance and knew how to treat a lady with respect.

It's no wonder my mother fell for him.

There was only one problem. Surely, being arrested for murder is a complication that would take a gal's breath away, but that pales in comparison to this new predicament. Jack and Sallie were related.

Here's how it worked. My father's uncle, John Thomas Hunt, married Sallie's aunt, Mary Elizabeth Stewart. They gave birth to Stewart Hunt. So my father and Stewart were first cousins. And my mother and Stewart were first cousins.

Some people in my family didn't think it was right that they were seeing each other in a romantic way, and marriage was out of the question. You don't marry people in your own family.

Sallie and Jack could not have cared less. Even though Jack and Sallie were related, it was not directly by blood.

They were in love. That's all that mattered.

7. Trials and Tribulations

Jack and Sallie's whirlwind romance filled their heads through October 1917. Then along came November and the preliminary hearing on murder charges for my dad and my uncles, Joe and Sam.

Uncle Jim Hunt, the eldest brother, was called to testify. No one seems to know why since nobody placed him at the shooting. Uncle Jim was a hardworking rancher devoted to family, and in the face of injustice had an explosive temper. According to his daughter Betty, he got so mad at the prosecutor for saying something rotten about his brothers that he picked up a chair and threw it at him. There's no record on whether the chair hit its intended target. Nevertheless, Uncle Jim was not called as a future character witness.[1]

The outcome of the prelim was that Sam, Joe and my father were indicted for first-degree murder and bail was set at $25,000 *each*. That was an enormous amount of money, the equivalent of more than $400,000 today for each of them.[2] Nothing romantic about that. With that hanging over my dad's head, mom may have wondered what kind of catch Jack would make.

The brothers certainly didn't have that kind of money. They had to pay the bail bond company 10 percent of the bond or $2,500 each (more than $40,000 in today's money)[3]. And no matter what happened, whether they were convicted or not, they would lose that money. At least they would be free on bail to defend themselves and continue working the ranch.

Since the bonding company put up the full $75,000, the Hunt family had to cover the total amount with assets. They pooled all of their money and guaranteed the rest with collateral such as land, cattle, horses, wagons, trucks, chickens, whatever they possessed. Even so, that wasn't enough.

Luckily, their friends contributed funds to ensure the balance. But the Hunt brothers still had to hire a crack defense team and somehow find the money to pay them.

It's a strange irony that the indictment may have saved Uncle Joe's life. He was twenty-two years old when the United States declared war on Germany in April of 1917 and entered the Great War. In August he had volunteered for the U.S. Army. One month later, before he was called up for duty, he was accused of murder and not allowed to go to war.[4]

Almost 126,000 American soldiers died in that war and 365,000 were wounded. With those numbers, there was a good chance he would have become a war casualty or a victim of the influenza pandemic that killed thousands of Americans fighting in Europe. But he was home, charged with murder... and safe.[5]

To put the impact of the murder charge in perspective, here were the Hunt brothers at the height of their earning potential with a war on and a market gone crazy for their beef cattle, and they were forced to sell off much of their ranch property and cattle to raise funds to pay for lawyers and their bail bond.

As if the murder charge wasn't enough to sap anybody's strength, 1917 had another dangerous surprise for them.

Although the Hunt brothers had moved to the Animas Valley, they still had an interest in the Rancho Sacatal with Cousin Stewart in southeastern Arizona and owned land over the border in Mexico where they grazed their cows on Mexican territory.

Since 1910, Mexico had been involved in a civil war, a fight that had nothing to do with the Hunt brothers. The most serious outcome of the conflict was the Agrarian Reform Act of January 6, 1915, which demanded that foreigners be prohibited from owning land in Mexico and their property, including cattle, be confiscated.[6]

This was nothing new, as there had been other agrarian decrees dating back to 1913. This was just the most boisterous declaration and the handwriting was on the wall. Their only choice was to become Mexican citizens like Stewart. He had married a Mexican woman and was thriving down there. At one time, he owned a big lumber business, a store in Guadalupe, a parts store in Agua Prieta, and ranches in Mexico and in Arizona.[7]

But the Hunt brothers were not willing to give up their American citizenships just so they could save their property and they ignored the warning signs. Then on February 5, 1917, things took an ominous turn. The Mexican Constitution officially formalized the seizing of property owned by foreigners.[8] According to Cousin Betty Hunt, her father, my Uncle Jim, the brother with the temper, said, "By God, they can take the land but they can't have my cows."

Jim knew that their cattle grazing on the Mexican side of the border were being watched by rustlers and Mexican federal troops waiting for a chance to snatch them. Under cover of darkness, on Christmas Eve 1917, Uncle Jim and some cowhands saddled up, rounded up as many cows as they could find and drove them toward the border.

Betty says they expected to be ambushed and her dad went ahead to see if the way was clear. He was gone a long time, and when he returned he was leading two saddled horses. He never said what happened, but everyone assumed the horses' owners did not give up their steeds willingly. A friend of my father's, Benny Snure, told Betty when she was very young that "your father is about the only man I know who I believe could just pull a gun and shoot you."

Do I believe Uncle Jim shot two men? Yes. In those days the law was not going to protect you when you were out in the rural areas of Mexico during a revolution. You took care of yourself.

After the attempted ambush, Uncle Jim and his men ran the cows all night until they were over the border in the safety of the Rancho Sacatal. He eventually moved them to the ranch in the Animas Valley.

The fall of 1917 was quite dramatic for my family. In September, my dad and his brothers were charged with killing a man. In October, dad met my mother. In November, my dad, Sam and Joe were officially indicted for first-degree murder. In December, Uncle Jim shot two banditos and ran his cattle out of Mexico over the border. *What did 1918 have in store?*

On Monday April 1st, 1918, the murder trial of Jack, Sam and Joe began. It ended the following Monday when the jury announced its verdict. My dad was set free, but Sam and Joe Hunt were found guilty of second-degree murder, and the court ordered them locked up in the Grant County jail pending sentencing.

Twelve days later, Sam and Joe were sentenced to forty to fifty years in the New Mexico state penitentiary.

Their defense team quickly filed a motion for a mistrial that the judge rejected but an appeal to the New Mexico Supreme Court was granted, and pending the outcome, Sam and Joe were freed on the same bond as before, $25,000 each.

The family worried that if the appeal didn't work, Sam and Joe might spend the rest of their lives in jail. This possibility was too horrifying to imagine, and the brothers considered going on the lam to Brazil where there was no extradition treaty with the U.S.[9]

After Chester Bartell's death, the threats against the Hunt brothers stopped for a time. According to Cousin Ken, it was not only as a result of the shooting but because of a confrontation my father had with Ben Robertson, the manager of the Gray Ranch. During the fall roundup in the Animas Valley, my dad met up with Robertson and warned him in unequivocal language that if there were any more attempts to hurt him or his brothers that my dad would personally hunt him down and kill him. Dad was very sweet, but nobody should have underestimated what he was capable of doing to defend his family.[10]

Despite this period of anxiety, the family tried to act normally and do normal things, like plan a wedding.

On September 12, 1919, mom and dad got married in Douglas and for a brief time everyone felt hopeful and happy. It was two years since my parents had met.

Even though my dad had threatened Ben Robertson with a horrible death, the harassment started up again. On more than one occasion, somebody fired shots at the Guadalupe Canyon ranch house from ridges above the house.

Then one day, somebody fired a shot through a window inches from where Jack's father was shaving. Ken says that my father armed himself and set out after the bushwhacker. He told Sallie that if he found the man who shot at his dad, he would kill him and light out for Mexico.

He said he'd tie his handkerchief on the gate to the ranch so Sallie would know she should join him. As Stewart had lots of influence, it would be an easy matter to set up life south of the border. He never did find the shooter.[11]

Jack and Sallie stayed a little while longer at the Guadalupe Ranch, but then moved to Southeastern Arizona. New Mexico no longer felt good to them.

In Arizona, Jack and Sallie bought the old Miller Ranch, which is about 10 miles north of Douglas. It was more like a homestead than a real ranch. It had a house and a little land, not much else. Even today it's called the Hunt Ranch.[12]

When my parents got married, World War I had been over for nearly a year. Cattle prices had slipped because prices depended on soldiers needing to be fed, but ranching was still a lucrative business. By 1920 prices had collapsed, along with the rest of the economy, and the United States wallowed in its first recession.[13]

Men back from the war were looking for jobs that weren't there and few had money to buy meat. And there were few government contracts requesting millions of pounds of beef.[14] For the Hunts, this meant a downturn in their fortunes. They could no longer sell their beef cattle at a high price, if they could sell them at all.

Despite the recession, Jack and Sallie were happy, even though the prospect of Sam and Joe going to jail was constantly gnawing at their thoughts. They feared the future. Would the family lose everything? Would Sam and Joe take off for Brazil? Would they end up in prison for the rest of their lives?

They got their answer on June 30, 1920. Sort of.

The Supreme Court of New Mexico reversed the second-degree murder convictions and set the case for retrial.

This was a first step toward freedom, but things could still go terribly wrong. Because it was a mistrial, Sam and Joe could again be charged with second-degree murder and go to jail for forty to fifty years.[15]

8. Having Babies

A couple of weeks after word of the mistrial, with the family anxious to find out what direction their lives might take, mom began having labor pains. It was Tuesday, July 13, 1920.

Dad immediately jumped in the car, barreled down to Douglas, picked up the doctor and brought him back to the ranch. Mom's mother was there to hold her hand and comfort her. She was an old hand at delivering babies and knew what to do. Dad didn't get upset or pace on the other side of the door like many expectant fathers, so I was told. He was calm, cool and resigned. He thought what women did was have babies. That was our job.

Without any trouble, I was born and I like to think that my birth represented a turning point in my family's fortunes, when *the troubles* loosened their grip, and my family began to grow and thrive. We just had to get over the recession and the next murder trial.

Almost a year after I was born, my uncles Sam and Joe were retried. The trial began on Monday, May 23, 1921, and they were yet again charged with second-degree murder. On Friday, they were found guilty of manslaughter and sentenced to seven to nine years in prison.[1]

The defense appealed to the Supreme Court of New Mexico and Joe and Sam were freed on $5,000 bail each to await the outcome. Seven to nine was better than forty to fifty years, but nobody wants to spend a day in jail.[2]

And the waiting resumed.

Up until this time, the Hunt brothers had engaged in a number of cattle business dealings with Cousin Stewart. In spite of the uncertainty about Joe and Sam, the brothers decided to end their business relationship with Stewart and go out on their own. To pay off a debt he owed them, Stewart gave them a ranch in the San Bernardino Valley called the *Malpais*. In December 1922, when I was two and a half years old, we moved.

My mom was pregnant again, and dad had put her in an apartment in Bisbee to be closer to the doctor. Very soon after the move, or because of it, she went into labor with my sister Nellie. They called my Uncle Charlie who was at a New Year's Eve party. He put down his glass of champagne, rushed over in his tuxedo and delivered my sister.

My mom was healthy and strong and recovered right away from giving birth. Heck, she lived to be ninety-two. She stayed in town until the baby was about a month old. Her mom helped her and she was close to the doctor if she needed him. After that, she headed back to the ranch where my grandmother continued to help out, and my dad and the cowboys were at her beck and call. She liked that.

9. My Childhood Ranch

I spent my childhood on the Malpais Ranch, also known as the IV Bar, its cattle brand. We were up in the mountains about 4,500 feet, and it never got hotter than the mid-80s. That was a blessing considering Phoenix could hit 110 to 120 during parts of the summer.

The ranch, located in southeast Arizona about 23 miles northeast of Douglas, was called the Malpais (pronounced *Mal-pie*) because it was near the Paramore Crater and the ground was permeated with a substance common to volcanic areas, *malpais.* Also called the *Badlands*, the land was a carpet of dark-gray to black fine-grained basalt rock where hardly any grass grew.[1]

We lived just west of the crater. A road ran north from the ranch house about 3 to 4 rough miles out towards the Chiricahua Siding, a railroad siding where my dad could pour water into containers and haul them back to the ranch.

The ranch had no wells, and water from the railroad was our main source of drinking water, bathing and washing our clothes. The cattle, horses and other creatures drank out of dirt tanks. These were big mud holes filled with water that accumulated after the heavy monsoon summer rains and sporadic winter rains.

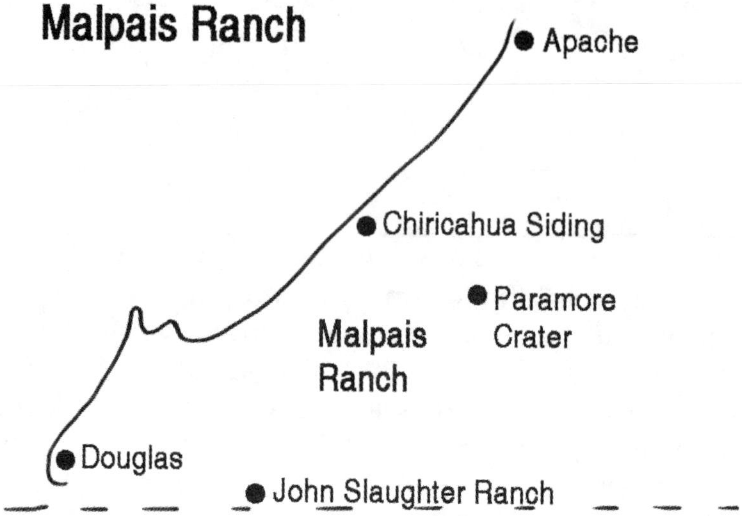

The dirt or surface tanks didn't happen by accident. My father, his brothers and cowhands dug them with mules pulling plows to turn the dirt. Then they used a *fresno*, also called a buck scraper, that scooped the dirt up and dumped it on the dam around the tank to make the banks that held back the water.[2]

We had several dirt tanks, two were enormous, each about a mile across, and they were positioned to take advantage of draws that brought water down like huge funnels. One draw came out of Chiricahua, the other came from the mountains. Altogether, we had four stock tanks above the house, three below, as well as more than a dozen galvanized metal tanks scattered around the ranch.

If you're not from the southwest, you are probably wondering what the heck monsoons are doing down here in the desert. Monsoons are usually in places like Vietnam or India. But starting in June, we watched dark clouds form, heard the thunder, saw lightning streaks, and felt the unbearable humidity shoot up from about 12 percent to 50 percent and more. Our shirts stuck to our backs, and 80 degrees felt like 100. After days of booming thunder, the rain began, and I'm talking deluges. I'm talking rain that beats so loudly on the roof that you can't carry on a conversation.[3]

The rain often followed a pattern, arriving in the afternoons, clearing by evening, and giving birth to the prettiest rainbows. Then it did it all over again the next day and the next for months until the end of September. Sometimes it rained all night, hard, relentless. The tanks filled up and overflowed, and we had to be careful where we rode our horses because sometimes torrents of water and debris including big rocks and dead trees suddenly roared down the washes, wiping out anything in their paths.

We relied on those rains for filling the dirt tanks. Without that pounding downpour, we couldn't water our cattle.

As well as building the dirt tanks, my father built us a house to live in. Cousin Ken says that the Malpais ranch house "was pretty crude." He believes that my dad built most of it himself and he wasn't much of a carpenter. He describes it as "a put together old ramshackle place." He says it was a "tough, bleak existence where the wind always blows in the valley."

I liked it, and I take exception to Ken's description of my father's carpentry skills. Maybe he wasn't a professional, but the roof never leaked, at least not all the time, and nature wasn't meant to have straight lines.

I was very young when dad was working on the house and digging the dirt tanks. I wasn't aware of the lengths he had to go to in order to make the ranch viable as a business and as a place to live. Years later I learned to appreciate his astonishing efforts under abysmal conditions. Some would have called his labor a form of madness. After being charged with first-degree murder, being set free, then watching his brothers endure year after year of torment, I think it was his therapy and his own piece of heaven.

The house suited our needs. Getting enough water, crucial to our existence, was a problem. We relied on the monsoons to fill the dirt tanks and our cistern, an underground tank that collected "liquid gold" from the gutters along the roof. An old man built it round and big and he made it slick on the inside so you could wash it. He plastered the inside walls with a mixture of buttermilk and cement and that made them like glass. To go inside, you climbed down a ladder through the opening.

After the cistern was built, mom and dad build a tower, slung two water tanks on top and at the bottom they hammered together a little shed. They put a Briggs and Stratton gas engine on the cistern and it pumped the water up to the tanks. When water ran through pipes from the tanks down into the house, it created water pressure. That's how we got running water in the kitchen and in the bathroom sink.

The pressure wasn't enough for flush toilets, however, and we had to traipse out to an outhouse far down by the chicken house. Most of the ranches in the area did the same thing. They installed tanks to get water pressure, unless you were lucky enough to have a hill and ran pipes from your cistern downhill.

Our big concern was the water going stale in the cistern and tasting bad. To keep it fresh, my dad ran a narrow copper pipe from the bottom of a tank down into the cistern. It trickled water all the time and that little bit of running water kept it fresh.

To fill the cistern, we ran water from the gutter, which ran all the way around the house. First we let the rain clean out the gutter for a few minutes and then redirected the water into the cistern. Still, a lot of dirt and other stuff ended up in the water.[4]

Regardless of what things may have looked like to outsiders, as a child I felt that the Malpais Ranch, despite its shortcomings, was magical. From our house we could see the Sierra Madre mountains in Sonora, Mexico, and knew if it was going to rain by watching the lightning move across the border. A week or ten days later, it always poured.

For a little kid like me, ranch life was like a fairy-tale. My mother celebrated everybody's birthday big time. There were cakes and guests and gifts. Dad joined in the festivities because he thought everybody should have birthday parties, even though he didn't want one for himself. He didn't like the attention.

From the time I can remember, I was on the back of a horse checking for stray cows. At four years old, I was milking cows twice a day, in the morning and at night. I suppose other kids might consider milking a cow a chore. To me it was fun. And I fed the chickens. I scattered corn and wheat seeds on the ground and the chickens fought and scratched for every morsel. I gave them lots of water, and I gathered the eggs if mom hadn't gotten them in.

My father stacked up cords of wood that he bought from the wood chopping camp up in the Chirachahuas, and each piece was cut in about 12-inch lengths. As one of my duties, I lugged in wood and put it in the woodbox for the fireplace and the stoves. No matter our size, skill or inclination, my father thought we could do anything and expected us to.

Since we didn't have electricity, we relied on kerosene lamps. The Coleman lamp had only recently come into style, and its gas smelled better than kerosene. The Colemans were good, but we didn't have enough of them and still had to use the others.

I hated cleaning the soot out of the lamp chimneys. I washed them with a cloth or a sheet of newspaper until every speck of dirt was off. You needed a clean chimney to let all the light in.

One of our jobs was doing the dishes in the sink after dinner. Without fail, we got to horsing around, giggling and popping each other with the dish towels. Dad came in with the kerosene lamp, set it on the pie safe, then dragged a big barrel that held about 100 pounds of flour over to the sink. He sat on the top and read his paper. He didn't say a word; he was the enforcer. The dishes got done rapidly after that.

I had other chores, too. One was ironing. Mom washed on Mondays and on Tuesdays we ironed up a storm. She slung an ironing board across the seat of a couple of chairs just the right height for me. I didn't start ironing in earnest until I was older, maybe six. We took the hot iron from on top of the woodstove and ironed tea towels, pillow slips, napkins, kerchiefs and my father's handkerchiefs. When an iron got cold, mom took the handle off and clipped it onto the next hot iron.

Then my father heard about a new Coleman iron called a *self-heating* iron that ran on white gas. He bought one for mom and it was much better than the stove heated ones. To start it, she shoved a match down into the iron to light it. The real advantage for mom was she could turn the iron up to whatever heat she wanted.[5]

I tried washing clothes like my mother using the old scrub board, but it was very hard on my hands. For the majority of the washing, mom made a big production out of it. She built a wood fire outside and suspended copper pots full of water she called boilers over it. She stuffed our clothes in, got the fire very hot, and boiled the clothes. Then she put our sheets in, boiled them, and then added bluing to whiten them. If she was going to starch my dad's shirts, she boiled the starch on the stove in a tub, dipped the shirts and without rinsing hung them on the line.

The shirts came out a brilliant white. Everyone admired them including our Shetland pony, Prince. He thought the clean clothes were tasty and chewed them right off the clothesline.

One day, dad was milking and I was supposed to ride Prince out to the pasture to round up the horses. I saddled him, mounted up, but then he backed up against the fence in the yard, and I couldn't get him to move. What I didn't know was Prince had taken a deep breath, deliberately bloating himself with air while I was saddling him.

Dad saw Prince against the fence and figured he'd rectify the situation. He hopped up behind me on the pony. Now that must have made quite a sight. A typical ranch horse is about 5 feet tall, but this little pony was only about 3½ feet tall. My dad was nearly 6 feet. And little Prince had a saddle, a child and a grown adult on his back.[6]

Dad took the whip and whapped him. Prince didn't like that much, put his head down and let out his breath. That loosened the cinch strap and the saddle flew off.

My dad and I were suddenly rolling around on the ground, and he was mad. He got on a horse and went out to the pasture himself and rounded up the horses. I took the milk in the house, and Prince wandered away.[7]

My brother Tom says Shetland ponies are only good for dog food. That's not a nice thing to say, but if you saw Prince eating your clean laundry like a billy goat, I'm sure you'd be beside yourself.

Mom eventually rigged something where she could put the clothes on the line and then push the line up with a pole where Prince couldn't reach the clothes.

Washing clothes by hand was hard work. One day my father was in town having the car worked on and a Maytag salesman came round and demonstrated a new metal tub washing machine that ran off a teeny motor filled with white gas. My dad had to have one.

Mom loved it. She filled the tub with water, stepped on a pedal that ignited its sparkplug and it started up and went *putt putt, putt*. She tossed soap and our clothes in and an agitator in the center swished back and forth, slapping against the clothes. Then she rinsed out the clothes a few times.[8]

After that, she squished the clothes between two rollers on the wringer to get most of the water out and hung the clothes on the line to dry. It was more complicated than that. She had to swing the wringer over two wash tubs, one with bluing agent, another with starch... but you've got the idea.

Golly, my dad was proud of that washing machine. He told everybody about it and a bunch of neighbors came over to see what the big deal was. Several of the men went to the store and bought their wives Maytag washers right away. Ranchers couldn't let someone outdo them.

Mom wouldn't let us work the washing machine. She worried about us getting our hands caught in the wringers. Instead she let us hand wash our underwear and fancy blouses.

She taught me tatting, how to make lace and crocheting. I learned to sew almost before I could walk and we made a lot of our own clothes using an old Singer sewing machine where we pushed a pedal with our feet.

Besides ironing and sewing, one of my jobs when I was small was picking beans. My father brought home pinto beans in 50-pound sacks that he bought in Douglas. Mom scooped out two cups of beans and I picked the beans out of the chaff, rocks and dirt. Then she washed and soaked them to soften them up for easier cooking in a traditional Mexican dish called *frijoles*.

Mom mashed the beans with lard, and there's nothing like lard for flavor. To spice up the beans, we added garlic, onions, cloves, green chiles, cumin, and cheese. We often cooked the beans with ham, fat back or salt pork.[9]

We kept one sack of beans in a barrel, cleaned and ready for cooking, and at least one extra sack for picking later because we always had company at dinner time. And they were hungry.

My poor mother made food out of nothing. She stirred up biscuits on the woodstove and plunked down beans with meat. Without refrigeration, it wasn't all that easy. Of course, things were eaten so fast around my place they didn't have time to go bad. My mother never complained. She came from the Goodnights, a Texas ranching family, and she learned from an early age that when you ranched you made do.[10]

My life as a kid was not all work. The ranch hands, section foreman, pump station people, farmers and highway crews had kids we could play with. We had races, and one of our favorite games was spinning tops. Mom bought slabs of Swift's bacon that dad loved to make for breakfast, and they were wrapped with butcher paper and heavy blue twine. I wrapped the blue string around the top, tied a slipknot on my finger, pulled it hard and *bingo*, it spun like crazy. First one kid set a top spinning, and then I spun my top and threw it, *kachung*, right on top of the other kid's top. With a good sharp nail on the bottom, it split the other kid's top open. We were ornery and got into fights.

Besides mortal combat using tops, we hiked, walked or rode our horses. I wasn't bored. When kids today say they're bored, I can't understand why. We played board games like Checkers and Parcheesi, and Mumbly Peg, where we threw our pocket knives at a board to see who could make it stick.[11] I never played much with dolls. I was more interested in catching and dissecting bugs. Our goal was to find the heart.

Just when my family was settled into living on the Malpais and following routines, things suddenly changed and our future was not so certain.

10. *Fleeing the Drought*

We still didn't know the results of Joe and Sam's appeal. Anything could happen. Prison was the biggest fear, and that would be catastrophic enough. But another calamity was looming. To say that it suddenly struck would not be accurate. This new misfortune sneaked up on us.

From May 1924 to April 1925, the entire state of Arizona saw only a little over 3½ inches of rain. At the end of August 1925, only .03 of an inch of rain was recorded for the whole summer.[1]

The state had had a drought for a couple of years, but the summer of 1924 began the worst drought in the west's history.

My dad saw it was getting bad. The dirt tanks had nearly dried up and the cattle had little water. We couldn't dig wells on the ranch because if you drilled a little ways into the malpais, the bit dropped down into a hole. There were holes under the surface everywhere.

At least the recession was over, the cattle business was flourishing again, and in June we had more good news. My brother Tom was born. The birth went well, and my mom spent another month in an apartment in

Douglas tending to him until she returned to the ranch. However, the drought was not going to let us rejoice for too long.

In the latter part of 1924, dad rounded up the family and the cattle, and we left the Malpais behind and traveled about 35 miles southwest to greener pastures on a ranch 15 miles east of Douglas called the John Slaughter Ranch, built by the famous lawman who died in 1922.[2]

The Hunt brothers leased the land from Slaughter's widow, and what was unusual about this ranch was that the border ran right through the main house. Part of the house was in Mexico and part in the United States. Our bedrooms were in Mexico and the kitchen and dining room were on this side of the border.

The ranch came with a lot of conveniences that we didn't have on the Malpais. Made out of thick-walled adobe, the five room ranch house was always cool in summer. It had a large pantry, kitchen, bathroom and a cowboy dining room. The property contained a stone ice house, a stone washhouse, granary, a commissary from which my mother sold groceries, and a car shed. My mom ironed clothes in the washhouse. The ice-house stored 300-pound blocks of ice hauled in by truck. A porch extended the length of the south side and the house had a hipped roof.[3]

The drought affected this ranch, too, but we didn't have to truck in drinking water or rely on surface tanks for the cattle. The ranch had a natural and plentiful supply of water from the Yaqui River drainage and from natural artesian wells.

Artesian water is often thousands of years old. Ranchers don't have to spend hard-earned cash drilling deep into the ground hoping to strike water. With artesian wells, pressure builds up between layers of rock, and when you drill even a small hole, it pushes the water to the surface. You don't even need a pump. The water, filtered through rock, is cold and sweet.[4] Artesian water is the best you can get anywhere.

John Slaughter's ranch was a cattle empire of 100,000 acres. My mother Sallie said that Slaughter owned the land on our side of the border, but not on the Mexican side. Yet he used the land on the Mexican side as if it were his.[5]

Dad grazed our cattle on the Mexican side and frequently went down there at night to tend to them. After the attempt by the Mexicans to confiscate the brothers' cattle over the border near the Rancho Sacatal years before, dad swore he'd never have anything to do with Mexico again. Sometimes you shouldn't swear because you might have to change your mind.

This time the Mexican government allowed the brothers to bond their cattle into Mexico and they could take them out at any time. Running cattle in Mexico was much the same as it was anywhere else. Dad used Mexican cowboys called *vaqueros* to help him with roundups and branding, and although the Slaughter Ranch had its own brand, we used the IV Bar brand from the Malpais.

My mom said that Mexican cowboys did not like crossing over to the U.S. side to work because they were afraid of being jailed as illegals. On the other hand, the Yaqui Indians on the Mexican side of the border often came across. Sometimes the authorities tried to catch them crossing the line (not that you could actually see the line separating the countries), but mom said she never turned them in.

"They would trust me and I would never do anything against them," she said. "Because those Indians... fought for our country... in World War I. But yet they weren't allowed to come over because they didn't have passports."[6]

The main reason mom didn't want to turn in the Yaquis was because they bought groceries from us. We often went to a grocery store in Douglas, stocked up on Mexican food and traditional American food, and sold goods to the Yaquis and Mexicans from the ranch's commissary, which was nothing fancy, just a room in the house.

Mom admired the clothes the Mexican women wore when they came across. They had big full colorful skirts, brightly-colored cotton blouses, and long *rebozos* or shawls with the ends hanging down over their backs. They often wore colored ribbons in their long hair.

Sometimes the Mexicans stayed for a while and cooked food. My mother loved Mexican food, but one thing she wouldn't eat was javelina. A javelina looks like a hog or wild pig, but is actually a peccary.[7]

The Mexicans showed my mom how to fix javelina. They cleaned it, stuffed the meat in two burlap sacks and then put it in a hole in the ground over hot coals. That barbecued it. She said no matter how much they cooked it, it was never done to her liking. Alongside the sacks of meat, they put a bucket full of beans. She liked them. After about 24 hours, they dug up the pig and put lots of pepper on it (they didn't care for salt), and ate it.

I've eaten it. Some people in Arizona hunt and eat them. Some say they taste like steak. I think they taste like pork loin. I had it done Mexican style, cooked in the ground, but it was well done and delicious.

Whether it was Mexican food or American, we ate well when we ranched. Maybe javelina wasn't to everybody's taste, but breakfast in our home was a big deal. This was dad's specialty. We ate oatmeal and cream, and I mean cream you had to dip with a spoon. And we had fruit, biscuits and meat. We made eggs every possible way. And we ate everything with a red chili pepper powder.

Making the powder was one of my chores. I put a red chili pepper on an anvil like you see at a blacksmith's shop, smacked the pepper with a mallet and popped the chili pepper open. I took out the seeds, and then pounded the chili peppers on the anvil until they were powdery. Then I pounded strips of dried beef we called jerky until they were powdery, too. For breakfast, mom or dad spooned bacon grease from the big can they kept at the back of the stove and put it in the skillet, browned it with flour, added the pounded pepper and jerky, stirred in milk, and made a gravy we poured over biscuits. We flavored it with seasonings from Mexico like oregano. Boy, we loved it.

And that wasn't all we ate for breakfast. Dad cooked hash browns, and served meat like ham, bacon or steak. We also liked what we called *mush*, which was cream of wheat. There were lots of biscuits, with butter, jam and coffee. Even as kids, we had coffee, mostly filled with milk.

Life on the Slaughter Ranch was like life on the Malpais, except with better water and more rattlesnakes. We had a cellar where they hung meat and a whole den of rattlesnakes took up residence. When we'd first moved there, my dad was in the kitchen at the table reading a book and my mother was in one of the back rooms with my sister Nell, she was just a baby, when a rattler slithered up the front steps from the basement and through the front door. It was about 10 feet from dad when he realized it.

"Oh, my God. That's a rattler," he said and pulled his single-action six-shooter from his pants and shot that snake's head right off. He said, "If you get into a bad situation, don't mess around with the rattles. That's the noisy part. Go for the head."

My dad was aware of everything that went on. You had to be to stay alive. By the way, it's a myth that cowboys always swaggered around with their guns stuck in their holsters. Where I lived, they stuck the pistols in the waistband of their pants.

Along with snakes, we had to deal with another vicious predator, the roadrunner, that large, long-legged ground bird with a head crest that fans up and down.[8]

That bird can run down its prey and jump up to catch grasshoppers or small birds. With its beak, it will grab a rattlesnake behind its head and smack it on a rock until it's dead. Okay, maybe a roadrunner is not as vicious as a rattlesnake to humans, but it was vicious to me. Here's what happened.

At the Slaughter Ranch, we had chickens, and I was out playing around the chicken house one day and heard squawking. I saw a roadrunner trying to get in to get the eggs. I sneaked up on him, grabbed him from behind, and he turned around quickly and clamped onto my finger with that treacherous beak. I screamed bloody murder, but he wouldn't let go. My mother ran out of the house, grabbed the roadrunner, rang his neck and threw him down.

He had lacerated my finger, and my mom took me into the house and washed it, wrapped it in gauze and taped it. She thought I was a hero for saving the eggs. I just wanted my finger back.

At the time of the Roadrunner versus Dorothy fight of the century, Uncle Joe was staying with us at the ranch. He was fourteen years younger than my dad, and the last of ten children, born in 1895 in Texas. The Arizona Republic newspaper described him as "nearly six feet tall, strongly built, athletic and handsome. He was also personable, well-liked, and, unlike most of his siblings, a gregarious extrovert."[9] The thing he loved most was a good glass of iced tea.

To me, Uncle Joe was a clown. He teased and teased and when he thought he'd teased me too much, he apologized, and then started all over again. He teased us about our freckles, he teased about anything. One time when I was older, I was in the kitchen preparing a button garlic to put in our dinner. He said, "Have you ever tasted it?" He told me to peel it and put it in my mouth and I did. I jumped around and spit it out. He thought that was funny.

Joe worked with my father, and they moved cattle back and forth between the Slaughter Ranch and the Malpais, changing the size of the herd on either property as the water and grass increased or decreased in volume.

Living on the Slaughter Ranch was not without its dangers. The brothers hired a Chinese farmer to tend things at the ranch, and one day a bunch of renegades killed him. They slashed up his mattress trying to find where he hid his money. You can see why my dad carried his pistol everywhere he went.

Uncle Joe must have felt like he was living in a nightmare. Everywhere he turned was peril. Renegades raiding and killing, Mexican bandits, rogue federal troops, and, if he survived them, he might still have years in the slammer ahead of him. He was doing all the difficult things you do as a rancher to build for the future, and all his efforts could be for nothing.

Uncle Joe was twenty-two when the shooting occurred. Now he was about thirty. I never saw him act out the stress he was under, but I can only imagine how worried he must have been. Jail? Freedom? Which one was it going to be?

More than seven years had passed since the killing. Although the second trial had ended nearly four years before, there had been no word on whether my uncles would go to prison or be able to go on with their lives.

When all of this started, Uncle Sam was thirty-two years old, born in 1885, four years after my dad. Now he was almost forty. Cousin Ken describes him as "a good-looking man, but a little shorter and stockier than his younger brother Joe. Sam was apparently rather shy."[10] Sam went to civil engineering school, but the only time I know he practiced his profession was in constructing houses on our various ranches.

As a child, I noticed that Sam was precise in how he dressed and how he kept himself. He always wore dress pants, had his shirt ironed and wore a tie.

He was the only one of the brothers who lost his hair on the top of his head. He started to lose it about forty-five or fifty. They say it's hereditary, but I don't know who else in my family ever lost hair. They used to tease my father about using color dye because he had a good head of hair, but he never did. All of us had good hair.

The brothers are the spitting images of each other so I can't imagine why Uncle Sam went bald. Maybe it was the stress from the trials.

I never knew him to work around the ranch. He was sensitive to people's feelings and thought about how they might take a certain statement. He never married and maybe that was because he felt for such a long time that his life was uncertain.

Everyone in my family was afraid about what could happen to Joe and Sam. I noticed the fear in their mannerisms, facial expressions and conversations. The apprehension affected everyone: the five brothers, their parents, their five sisters, cousins, spouses and children. Even though they tried not to talk about it, *the troubles* interfered with plans for the future. What do we do if Sam and Joe are freed? What do we do if they are sent to prison?

In December, 1924, my uncles got the final verdict. The judges in the Supreme Court of New Mexico declared they were *not* guilty of manslaughter and ordered them discharged. That night, Joe Hunt's friends in Bisbee threw a big party to celebrate their release. The rest of us celebrated at home.[11]

This whole episode raises a lot of questions. Why were my uncles and father charged in the first place? Why wasn't the shooting declared self-defense? Why were the Hunts made an example of? Some think it was political. Crime was out of control in the Old West, and the shooting was an incident that politicians, judges and prosecutors seized on to make a name for themselves, to make it look like they were tough on crime. I think they were irresponsible and my family suffered as a result of their grandstanding.

When Sam and Joe were set free, I was nearly five. The trials and my life on the Slaughter Ranch are a blur now. My cousin Ken (Norman Ken Hunt) wrote the ultimate book about the shooting and trials titled *The Killing of Chester Bartell*, an exciting and exhaustively researched piece of western literature.

After we got the final order about Joe and Sam, the year 1925 continued to feel like we were treading water, if you will pardon the irony of that comment. Because it was the worst year of the drought, and the worst drought year in the history of Arizona.

But in the summer of 1926, it started to rain. It rained in long dark sheets that streamed from the clouds. It rained all day and all night. It rained so long and so hard you thought Noah in his great boat would come around the mountain at any moment. The monsoon rains were torrential and unrelenting. Then in September, a tropical storm dropped an additional 5 inches of rain in southeast Arizona.[12] The rains flooded the washes and the draws and filled the surface dirt tanks at the Malpais.

The drought was over and we made plans to go home. We had been at the Slaughter Ranch about 20 months. I was four when we arrived, and six when we headed back. To me, going home was a continuation of my wilderness adventure. For my dad and his brothers and the adults in the family, they could breathe again and make real plans.

11. School Days on the Malpais

In June 1926, we headed back to the Malpais. I turned seven one month later and was looking forward to going to school. My mom was pregnant again, and dad didn't think I should start school in September until our new brother or sister had entered the world. So I worked on the ranch and prepared for the new arrival.

In November, mom went to Douglas to stay in an apartment as she usually did to be near the doctor. Tom, Nell and I went with her, dad stayed on the ranch, and in December my beautiful sister Elizabeth Mary Hunt, who we called Bess, said hello. She was a great Christmas present, just like my sister Nellie who was also born in December. Tom was born in June, which welcomed the monsoons, and the rains that made the ranch grow.

Now it was time for us to start school. Since there was no school building for miles, the railroad foreman had one built in a pasture near the Chiricahua Siding, the same place we got our drinking water for the ranch. The schoolhouse was humble in size, consisting of one room.

People referred to our school as The Chiricahua School, but we called it *Chiraca.* And it was not only for our family. The Yaqui Indian children of the men who chopped wood for the railroad attended with us. The Yaquis had big camps nearby, and they were often back and forth across the border. Their children were our neighbors and friends.

One day in January 1927, I got up early in the morning, as we always did, my father made breakfast, as he always did, and my mother fixed my lunch and got me ready for my first day of school.

We wore boots on the ranch, but dad said, "You don't go to school without your shoes. You don't go to school without your dress on."

He said I had to look ladylike, and not only did I have to wear a dress, I had to wear stockings or socks. Well, the boys wore jeans. I wanted to wear my jeans. I can remember lying in bed and thinking, *I'm gonna run away from home because my father said I can't wear them.*

Dad drove me in the Model T the 2 to 3 miles to Chiraca. Everything was new to me. We had to be at school on time by 9 AM. Even the Yaqui children had to be in school on time. The man who hired the woodchoppers, Mr. Rodman, made sure of that. If he didn't see their kids in school, he went to their homes to see why not.

We started school with the salute to the flag, sang a song, and then began our classes. We studied spelling and math, and you had better know your reading lesson.

We read books like *The Little Red Hen*, *This Little Chick* and *Three Little Pigs* and their moral lessons applied to living on a ranch. Work hard, don't be lazy, do the best you can.[1]

I got out of school in the afternoon around four, went home and did my chores. In the dead of winter, I couldn't do much because it was dark when I got home, but in the evenings I helped milk the cows and bring in firewood.

Then I did my homework and there was no tom-foolery. I sat at the table after dinner and my grandmother or my dad or mom sat with me. After Nell and Tom were old enough to go to school, the adults sat with all of us. They threw out words for us to spell and helped us with our math. If we had no homework, it wasn't fun and games. Then we had to help with the dishes.

One of my favorite subjects was history, but when Grandma Susan, my father's mother, helped us, *look out...* She knew history, she had lived it, she had gone to college and studied it. But when we got to the American Civil War in our class work, she refused to discuss it. She was from Virginia and Mississippi, and never forgave the damn Yankees for what they did to our family.

Not only was she unforgiving for Lucy's death, the loss of the family's plantation and our livelihood, she was also angry because of what happened to her father, Captain Sampson Leroy Harris. He was killed in action in Sharpsburg, MD, at the battle of Antietam.[2]

Grandma Susan and my parents were not the only taskmasters in the house who looked over our shoulders and corrected our mistakes. After we moved back to the Malpais, dad remodeled the house and added extra rooms. The teacher at Chiraca didn't have a place to live, and since we had an extra bedroom, she lived at our house. Now wasn't that a drag? Could we get away with anything?

And there was rarely an excuse not to go to school. In bad weather, it was too muddy for us to go in the Model T. Dad or mom then took us into the garage, put us up on a horse and covered us up with a big yellow slicker. A handyman took the reigns and led us to school. I could ride, but he had to take us because horses tend to shy when there's a slicker hanging over their backs. At the end of the school day, the handyman came back to take us home.

When it rained, Nell and I wore our dresses and shoes under the slicker, and the shoes got wet and were often ruined. It's too bad. We should have worn boots. *And jeans.*

For many years, we never missed a day of school. All the students used the same bucket of water, drank from the same dipper and never caught anything really infectious. If we caught a cold, that was no reason to stay home. A little cold never hurt anybody. You had to be really sick, I mean, violently ill to miss school. When my sister Nellie had rheumatic fever as a little kid and her nose bled all the time, she stayed home. That was a good reason not to go.

I enjoyed school, I loved learning, and especially loved recess. There was a watering trough out behind the schoolyard, and the teacher didn't care what we did at recess. We scooped snails and lizards out of the trough, sneaked up behind the new kids and stuck them on them. They screamed and yelled.

We played lots of games, but the most fun game was the most dangerous. Otherwise, why do it? We called it the *Johnny Stride* or *John-A-Stride Pole.* It was a rotary swing that was as death-defying as anything you can imagine.

Picture a tall metal pole cemented into the ground. At the top of the pole connected to a swivel were pairs of metal chains, and each pair was separated by metal bars attached horizontally. Each apparatus hung down just enough so we had to stretch our arms to reach it. The whole thing resembled a trapeze.[3]

We held onto the metal bar with both hands, ran around the pole and swung up and down. The object was to go higher and higher with our feet far off the ground. Then on the way down, we cut back and tried to get as close as we could to the pole without smacking into it. Good Lord... The teacher never said anything. Fortunately, none of us got killed.

A couple years after we returned to the Malpais, in 1929, my cousin Betty joined me at school. The Hunt brothers had purchased another ranch just northeast of the Malpais ranch house called the Webber Place, just 4 miles from Chiraca, for Uncle Jim and his family. His daughter Betty was two years younger than me and we palled around together.

At the time, my Uncle Charlie was the chief surgeon for Phelps Dodge in Bisbee. My father, as president of the school board, loaded all the students into trucks or cars and took us to Douglas. My uncle met us there and vaccinated everybody.

Uncle Charlie was an amazing man. By all accounts, he should not have lived past his teenage years. He was the oldest of the brothers, born on March 8, 1876, while the family was living in Como, Mississippi. When he was a teenager, he was accidentally shot in the chest with a small caliber pistol by his cousin, Stephen Leroy Hunt, when they were out squirrel hunting.[4]

The shooting occurred in the late 1880s or early 90s when surgery was very crude and sometimes barbers performed the most outrageous doctoring. They pulled teeth and performed minor surgery. The signs outside their shops often called them barber-doctors or butcher-doctors because many butchered cows in their spare time.[5] Lucky for Uncle Charlie he was operated on by an actual doctor, his uncle in Tulane, but he lost a kidney and his left lung.

As a result, he had a constant fever, was often seen bent over, and stood with a leftward slump. Nevertheless, he was so impressed with his uncle's medical treatment that he studied medicine at Stanford, and graduated in 1903 at the age of thirty.

He was a tall, slender man, and never was as physically active or robust as his four other brothers. Wherever he went, he carried a black valise filled with medical supplies and instruments. He nearly always dressed in conservative, vested suits and had a courtly manner and a good sense of humor.

Uncle Charlie did quite well financially, not so much from his doctoring or from infusing cash into his brothers' ranching enterprises over the years, but in mining stocks.[6] Although he did not provide physical labor on the ranches, he doctored everybody for free, including injecting all the school kids with the latest vaccine to fight off who knows what. It was not a procedure I looked forward to.

As it turned out, he didn't have to attend to the Chiraca children for very long. When I reached grade 4, the camp of woodchoppers closed down and the Yaqui children left, leaving only four or five of us to attend school.

As there weren't enough kids, dad shut down our one-room schoolhouse and sent most of us to Apache School in the little town of Apache.[7] The school was about 15 miles northeast of my house and about 10 miles from Betty's house. This was a much bigger school. It had *two* rooms.

In order to get to Apache on time, around 7:30 AM we shuffled up to the gate that led to the overnight pasture where we kept our horses and caught the makeshift school bus. The bus was a little old Chevy sedan touring car and was by no means luxurious. My father thought it was pretty crummy and used to cuss about that thing. It had two doors and a folding passenger seat in the front. They took the seat out to make access easier and then the only seat in front was the driver's. They put benches down the sides and along the back, and we could squeeze in seven kids.

I remember standing there with my little lunch pail waiting to get in while our dog Zip peed on a tire. Zip was a fox terrier with his tail lopped off so he only had a two-inch stub. He kept rattlesnakes away, and anything else that crawled. As far as his fondness for peeing on the Chevy's tires, perhaps he was expressing my father's negative feelings about the car.

The driver of the car often brought his young daughter. My brother Tom says he had a crush on her. "She was as big around as a TV set, but I thought she was pretty cute." That's what he says now, but we didn't have a TV set then. It hadn't been invented yet.

On the bus trip, we went to all the ranches to pick up the kids and it took about an hour on rough, rutted roads. Sometimes we got stuck in the mud, and the more the driver gunned the engine, the deeper he dug us into a hole. Everyone had to get out and push. If that didn't work, a rancher brought out a horse and pulled us out.

Happily, after I moved to Apache School for 4th grade, the teacher no longer lived with us. The school board furnished *teacherages* for them.[8]

We had two teachers, Mr. Coleman and Mrs. Keeling. Mrs. Keeling had her own little bitty house out in a pasture about a half mile from the school. Mr. Coleman lived on campus in the teacherage, located right on the playground. The teacherage had a bedroom, maybe two, a little living room/dining room combination, a kitchen, porch and a back porch. After a while, Mr. Coleman left and Mrs. Logan took his place.

You may not think it unusual today that we had *married* female teachers. Then it was very unusual. Often married women were not allowed to teach.[9] My dad and the school board ignored that restriction and offered a rent-free teacherage as an incentive, as not many wanted to live in a small community like ours and the salaries were appallingly low. The male teachers in Arizona received about $165 a month and the females about $119.[10]

At any one time, we only needed two teachers, one for each schoolroom. One room was for grades 1st through 4th and the other room was for grades 5th through 8th. There were about ten kids in one room, fourteen in the other. There were four of us when I was in the 7th grade, and when I got to the 8th grade, there were three, Benny Snure, Eula Olds and yours truly.

The teachers were usually kind and considerate. When it got cold during the winter, they made us hot chocolate on the cast iron woodstove, a big oblong thing. Occasionally, the wind blasted down the stovepipe and blew smoke and ashes everywhere. We had a metal plate underneath the stove, but the wood floor was oiled to keep the dust down. The ashes stuck to the floor and whatever you dropped on the floor, a pencil, eraser, paper, mitten, was dirty when you picked it up. Can you believe it, oil? The rooms were made of wood. With oil on the floor, the school was a dangerous fire hazard.

To make the rooms more presentable, Mrs. Keeling attached window boxes her husband had made and planted nasturtiums. We thought they were gorgeous. They brightened up the school with splashes of bright yellow and orange.[11]

For the most part, the teachers the school board hired were competent and we liked them. That wasn't always the case. My father once hired a teacher from Oklahoma and her husband was an insurance salesman. That was enough to turn my father off right away.

One cold winter day, my dad was driving down to meet another rancher, Gus Kimble, to take him to a school board meeting, and as he went by the school, he saw a kid sitting out on a stump of cordwood. He drove on and picked up Gus, and as they were passing the school, they saw a whole bunch of kids sitting out on the woodpile.

My dad and Gus drove into the schoolyard and got out of the car to find out why the kids were out there shivering, not learning a thing, their books beside them. They talked to the teacher and she said, "The kids won't behave."

My dad told her to get those kids back in and he never wanted to see that happen again. With only ten or twelve kids in the class, she couldn't keep discipline.

The school board started searching for a new teacher right away. I was fortunate she was not my teacher.

Most of the time, however, teachers seemed to like the kids. Otherwise, why be a teacher? They had to like kids because sometimes they were called upon to do things they'd rather have avoided, such as check our heads for lice.

They took a couple of rulers, pushed our hair apart and looked for something with legs. We called them nits, but those are actually the eggs. If the teachers found lice, they got the spray gun filled with kerosene, made you put your head over and sprayed the kerosene right into your hair. I had it done, but I don't remember if it hurt. I think I've blocked it from my mind.

One day my sister Nellie came home from school and my mother looked at her bangs and said, "You come here." She took her outside and saw a nit hanging from her bang. Well, you would've thought the world was coming to an end. My mother couldn't believe that Nell had a louse on her head. My mother got her nit comb and combed it out.

Lice are contagious and having them doesn't mean that kids are unclean or have poor hygiene.[12] We were very clean and yet sometimes we got lice, too. The Mexican kids who came in from Sonora sometimes had them. Just about everybody seemed to get them at one time or another no matter how much they washed their hair and took baths.

Every morning when I got on the bus with my brother and sisters, the bus driver and the other kids said all they could smell was soap and called us the Palmolive kids. That's because not only did we have the proverbial

Saturday night bath, but we also bathed during the week, which was not all that common then.

My dad regularly hauled in the bathtub and put it in front of the woodstove. Then he heated up the water in the stove, poured hot water in the tub, then cold water until the temperature was right. In a woodstove, there was a hot water tank in the fire chamber and that's where he got the hot water. Occasionally, mom heated up the water in a tea kettle.

Not only did we have frequent baths, we washed up every night. We had a foot tub to wash our feet and we did our hands and face in the sink.

I never wanted to be thought of as dirty and I abhorred kids who were grubby. I had a problem with one kid at school that never washed his hands. One day the teacher said this boy didn't have an eraser and I had to lend him one of mine.

"Dorothy, you have plenty of erasers," she said.

"No, I'm not going to," I said. I could be a stubborn thing.

"You lend him the eraser," she said.

I relented and lent him a pink one. They had only just come out in that color and I cherished it. He erased what he had to on his paper and gave it back. I threw it out the door.

"Would you like me to discuss this with your father?" said the teacher. I didn't want her to do that and went outside and picked it up.

When I got home, I told my mother what happened. "His hands are always dirty," I said.

"Maybe he doesn't have a place to wash them," she said.

I hadn't thought of that. I felt sorry for him, but I never lent him my eraser again.

12. Recess

We played a lot of games at school. One of them you may not think is a game, but we thought it was the funniest thing we did.

We had two outhouses at school, one for the boys and one for the girls. The moment we saw the boys go in, we picked up rocks and *bam, boom, bang...* we rocked the outhouse. Every time the boys saw the girls go in, they picked up rocks and threw them against the walls of our privy. We called it *Rock the Outhouse.* This may be too much country humor for you city folk.

We played real games, too, although some of us who attended that school might feel today that rocking the outhouse was the high point of our merriment. If you can believe it, we had an even bigger and better Johnny Stride Pole at Apache. There we flew higher, and we called that amazing achievement *Slicing the Pole,* although neither pole nor child got sliced or injured.

Amazingly, we were not allowed to have a regular swing set at the school. The powers that be (including my father) felt that swings were too dangerous. More dangerous than the Johnny Stride Pole? Maybe it was because we initially had swings at Apache, tried to see how high we could go and then jumped out of our seats when we reached the top. We even tried to get the swing to go over the top. Nobody broke a bone, but they took the swings out anyway.

We played a lot of less lethal games, too, like *Dodge-ball*, a game where you were encouraged to hit another kid.[1] Another game, one that was not banned, but should have been, was *Crack the Whip*. Everybody held hands in a long line and the leader started the line running in the schoolyard. At some point, the leader swung the others kids around in a semi-circle and the player at the end of the line usually fell on the gravel and skinned his knees.[2]

Like most kids, especially girls, we jumped rope during recess with three, four, even six kids participating. But these were no ordinary ropes. They were made of hemp that my dad had used and thought were worn out. They were old, dry, and sometimes broke due to rot.[3] They were fine for our purposes because we didn't put much stress on them. We weren't roping cows or tying up bundles of hay.

The tough hemp fibers, though, cut us behind the legs, and *whooeey*... they burned, and we went home with big cuts and abrasions. My mother put a yellow liquid called Caring Oil on the back of our legs, bandaged them up, and said, "Now, no jumping rope." "No, mom..." We did it anyway and never got infections.

Once in a while, we used a *reata*, which is a hand-braided cowhide rope about 100 feet long, for a jump rope, but they got stiff, not to mention heavy.[4] And if it ever caught you from behind, you were going down in the dirt.

Whatever game we played, we intentionally added more than a hint of peril. We played lots of baseball, and instead of those silly messes they call softballs, we used hardballs. We caught them with our bare hands and that is why my hands still have scar tissue. None of us threw the ball in that underhand girlie way either. We did it overhand and we threw it hard.

We played other dangerous games like *Anti-Over* where we had to catch a ball thrown over a building and *Red Rover* where you held hands with teammates and other kids tried to ram through your line. We ended up with sore hands, wrists and arms and lots of bruises. No one ever broke their arms, although I don't know why not. I often went home all banged up. Nobody said anything about it.[5]

As you can see, being a ranch kid was not all milking cows, roping steers and going to school. We made time for games and fun, just like kids in the cities. We raced, we played tag. Not kickball, we didn't have any kickballs. And we didn't play tetherball. We didn't play basketball at Chiraca. No baskets, no basketballs. Although we had one basket at Apache. We brought all the equipment we needed from home, and if we didn't have something, we couldn't play the game. No one ever thought of buying equipment for the school.

Not all our games were about seeing who could nearly get killed. I don't want to give you the wrong impression. We played peaceful games, too, like marbles.[6]

I kept them in white muslin tobacco sacks with yellow drawstrings. I got them from the cowboys my mother used to shop for. They gave mom money and a list of what they wanted and she went to Douglas and bought Tinsley chewing tobacco with the star on the top of the flat tin box and sacks of Bull Durham loose tobacco to roll their own cigarettes.[7]

According to urban legends, marbles are more than kid stuff. Squeezing an aggie is like a lie detector test that says if you are telling the truth (don't ask me how). An aggie supposedly improves memory and concentration, increases stamina and prevents insomnia.

Gosh, what did I do with my marbles?[8]

13. Readin', Writin', 'Rithmitic

I went to the one-room schoolhouse out in the pasture until grade 4 and then to the two-room schoolhouse up to grade 8. Don't let the size of the school or its location next to grazing cows fool you. Our hearts were big, our minds were bigger and the teachers didn't put up with nonsense.

They taught us the fundamentals well. We had to know our math, reading and writing. And we learned history, science and biology. Before I was allowed to graduate from 8th grade, we had to pass a test administered by the state. Among other things, we had to know the history of the state of Arizona, Arizona's Constitution, and the federal Constitution. We were not going to pass that test unless we were well taught, paid attention in school and did our homework.

Unlike bigger schools, we did not have a good library to help us with our studies. Apache had a tiny one that was only a few shelves of dog-eared books. But my parents created the next best thing. They furnished a lot of books for us to read, as well as an assortment of periodicals and newspapers.

When we went to Apache, everyday at noon we walked over to the store and picked up dad's newspaper and the mail that arrived on the train. Every evening after work, dad read the newspaper. Then he discussed stories and issues of the day. Like he'd tell us about something in the legislature and if it affected ranchers or parents or kids. He told us about unusual things from across the globe, what he thought about them and how we fit into the big picture. We were expected to read articles that he marked. He made us feel like we were part of the larger world, not only our stretch of sun-scorched desert in the state of Arizona.

We got *Time Magazine*, *Look*, *Life*, and *The Saturday Evening Post* and fought over them. We cut out pictures, hung them on a wall or put them in a stack. We got *National Geographic*, and I dreamed of going to some of those places. Mom got her periodicals like *Woman's Home Companion*, *Cosmopolitan*, *Red Book*, and *McCalls*.

McCalls had lots of recipes, but the main reason we liked *McCalls* was for the fiction stories called serials and the paper dolls and Betsy McCall clothes. Our newspaper was the late edition of *The Arizona Republic* out of Phoenix. Dad said it was the state newspaper. I didn't know that Tucson had a newspaper because the Republic was, as far as we were concerned, the *official* paper.

For a time, we subscribed to *The New Yorker*. It had the funniest jokes. Then dad found out and cancelled it. He thought it was pretty far-out, but we secretly ordered it again.

There was a little library in Douglas about 30 miles away partly over rough roads, but we didn't go there too often. Mostly, we exchanged books among family members. I loved books. I loved Charles Lindbergh's book titled *We* about his lonely non-stop solo flight across the Atlantic Ocean. I don't know how many times I read it.[1]

I loved short stories and history and often reread the books we had at home. I liked to read biographies about women and men that accomplished what they set out to do. I read about Madame Currie, who discovered radium and changed the way scientists thought about matter and energy; I read Abraham Lincoln's Gettysburg Address (forgive me, Grandma Susan). And I read poetry like *The Raven* by Edgar Allan Poe. "'Take thy beak from out my heart, and take thy form from off my door!' Quoth the raven, 'Nevermore.'"[2] We had lots of religious books, too. My mom bought whatever books we wanted.

Despite the remoteness of where I lived, I was not atypical in my desire to expand my mind and interests. All the ranch kids read a lot. Not the boys so much, but the girls, and sometimes we sat around and talked about books we'd read.

I often sat on the big porch in a rocking chair with a book in my lap. Sometimes I lay on a cot and dreamed of places and events I'd been told of like the American Civil War, which played a heartbreaking role in my family's life. That's why I was especially fascinated by *Little Women*, written by Louisa May Alcott who lived during the Civil War.[3]

I also read *Rebecca of Sunnybrook Farm*, the *House of the Seven Gables* and other books dealing with romance, mystery and history. I read *Daddy Longlegs*,[4] the story of an orphan girl growing up in an institution and how she eventually finds true love. The book's significance for me was the girl's lifelong letter writing.

I read those books on my own, but I'm sure many people wonder how I was able to learn anything in school when we had four grades combined. At Chiricahua, the teacher taught four grades in one room. Apache had two rooms, and the teachers taught four grades in each of those rooms, grades 1 to 4 in one room, and grades 5 to 8 in the other.

In grades 5 through 8, there were a lot of developmental differences. We could do some things together like our openings and flag salutes. After that, the teacher wrote the vocabulary for all four grades on the board and the students had to find the meaning. She started by introducing the vocabulary to one grade and then to the others.

We had a dictionary to look up the words, but primarily we had to find the words in our book or story. When we found the word, we tried to figure out what it meant from the way it was used.

Next, the teacher put questions on the board about the story and we answered them in our notebooks. Sometimes she made us put the words in sentences, but when she went over them, you better know them. I have to admit, I eventually became that kind of teacher.

After the teacher finished teaching one grade and got the students working on something, then she went on to the next grade. When she was done with all four grades, she went back to the first and reviewed their work. The kids learned because they didn't have a teacher there every minute to help them. They had to think like individuals and not rely on the teacher doing everything.

Sometimes the teacher had the 8th graders assist her in teaching. They administered spelling tests to the 5th graders, for example. We wrote down our words in our paper spelling tablet, and made the words big so we could hold up the tablet and show everybody. It was clever of the teacher to have the upper grades teach the lower grades. In case the older students forgot how to spell certain words, they were reminded and everybody learned.

Writing class was with all the grades. Math was individual. There was always a big assignment in the back of the math book and sometimes the teacher put problems on the board. At the end of the lesson, we went to self-help drills at the bottom of the page and the teacher timed how long it took us to do them.

Then there were the multiplication tables. Oh, my, yes... we knew our multiplication tables *or else*. We memorized them and repeated them so we wouldn't forget. Sometimes the teacher had everybody in all the classes repeat them together.

We studied history and geography and the teacher handed out map outlines for us to fill in the state names. Using our encyclopedia at home, we looked up what we needed to know to write articles. When we got to class, we gave our reports and answered questions about them.

Sometimes we got in discussion groups, and I felt that I got a lot out of listening to the students in the grade above me talk about things. That was one of the benefits of having combined grades. We got a head start on learning new ideas from the grades ahead.

It didn't bother me that the teacher taught another grade level while I was doing my work. That went on all the time. It improved our concentration and ability to focus. When you're in one room with different things going on around you, you develop good study skills from necessity.

As kids, we knew that we had a responsibility. Mom and dad's responsibility was to put bread on the table and provide a nice place to live. The kid's responsibility was to go to school, study, and achieve.

It's that simple. At least, it was then.

14. The Great Depression Strikes

After my uncles were acquitted of murder in the mid 1920s, what followed were a few years of great prosperity for my family. The demand for beef was high. Nobody talked about fleeing to Mexico or Brazil anymore, and it felt like a great black cloud had been lifted off our shoulders. Although my parents kept the worst of what had happened from us kids, I felt that everybody was happier and *the troubles* were over.

In the fall of 1929 a great tragedy struck the country. The New York stock market crashed. At nine years old, I didn't fully understand its significance, but when my father read the newspaper and discussed what was happening, I wondered if we would be affected. It wasn't like we were involved in the Wall Street stock market, although in one sense we were. We didn't have paper stock. We had *live*stock.

We were fortunate that, to an extent, the federal government helped us get through this awful time. The feds passed a law at the height of the Great Depression to buy our cattle or pay us a subsidy for them.[1] Although we now had water, we were still in a drought and few people were buying beef. It was not smart to have a lot of cattle and my dad sold off quite a few head through that program. Even though the price we sold the cattle at was low compared to what we were used to getting a year or two before, we knew things could get very bad if we didn't sell as quickly as possible. We'd lived through bad before and hunkered down to wait out the situation.

From 1932 to 1935, the newspapers and magazines reported on the dust bowl in the Great Plains that was driving people from their homes. They showed pictures of people with mattresses on top of their cars traveling to get someplace. Often they didn't know where they were going, just someplace other than where they'd been. I felt sorry for them as they didn't know what they were going to do when they got there.[2]

The papers told stories of thousands riding the rails and I was horrified that people were going hungry and didn't have a place to live. They told of teenagers, kids who should have been in school, their families too poor to feed them, taking off and riding trains, some to pick vegetable and citrus crops in California, cotton in Texas and Arizona, corn and wheat in the mid-west, many to nowhere. As many as 250,000 teenage hoboes roamed America. About ten percent of them were girls, often disguised as boys so they wouldn't be raped.[3]

I was ten in 1930, but by 1933 had become a teenager like so many other children across the country, and I couldn't imagine what it would mean to leave the ranch, leave my parents, leave the life I had known, and suddenly be thrown into a world of danger riding boxcars, meeting strange people, going hungry, not going to school, and focusing all my energy on trying to scrape up a meal.

I knew how lucky I was to have a place to live, with food on the table, and a family that had land and worked hard to keep it. I knew how lucky I was to be loved and surrounded by family that cared about me.

We didn't see a lot of wanderers where we lived, and we didn't need any more ranch hands. We were trying to ride out the Great Depression that President Hoover promised would end any day now. We were nearly self-sufficient and able to look after ourselves. Some of our neighbors and friends, however, needed help.

Dad was especially sensitive to people in trouble. He often patronized the Kress Five and Dime Store in Douglas and had become friends with the manager, Bill Gidley. Bill got appendicitis and had to go to the hospital to get his appendix out. When he was well, the store management just up and fired him.

These were hard times and a lot of stores were laying off or firing employees. But firing Bill because he had a medical emergency seems hardhearted. So you get a better appreciation for what I mean, Samuel H. Kress was a millionaire who made his fortune around 1900 on five and dime stores. Retired at the beginning of the Great Depression, he didn't know what to do with his money and thought starving folks would benefit from seeing his multimillion dollar art collection, which included 1,400 Old Master paintings.

In 1932, at the height of people's misery, Kress sent his collection on the road to dozens of cities across the country. I'm all for art shows, but with his vast fortune, why couldn't he continue to employ one devoted, competent manager who was ready to go back to work after his illness?[4]

Understanding the situation, dad invited Bill to the ranch and he lived with us for a few years until things got better and he could find a job. He was eventually hired by Phelps Dodge in their Assay Office, and in 1936 he married Josephine Jeffery, who was a nurse, and they had two boys. One of them joined the Merchant Marine.[5] If mom and dad had not given Bill a hand up, what would have become of him? Would he have gotten married? Would he have had children? And to think there were many thousands like him.

Bill was but one of many people my dad helped out. On the west side of our ranch lived the Krentz family. They had no place to water their large herd of cattle, but our huge surface tanks were still full from the monsoon rains. The monsoon rains can be fickle. It can rain on your property, but not on your neighbor's.

The Krentz's daughter told my dad they had no water and their cattle were going to die. Dad immediately took down the barbed wire fence between the two properties and let their cattle in to go to the water tanks. That's what you did for neighbors. We all helped each other. That's how we survived. At the same time, you didn't go to somebody's ranch and think you could just demand help. That's not how it worked. And you didn't take down a fence without asking.

During the Great Depression, my parents helped not only friends and neighbors, but, as you might expect, family members as well. Our relatives who lived in the cities came out to have a good meal and live with us anytime they wanted, but they were not allowed to sit on their duffs. Not on a ranch you didn't. Everybody had to work.

You might say my dad had a *food-for-work* program. We had meat and eggs and chickens and fresh vegetables, either from our garden or the neighbor's. In the winter, we had canned vegetables. We never bought meat at the market. We butchered our own beef, and, at one point, we raised pigs for pork and bacon, not something cattle ranchers did much. And mom canned everything, fruit, meat and vegetables.

Anybody who visited was immediately greeted with the refrain: "Are you hungry? Have you eaten?" We always had beans cooking and fresh bread in the oven.

The Great Depression didn't affect us as much as the people that lived in town, but we were careful. We didn't spend money for nothing and didn't waste a thing.

We got 100-pound sacks of flour, and with all the bread and pie baking mom did, we went through the sacks quickly. Then my mother cut up the empty sacks, soaked them in salt to soften them, bleached them, and made tea towels out of them. And, by golly, you didn't mess with her tea towels. You couldn't get large cotton tea towels that big in the store, not to mention that the price was right. Once softened, they also made good diapers

Like my mom, Betty's mother also bleached out the flour sacks, and used them for diapers and anything else that needed a soft cotton fabric like curtains or clothes. With all her baking, she had a lot of sacks, and between Betty's mother and my mother, they cornered the market on tea towels. They should have gone into business.

15. Food, Glorious Food

The newspapers were full of stories of people going hungry around our nation, and we were grateful that we didn't have to rely on anybody except ourselves for food.

We weren't sophisticated in our eating habits and neither was anybody who visited or stayed with us. We didn't serve any of that citified, pasteurized, over-cooked, low fat, no fat, tasteless chow. Our food was good, heavy, nutritious, and there was lots of it. It put meat on your bones for the heavy work expected from a ranch family.

In the morning, we usually had biscuits, butter and jam, oatmeal, milk, eggs and meat like bacon, ham, sausage or steak, and lots of coffee and milk. It was a hearty breakfast and everybody needed it for the workday ahead.

Breakfast was the big meal of the day, but by noon we were hungry again and wolfed down beans, potatoes, meat, bread, biscuits and milk. If we were planning on working cattle all day out on the range, mom packed us a lunch, stuffing our saddlebags with sandwiches or biscuits filled with meat.

After lunch, we went under a mesquite tree for shade, dad unsaddled the horses, and we opened our canteens and had a drink. Dad made everybody, including the horses, take an hour's *siesta.* We put our heads down on our saddles, closed our eyes, and before long we were saddling up and going back to work.

We started out early so by noon we'd already worked six hours or more. If we were rounding up cattle in the pastures, we couldn't stop for a rest. We rode the whole time and ate our sandwiches on horseback. We ate anything and everything. Sometimes we got down on our bellies and drank out of the dirt tanks, the cows slurping up water nearby.

We didn't always bring our lunch. Sometimes my mother cooked for the cowboys, put the food in the back of the pickup truck and drove down to where we were gathering cattle. We ate off the tailgate, devouring feasts of frijoles, short ribs or a big roast and vegetables like peas and corn. Then we really needed a nap.

As always, we worked until sundown, and when we got back, we milked the cows, fed the horses, carried in firewood and did anything else we hadn't done while out on the range.

Something else mom did in case we got hungry while on horseback was cram our pockets with beef jerky. Jerky is more than meat. It's legend, handed down over centuries. Native Americans originally made it from buffalo, elk, deer, and caribou, and used it to sustain themselves on long hunting trips through the backwoods. It never spoiled and they always had a quick meal.[1]

My father made jerky in the wintertime. That's when we killed the beef. Betty says when they butchered, they split up the meat among the families, hung the beef at night and wrapped it in a tarp during the day.

To make jerky, dad strung wire back and forth near the ceiling on our big screened-in porch. Then he cut the meat in real thin pieces using a skinning knife he'd sharpened on a whetstone. He discarded the fat because that would soon make the jerky taste rancid. He sprinkled salt and pepper on the thin strips and hung them over the line to dry.

We put a toothpick between the two ends of the meat so they didn't meet and stick together. The time it took to dry depended on if the weather was damp or dry, but it usually took a week. Afterwards, we put them in sugar sacks. They were like flour sacks, but about a foot wider. To keep the jerky from going stale, we hung the sacks where the wind got to them.

Sometimes we used the jerky for biscuit gravy by pounding jerky strips on an anvil until they had the texture of salt. The Indians called this concentrated stage *pemmican*, which means, roughly, "travel food made for long trips." They mixed the powdered meat with bear fat and stuffed it in a pouch.[2]

The best way to make jerky gravy is by mixing in pure lard. We never used artificial store-bought stuff like *Wesson Oil* or *Crisco*. We used lard that we had rendered up ourselves or bought in a 5-pound bucket.

For you city folk who don't know anything about lard, it comes from pigs and it's every cardiologist's nightmare. It's a shame that something so delicious is so bad for you.

You make lard by cutting up pork into small pieces and putting the chunks in a pot in the oven or in a pan on top of the stove. You keep turning up the heat until the fat renders out of the pork, fills the pan with lard and boils.

At this point, you can make *cracklins*. Cracklins are skin, fat and a small bit of meat. The lard deep fries the remaining skin and meat and turns the cracklins into crispy curls of golden pork.[3] You pour off the lard for the jerky, and then you take the cracklins out, lay them on napkins to dry, and salt them.

Cracklins are not good for you. They are high in fat and sodium. I didn't eat them; they are too greasy for my taste. But you can buy pork rinds or pork skins in the store today. They're similar, but don't taste as good as fresh cracklins from the stove, or so I'm told.

We put the cracklins in dog food. When we raised cow dogs in the White Mountains years later, my mother mixed a coarse cornmeal with lard, added in cracklins, salt, eggs, water or milk, whipped it up and baked it. It came out looking like cornbread and the dogs loved it.

Jerky was our thing. My brother Tom says when we were working the cows, we ate onion and beef jerky with cold biscuits, but it didn't do much for our halitosis. He says we washed them down with lots of coffee and never cleaned the pots, just added more grinds and water, and sometimes drank down baking soda to fight the acid stomach.

In case you haven't guessed, a cowboy's diet was pretty bad. We ate lots of beef, but few if any greens or milk. We had onions, maybe some dried fruit, but mostly meats and breads, and that's not enough. A diet like that can cause stomach problems. My Cousin Stewart down in Mexico had bleeding ulcers. To cure them, he ate nothing but rice and milk for a while and lived to a ripe old age.

When we were home at the ranch house, we ate good, healthy food. Maybe doctors would disagree because we used lard, but to supplement our fresh meat, we ate fresh vegetables and fruit. When they weren't in season, we ate them canned. My mother canned peaches, pears, strawberries, figs and apricots, and one summer when I was ten or twelve years old, I helped her put up 52 gallons of vegetables and fruits. Another summer, my mother canned 16 gallons of peaches alone.

Mom canned a whole lot of meat, too. Dad killed a beef calf, and then a pig, and mom made sausages. She got her big skillet real hot, (we only cooked on iron skillets, which are healthier for you), and she browned the sausages on both sides, added gravy, stuffed them in number 3 cans, poured the drippings from the sausages over them, and then put them in a pressure cooker to seal the cans. We ate them during the winter, and man they were good.

Our garden was essential for fresh vegetables and good health, but it began as an educational project for my brother Tom. When he was about seven, we went to my Aunt Lucy's house outside of San Antonio, Texas, for a visit. She was my father's oldest sister. One day Tom ran in and said, "Oh daddy, come out here. There's a tomato growing on a weed."

When we got home, my dad said, "I'm not going to have one of my kids that dumb."

And he put in a vegetable garden. Dad hauled water and poured it in tanks so we could water our tomatoes, green peppers, chilies, squash, and green beans.

Tom never said he thought a tomato grew on a weed again.

Our garden came in handy when it was time for our evening meal. We often had fresh vegetables, hominy and potatoes with our meat, sometimes what was leftover from lunch. We had beans every meal except breakfast and augmented our dinner with hot, pickled or plain peppers. Mexicans generally have beans for all three meals.

Best of all, mom baked a hundred different kinds of bread. I especially liked what we called "light bread," made from pancakes, muffins and cornbread. When we came home from school on the day she baked, we could smell the bread way up at the gate as we got off the bus and we ran toward the house to get some.

Mother baked bread two days a week and it was hard work. Dad dumped 100-pound sacks of flour in a big bin where rodents and weevils couldn't get at it and mom scooped the flour out of the bin and mixed her dough on a big sideboard. She put dried yeast in warm water to start it working, put it in the bread and kneaded the dough.

Then she put the dough in the warming oven on top of the woodstove and watched it rise. She poked it down, then it rose again and she baked it. She did it early in the morning and by late afternoon it was ready to bake. She stoked the oven with wood and shoved in her loaves of bread on 6 inch by 4 inch bread pans.

The best part of the bread when it's hot is the heel. And she didn't make just bread. She made cinnamon rolls and what we called *rusk*. She mixed sugar, cinnamon, raisins, and sprinkled them into the dough.

Today it seems impossible, but she learned to bake and cook on a woodstove. Woodstoves hold heat evenly and she learned when to stoke it with wood and when not to. She made fried chicken using a cast-iron skillet for deep frying. On Sundays we had chicken and dumplings. She killed the chicken and dipped it repeatedly in boiling water until the feathers came off easily. Then she picked out the feathers, especially the pin feathers, and when it was clean, boiled it. She rolled out biscuit dough and dropped pieces into the pot until they cooked.

We raised our own chickens, mostly Plymouth Rock and Leghorns. My father didn't like the Leghorns because they didn't have as much meat on them, but they are great egg layers and can drop about 300 eggs each year. That's a lot of eggs for one hen and we had lots of hens. No wonder the foxes and roadrunners tried to get into the hen house.[4]

Even though we had an abundance of eggs, we never sold them. With so many people visiting and staying, particularly during the Great Depression, we used them for our own meals.

Mom also cooked wild duck that we raised for that purpose, and fed them corn and wheat. Mallards are especially tasty, but only if you soak them in a marinade. Otherwise, wild duck will taste muddy.

We raised turkeys, too, mostly for the holidays. We had one old mean gobbler who put his head down, tried to bite us and chased us out of the yard. Then we had guinea hens resembling big partridges that hung out at our huge woodpiles.

We never ate the guinea eggs or the guinea hens. Because if anything came around like skunks, coyotes or foxes to get at our chickens, the guinea hens made loud, harsh, piercing sounds and either scared them off or alerted us to the problem. They are a great help around the ranch. They eat flies that the cows attract and gobble down worms, ants, spiders, and ticks that the dogs could bring into the house.[5]

We ate a lot of Mexican dishes. Mom made empanadas out of dough with cooked fruit inside like dried apples or apricots. We called them fried pies, but they're a Mexican specialty and you could have them for dessert or breakfast with fillings like pumpkin, yams, sweet potato and cream. Instead of fruit and vegetables, you can add beef, chicken or cheese. Anything goes.[6] Sometimes we took them with us on horseback during roundups for lunch or snacks.

Mom cooked outside a lot in summer so the house didn't get too hot. One of our staples was *tortillas*. Tortillas are not tortillas unless they are made with lard and show dark brown spots after you cook them.[7]

Mom made green corn *tamales*,[8] too, but a *sweet* tamale, well, you must... Come Christmas, my mother made what Mexicans call *tamales dulces*. Why only then? Because even with help, it can take two days to prepare them.

First, the corn had to be shucked and the kernels cut off the cobs. Then you separately prepared the masa (corn flour and lard, soaked in mineral lime water) and the sweet filling. The filling can contain ingredients like raisins, crushed pineapple in heavy syrup, honey, nutmeg, ginger, cardamom, coriander and Mexican vanilla (the only kind to use). The filling is not the only thing that's sweet and savory. The masa can contain roasted pecan meal, lots of brown sugar, lard (of course), and cinnamon.[9]

Most Christmases we returned to the John Slaughter Ranch, and the Mexican women brought sweet tamales in oversized enamel wash pans to the house to repay dad for giving them beef. My brother Tom said that he can never find a tamale that tastes as good as those we had for Christmas or those my mother made.

The tamales were superb, but when we were kids, tamales didn't hold a candle to the ice cream and custard we made. In the summer, we went to the Ice House in Douglas and mom bought two 100-pound blocks of ice. We wrapped them in old Army blankets, swathed the blankets in newspaper and shoved them into the back of the truck. When we got them to the ranch, we lifted them out of the back with tongs we used for lifting hundred pound loads of hay. No wonder everyone in my family had a bad back. We wrangled the ice into the bathtub or a cool spot and then broke off chunks with an ice pick.

It was a lot of work making ice cream. Mother used heavy cream from our cows' milk to make the custard, and then we had to crank a gizmo like a butter churn for what seemed like hours.[10] But it was worth the effort, for more reasons than you can imagine, as I relate the next story.

The JC Penney department store in Bisbee was having a fall show and my cousin worked at Penney's as a comptroller. She told us that a wool blanket was frozen in a 100-pound block of ice and the person that was the closest in estimating when the ice would melt would win the blanket.

I was in 7th grade and made a calculated guess. After all, I'd had some experience with melting ice. I won. Or so I thought. My aunt, Uncle Charlie's wife, said that a kid shouldn't have won. My cousin from Penney's became angry, and said, "Dorothy is the one that entered, and it's in the newspaper about how long it took to melt. She guessed right."

I think this started a family feud. Anyway, that was the first thing I ever won and my parents were happy for me. I don't know what they did about my aunt. After that, I don't remember getting a Christmas card from her.

16. Mom and Dad

I know I've made my father seem like a candidate for the Best American Father Award, but things didn't always go smoothly between us. One encounter, in particular, became a turning point in our relationship.

My father always told the truth. He believed it made you a better, more moral, person. I took this seriously, so when I was accused of lying, I was crushed.

We had a 50-gallon barrel of fuel on the ranch in order to fill the gas tanks in the cars and run the water pump. Since we had no other source of energy, the fuel was our most essential power source. The barrel sat on a stand, and in order to fill up a car's tank, we put a gas can up to the spigot and turned it on. After we filled the can, we turned off the spigot, and then took the can over to the car and filled it up.

I was about ten years old on this momentous day. My dad called me over because somebody had left the spigot on and all the gas had run out onto the ground.

"Have you been playing around the barrels?" he said. "Why did you turn the spigot on for the gas? Were you getting gas?"

"No, I didn't do it," I said. "I never touched it."

"But you did," he said. "All of it has leaked out and you're the only one that could've done it. You were out there."

Then he spanked me with his hand like I was a three-year-old who had put her hand on the hot stove. He'd never done that to me before. My mother had swatted me on my legs with a flyswatter if I'd defied her, but my father had never disciplined me physically.

I was humiliated because I was a young lady and a conscientious kid. Our relationship was built on trust. If he couldn't trust me anymore, what was I going to do? I was sullen during dinner, did my homework and went to bed.

The next day, Uncle Jim came to the ranch. He'd been in Douglas and this was the first opportunity he'd had to talk to my father.

"You know what, Jack," he said. "I got into town, and I remembered I hadn't turned off the gas and I'm sure it all went out on the ground."

After he heard that, my dad grabbed me and hugged me and said that he would always remember this incident. That he didn't want me to be angry with him, and that for now on if I told him something, he'd never ever not believe me. He felt so bad that he cried.

That was a defining moment in our relationship. I knew I was no longer a kid. Now he knew it and we began an adult friendship.

One of the reasons that incident happened was because my dad was prone to flying off the handle before checking the facts of a situation. He wanted things to go his way, and when they didn't, he got upset. My mom was the calming influence in the family.

She batted her eyelashes at him and he melted. She had long black curly hair down to her waist or done up in a knot on the back of her head. She braided it sometimes and wrapped it around. Her hair was thick and heavy, but she started getting gray when she was young, in her forties. She wore little turquoise or black or brown combs in her hair on the side to hold it back and keep it in place. Dad was still infatuated with her.

She didn't have her ears pierced, but wore clip-on earrings. She never wore them at the ranch. With all she was doing, they'd probably fall off and end up in the bread dough or jerky gravy. She wore the earrings when she went to town or got dressed up to go someplace.

She sometimes wore plain cotton dresses, but also a lot of pants and work shirts because she rode on horseback with my father so much. While taking care of the house and kids, sewing clothes, making food, and doing the laundry, she made time to go out on the range, although not as much as Tom and I went out with my dad. She cooked for everyone, including the cowboys, and for a while she was a little on the heavy side from tasting her own good food. Then she lost that weight.

My mother was cheerful and took the bright side. She said things to my dad like "Don't let that upset you," and, "Sure, it'll work out." My father, on the other hand, worried about everything. My mother didn't, and I think that's why they did well together.

It also helped that my mother was gifted mechanically and could take apart a motor, put it back together and it ran. My father didn't have the patience for it. If my dad took something apart, he usually had a piece left over and the darn thing wouldn't run. He had quite a temper, and fumed and cussed and when he was totally exasperated called for my mother.

My mother put down her dishcloth or the paper and came outside and took over. "Now, Jack, calm down," she said. "I'll take care of it." She took out each part, cleaned it, put it back in, and the pump motor, fan or car engine worked fine after that. She had the knack.

Another time, we had to build chicken coops for the old biddy hen to lay her eggs. We knew you didn't ask the men to do it. They'd get a square and a leveler, and when they got through, the chicken coop was still unfinished or not level or things didn't fit properly. The ladies built the chicken coops a lot better. They didn't need the levels and all the tools men salivate over at the hardware store. The ladies, my mom and Aunt May, Betty's mother, got the lumber, held it up to the light, got the saw, sawed away, and everything fit.

My mother was good at delivering calves. My father was quite a veterinarian. He could doctor a horse or cow and we didn't lose any from sickness. A lot of people did. Like if the cows ate something poisonous like locoweed my parents knew what to do with them. They were a good team.

Apart from being mechanically challenged, my dad interacted well with my mom. They talked over the things they were going to do. Mother knew what dad planned for the day and dad knew what she planned. They visited each other frequently during the day and spent time together. They liked each other and got along well. I don't remember my mother ever being mad at my dad. Well, I shouldn't say *ever*. She used to get aggravated because he ate crackers all over the house after she'd cleaned and there were crumbs everywhere.

According to my mom, there were a few things that you just didn't do. You didn't wear your spurs in the house. You didn't wear your hat in the house. You came to supper when you were called and you didn't dillydally. They didn't have big fights. And if dropping crumbs was the only thing they fought about, their relationship was pretty sound.

Sure, he had a temper sometimes, but never directed it at my mom. He directed it at machines that couldn't fix themselves and at people that weren't honest. He would have a snit about that. If you made an arrangement with him, he took you at your word and you shook hands on it.

He believed in the basic decency of human beings and never locked our house. After my father bought his first house in Tucson many years later, he couldn't get over the fact that you couldn't leave your house open.

The only thing that rankled my mother, besides dad dropping cracker crumbs on her clean floor, was what my father did when they went to big parties. Although there were lots of people to talk to, before you knew it, my father, Uncle Jim and Uncle Joe were over in a corner chewing the fat instead of visiting other folks.

Mother cornered them and said, "I do not want to see you people standing together. You should visit with everybody else."

To please my mom, they broke up their little summit and started to mingle. Five minutes later, they were back in their corner arguing about something. My father's favorite topic with Uncle Jim was about Los Angeles stealing all the water.

Los Angeles stole the Owens River water, diverted the snowmelt that flowed from the Sierra Nevada, and then set its sights on the Colorado River where Arizona gets a big portion of its water. That enraged my dad's sense of fair play and they really got into squabbling.[1]

My uncle and dad endorsed Mark Twain's saying that "Whiskey is for drinking, and water is for fighting over."[2]

17. Preachers, Salt Licks and Bugs

Another topic my father liked to talk about was itinerant preachers who wandered from town to town punching the Bible and looking for handouts. Just like everybody else, preachers on the pulpit circuit were having hard times during the Great Depression. My father tried to make them feel welcome, but his heart wasn't in it.

An old itinerant preacher turned up at our school every now and then on a Friday and announced if there was going to be preaching on Sunday. Though not religious, we regularly went to his sermons. I don't remember much of what he said. I knew when to say *Amen* and it was a lot of times.

When an itinerant preacher preached, he tried to represent all denominations from Catholic to Baptist to Methodist and Presbyterian, or so it seemed to me. And he was prepared to preach on any subject at any time for any audience.

One preacher I remember did a regular sortie on Apache and Chiricahua. The mothers scrubbed their kids' faces and took them to the makeshift church at the two-room schoolhouse in Apache. There weren't many social events out in the boonies and this was an event that allowed everybody to dress up in their best clothes. For the boys and girls who had entered puberty, this was an opportunity to check out the opposite sex.

After the collection plate was passed around, the preacher filled his pockets with change and greenbacks. When you add in the extras like gas, food, and lodging in our homes, he made out like a bandit during very tough financial times for the area's inhabitants. I'm not saying that the preachers became rich, although I'm sure some subsisted handsomely.[1]

In fact, some towns banned itinerant preachers because they horned in on the local pastor's bounty and drained the collection plate. That didn't happen in our little town because we didn't have our own pastor and relied heavily on the itinerant preachers for salvation. Based on the number of preachers who came through, we were saved so many times the whole community would have had no problem marching into heaven with a brass band at the head of the line.

I started going to these little revivals when I was about ten. Mother baked bread and other goodies for the event and the preacher took home what was left over. The sermons were about an hour, which wasn't too bad. To keep the little kids from squirming in their seats, they were allowed to scribble with crayons in coloring books. After the sermon, we went to Sunday school where the preacher read us a text and we discussed it. That was okay. I didn't have to say *Amen.*

Some of the sermons were fire and brimstone with lots of Bible thumping and shouting. There were two or three regular preachers that ranted and raved. Some ranted and raved more than others. And the stories were mostly of hope, which uplifted many people during that difficult time.

We had a banged up piano at school and my father arranged for somebody to tune it up for the revival. The preacher's wife played the piano and led us in singing religious songs. Dad thought it was all right if Tom and my sisters and I attended and got religious instruction so my mother and grandmother took us. Dad was too busy. In truth, he couldn't stand it.

Often the itinerant preacher and his kin came to the house for dinner. We didn't invite them. They just showed up at dinnertime and invited themselves. Then they needed gas for their car and dad pumped the gas out of the barrel and filled up their car.

Whether they were preachers or just plain folks, we felt sorry for the people caught in the grip of the Great Depression. We talked to people who had lost jobs or came to the ranch needing food. That made it personal.

We did the best we could to grow up like normal kids during an abnormal time for the nation. It's one of the reasons we were interested in nature, so we didn't have to think about how bad off people were. Sometimes I sat and watched bugs or ants move a blade of grass or a snake dig a hole. The simple things amused and intrigued us.

I watched cows chew their cud. The juice spilled out of their mouths down over their chins. Sometimes it was green, sometimes purple, depending on what they were eating. I thought, *Oh, that looks good.* So I chewed up some grass and it was awful. Cousin Betty got down on all fours and licked the salt block we put out for them. She said it didn't taste half as good as it looked.

My brother Tom and I aspired to be cowpokes. When we were quite young, we watched the cowboys branding.

We cut the bottom off a clothes hanger and bent it with pliers to look like a branding iron. We put it in the same fire the cowboys had their irons in and got it red hot. Then we branded our cattle, which were corn cobs.

There were a lot of insects on the ranch. Glowworms, ants, beetles, and not all were benign. When I was nine, I was stung by a venomous Arizona Bark Scorpion and I darn near died.[2]

I had gone to the outside privy and sat on the seat and that's when the little scorpion got me right on the hip. You want to laugh about it now because of where I was when it happened, but I wasn't laughing then. It didn't just hurt, it burned.

I screamed and ran to the house. Luckily, my father was home. My parents put me in the car and we started for Bisbee where my Uncle Charlie was. I was in such pain and it spread through my body.

When we got to Bisbee, I told my mother, "I can't breathe."

"You have to," she said. My throat was swelling up.

We got to my grandmother's house and my uncle came right out. He said, "We've gotta get morphine in her. And get a pitcher of ice water. She has to continually drink. It's the only way we're gonna get the poison out of her system."

Every few hours throughout the night Uncle Charlie gave me a tablet of morphine for the pain and swelling. Mom kept a glass of water by the bed and I drank gallons. Finally, I got to feeling better. But for months if I sat down to milk the cows or do anything, my knees hurt bad as a result of the poisoning.

Years later when I was living in the White Mountains, I was saddling my horse, stuck my finger under the saddle and a big scorpion bit me on my middle finger. I started screaming because I knew what it meant. It was a lot harder to find a doctor this time.

My mother said, "Wait a minute. I know what to do."

She submerged my finger in a glass of cold, sour milk, and I kept it there for more than an hour. My mother said the sour milk would draw out the poison. Sure enough, it worked.

We dealt with bugs all the time. But we had to find ways to eliminate them around the ranch so they didn't kill us or drive us insane.

Every morning after breakfast, especially during the summertime fly season, mom filled a tank connected to a FLIT Gun with insecticide. She pumped the plunger on the back of the gun and sprayed the corners of every room. Then she swept or mopped the floors and found dead flies, mosquitoes, sugar ants, centipedes, and stink bugs. When Black Leaf 40 came out, my mom thought she had died and gone to heaven. After she sprayed with that, we never had any more ants.[3]

We didn't have a refrigerator, so we kept insects off our food by putting leftovers in a pie safe that sat on the kitchen counter. It was a high box with shelves, had tight joints and a close-fitting door, yet had enough humidity to keep pies and other food moist. And it had tiny perforations in the door that were so small that ants and gnats couldn't get in, but air could still circulate to prevent mold.[4]

We all have milestones in our lives from which we mark time. Age nine was my year for the Arizona Bark Scorpion sting that nearly killed me. However, age nine was not through with me yet.

It was also my year for an unexplained illness. In the spring after I had finished grade 4, I got very sick. I couldn't get out of bed. I had no energy. The whites of my eyes turned orangey-yellow. Even my hands turned yellow.

Uncle Charlie came out to see me, told us I had Yellow Jaundice[5] and it was quite contagious. My poor mom had to boil everything that I touched, anything I ate from or drank out of. And everybody stayed away from me. I don't know how I got it, but nobody else in the family came down with it.

I lay in bed for six weeks. I didn't feel like eating and got quite thin. Then one day I smelled string beans that my mom was cooking on the stove. That was the first time I felt interested in food since I got sick and I ate some string beans, drank lots of soup, and from then on didn't have a problem eating.

After I got over it, the skin on my hands peeled. Gross, huh? I don't know if I really had Yellow Jaundice. Nothing explains the peeling hands.[6]

Years later I went to give blood, I wanted to be a good Samaritan, and the nurse asked, "Have you ever had hepatitis?"

I said, "I don't know. I turned yellow once."

She didn't think that was very funny and said they didn't need my blood after all.

18. Roundups and Mountain Oysters

After my sickness, I quickly got my energy back. It was the summer and we had work to do on the ranch. And no matter what job we did, we were expected to tough out any situation.

Like the time Tom and I were driving a bunch of cattle toward the barn. A cow shot out of the group and off I went to cut the cow back. My horse stepped in a gopher hole, I saw his neck go down, and he rolled over to the right side and I fell with him. I hurt my back, but I got back up on him and we finished our job.

Those gopher holes were dangerous, and they wrecked the dirt tanks. The rodents burrowed down into the earthen dams, made little holes, and the water streamed out. Before you knew it, the whole mile long tank was running into the ditch. If there was Bermuda grass around the tanks on the dams, one of our jobs was to pull it out because the grass attracted them.

If we spotted a hole, we put mothballs in it and covered it up. Gophers won't come back. Another thing we did was stuff poisonous castor beans in the hole, cover it up, and tamp the dirt down.

We often rode along the dirt tanks checking for gopher holes to plug. If nobody was looking, we jumped in the water and went swimming. When we got out, we were always covered in black leeches. We just pulled them off. It was no big deal.

Sometimes we went out on the range in winter and it got cold on the Malpais. Temperatures got as low as 40 degrees or even below freezing.[1] No matter how cold it got, cows had to be fed. We bundled up by pulling on long johns, flannel shirts and a heavy denim jacket called a *booger red*, named after a famous Texas bronco rider named Booger Red who rode in the late 1800s up until the day he died in 1926. He got his name at the age of thirteen after lighting up a load of gunpowder he'd stuffed into a bored out tree stump. The resulting blast nearly killed him and he was so ugly after that people called him Booger Red because of his red hair and ruined face.[2]

The jackets were made out of denim or a reddish chap leather and adorned with metal buttons. They were lined, which made them real warm, had big pockets on either side, and had a corduroy neckpiece you could turn up under your Stetson hat to keep the rain off your neck.

They weren't ugly like Booger Red was purported to be, but I think they got their name from being red and durable like the cowboy. Nothing could tear them, shrink them, drown them, or wrench them out of shape.

To further complement our winter gear, we wore chaps and *tapaderos*, or *taps*, which are long, pointed, leather stirrup covers. They enclosed the front part of our boots and prevented our legs from being stabbed by cacti and thorns. In winter, they kept our feet warm.[3]

Wearing our booger reds and taps, we rounded up cattle in the fall and then again in the early spring after the new calves were born in February. Our neighbors helped and we went to their spreads to help them. That way nobody had to hire on extra hands.

When my dad and uncles branded cattle, sometimes Nellie and I sat on the fence and watched. They had two irons in the fire, the stamp iron and the running iron. The stamp iron had the full brand on it and the running iron had a hooked tip.

The cowboys burned the IV Bar brand into the back hip of the cows with the stamp iron. The brand was constructed with the "V" under the "I" and the "Bar" was drawn under them.

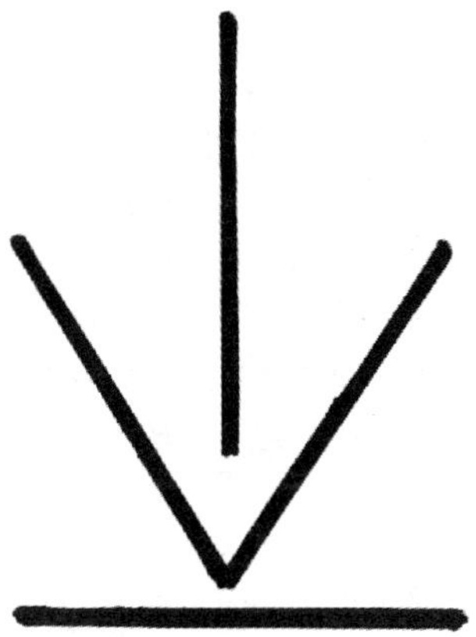

We preferred a complicated brand because that made it difficult to re-brand a cow if somebody stole it.

Cattle rustlers used a running iron to alter brands, but we used it if the stamp iron didn't come out clearly. In some places, having a running iron in your possession meant you were a thief and vigilante groups hanged you on the spot.[4]

I found out the hard way just how hazardous a running iron could be. To prevent screw worms or infection, we soaked a piece of burlap in a bucket of water mixed with creosote and a little bit of alcohol, wrung it out, and then rubbed the brand with it so the burn turned pink and scabbed over. My uncle Jim had just finished branding with a running iron, and as I leaned over the calf and started scrubbing, he threw the iron back toward the fire, but it caught me across the side of my face.

It seared my cheek, but I had my hand in the bucket and threw the mixture of water, creosote and alcohol on my face. He apologized, but I shrugged it off and went back to work. The wound didn't get infected and left no scar and I never had a tetanus shot until many years later.

Branding the new calves was one of the most important jobs during the roundup. One time, my mother's aunt's daughter, Ruth, and her kids came down to watch. I didn't say anything, but thought, *Wait until these city slickers smell the burning from the brand.* Uncle Jim pressed the brand against a cow's hide and you could hear the sizzling, see the smoke, and smell the singed hide. The oldest kid was okay. The eight-year-old screamed and ran for the house.

Cousin Ruth held up her camera to take pictures when Tom whetted his knife and then sliced the bottom off a bull calf's scrotum, cut out the testicles and threw them in a bucket of water.

"I hope you saved the testicles to eat," I said to Tom.

"Of course, I did," said Tom.

We were such brats. We ate all those things: testicles, brains. My cousin got queasy and never did take a picture.

Bull testicles are known as mountain oysters, prairie oysters, cowboy caviar, calf fries and a bunch of other names.[5] We didn't want the male calves growing up into bulls because you don't need too many bulls around pawing the dirt and getting into trouble. A bull can grow to over 2,000 pounds and he'll push through a barbed wire fence and not notice the barbs. By castrating them, the steers grow meatier and are easier to control.

The morning after a roundup, we peeled the testicles, washed them, rolled them in cornmeal, added salt, and fried them up in a skillet. In the Wild West, cowboys tossed the meat onto a hot iron stove, and when they exploded, they were done.[6] I don't think there's anything a human being won't eat.

Roundups were a lot of work. We roped and branded, castrated the males, counted the stock, and doctored. The calves sometimes got screw worms around the cord or on a wound as a result of branding, dehorning, or injury, and we put chloroform on a piece of cotton, placed it on the wound, and the worms fell off.[7] Then we washed the wound with a solution of half creosote and half water to prevent infection and to keep the flies away.

Another task we performed at roundup was cropping the calves' ears so at a distance we saw if it was our cow or our neighbor's. On the IV Bar, we undercropped on the left side by cutting a little wedge out of the ear.

Our work was still not done. With calves that showed developing horns, we dehorned them. Even heifers grew them. Otherwise, they could be dangerous during a roundup or doctoring procedure. A cow can easily injure another cow, ram your horse and tear open your leg or stomach with its horn.

Dehorning was demanding. When dad sawed off the horn, often there was blood. He had to quickly take a hot poker from the fire and cauterize the site of the horn. You have to dehorn the calf when it's young and not wait for it to get bigger. The more mature the animal, the greater the blood supply to the horns and it got very messy. If you were not fast enough with the hot poker, the animal could bleed to death.

Working cattle was not easy. These are very strong animals, even when they are calves and look so sweet with their big blue eyes and long eyelashes (if they're Herefords). Big or small, they will sometimes put their heads down and ram into you, or throw their heads to the side and hit you hard with the top of their skulls. Sometimes if they are along side you, they will kick up their back legs and hit you in the ribs, leaving bruises and sometimes broken bones. That's why we rarely got off our horses. If we had to get off to brand, we tied their legs and made sure they were down.

My father learned firsthand how crotchety they can be when a cow stuck a horn through his hand. It was bleeding profusely and he went to the house to get mom. The horn had sliced through just below the thumb. Mom poured a mixture of medicines in the hole and the liquids ran out the bottom of his hand.

To heal wounds, even big wounds, we mixed turpentine and laudanum. The laudanum relieved the pain. The turpentine burned, but it prevented infection.

Then, for some reason, mom couldn't find laudanum anywhere. Stores had stopped selling it. An alcoholic tincture of opium, Laudanum was widely accepted as a miracle drug for centuries long before anybody knew how addictive it was. Many famous people had become laudanum addicts like Lewis Carroll, Charles Dickens, Edgar Allan Poe and even President Abraham Lincoln's wife, Mary Todd.[8]

But those people were drinking it, apparently by the bucket. We were only pouring it on wounds. Now it's listed as a controlled substance.

Mom also used laudanum on big boils caused by staph infections that the cowboys got from the wool of their heavy jackets rubbing against their necks. Mother was a folk healer and used things doctors wouldn't dare consider today, like turpentine.

If we got a sore throat, she swabbed it with turpentine. We used turpentine on every wound, as long as we let it dry first and didn't wrap it until later. Otherwise, it stung.[9]

As well as turpentine, mom kept more traditional ingredients on hand such as Epsom Salts and castor oil. Sometimes she fed us castor oil mixed with orange juice to keep us regular. To this day, Tom can't drink orange juice because all he tastes is castor oil.[10]

We had other uses for these ingredients, too. For cows, castor oil and Epsom salts are good if they're bloated, have parasites or have eaten poisonous plants like locoweed. We mixed one cup of Epsom salts to one cup of castor oil into a gallon of water and poured it down their throats. That concoction could get rid of anything.

Turpentine, laudanum, castor oil, Epsom Salts... they made sense. But my mother practiced a folk medicine that was at times extreme. She employed a *healing stone* to cure bites, stings, and everything else.

My son John cringes when I mention this. He's a doctor and can't believe he evolved from such a superstitious lot. But is it superstition?

My mother's healing stone was not truly a stone. It was a highly polished, petrified wasp's nest cut in half so you could see inside.[11] It had pretty colors and she kept it in the drawer of her Singer Sewing Machine. When she needed it, she wet it, stuck it on the bite mark or cut and it took the sting away. If a rattlesnake bit you, it drew out the venom. I can't say for sure about that because we were never bitten.

Tom says you were supposed to heat the stone in warm milk and treat not only snakebite, but hydrophobia, better known as rabies. I shudder to think what could have happened if we tried that one on somebody bitten by a rabid animal.

My mother came by her folk remedies honestly. Her great grandfather on her father's side was an old country doctor and had a remedy for curing blood poisoning, which was a mixture of sugar, lead, lithium and sulfate of zinc, or something like that.[12] According to family anecdotes handed down through the years, it worked, but seems more like something you put in a battery instead of in a person.

Folk medicine was for people, cows and anything else that walked, ran or crawled on the surface of the planet. There was always a need to cure some ailment or infection.

Our cattle were exclusively red-hided, white-faced Hereford cows, a breed originally from England that often developed pink eye, which is contagious and can turn cancerous.[13] We had to constantly wash their eyes with a saline solution. Sometimes we blew salt directly into the eye through a straw and that cleared it up.

Tom and I didn't tackle the tough stuff like pink eye. On occasion, we sat on the fence and watched our fathers work the cows during roundups, but other times we rode fence on horseback to make sure nothing had fallen down, and if it had, we didn't go crying back to dad for help. We fixed it. We put up fence, filled troughs with water and didn't have to be told to do it.

Dad always said, "If I send you out to do something, don't come back and tell me you didn't do anything because it turned out that didn't need doing. Find something else and do it."

One of our jobs was watching the cows at the watering troughs. These were galvanized tanks with floats similar to what we use in the backs of toilets today. Dad installed the tanks near the railroad at Chiricahua so the cows were never without water close by.

Tom and I often rode down to a highway bridge and sat underneath to get out of the hot sun to watch the troughs. The cattle came to drink, jostled each other for a good spot and sometimes knocked the float off. When that happened, the trough kept filling with water and overflowed. If it got damaged, we knew how to fix it. We couldn't afford to waste water. Before dark, we checked the floats one last time, got on our horses and headed home.

Sometimes, instead of working on horseback, I had to drive the truck. I was ten or eleven when I learned how to drive on those muddy, rutted roads through the pasture.

Tom and I often loaded cottonseed cake and 100-pound bales of hay onto the back of the truck. It was not so easy when you were kid-size, but we grabbed the hay with a hay hook, boosted it up with a knee and threw it on the truck. Between the two of us, we handled it.

That truck was an old rickety flatbed Model-T. It was hard to drive because of the clutch, but that's what I learned to drive on. As soon as the cattle saw us coming, they chased after us.

The hay bales had two or three wires on them. We cut them with snippers, tore flakes off the bale and threw them down on the ground for the cows. After that, we broke up cottonseed cake, which is what's left over after oil is pressed from cottonseeds, and crumbled it over the hay.[14] You've got to train a cow or a calf to eat cake. It's foreign to them. By mixing it with the alfalfa hay, they get used to it and like it.

Cottonseed cake is real nutritious. While we fed it to the cows, we stuffed it in our mouths, probably with rat droppings mixed in, but it was tasty, like molasses. The cows sparked up on it. It gave them a lot of energy, they put on fat and their coats glistened in the spring. Can't say it did much for our complexions.

19. The Selling Business

Working cattle, branding and doctoring were part of growing up that defined my life and anchored me.

However, while riding around on the range, smelling the peppery grass, and enjoying the sunshine, it was easy to lose sight of why I was out there. We were involved in an activity as old as the human race. My family sold food for the dinner table.

Sometimes we rode around counting heifers in a little pasture my dad called the calving pasture that was about a mile square. At any one time, we had about 50 or so heifers in there getting ready to deliver. We kids tried to guess which one would deliver that night. We rarely guessed right. My dad, with all his experience, couldn't guess right either, so I never felt bad about that.

My dad and Uncle Jim sat in the kitchen and could describe what a cow looked like and where we would find it. They knew where they liked to hang out. A good cattle person knew where cattle had a tendency to graze and where they came in to water. He knew which one had calved and which one was about to calve.

When the heifers were ready, we led them into the corral, fed them well and checked them at midnight and in the morning. The Herefords are bred for their marbled beef, the meat is tender and tasty, and ranchers got the best return for their product. But the two-year-old heifers, the ones that hadn't given birth before, can't deliver by themselves because the babies are too big to come through the birth canal. The babies have big heads and big shoulders. We could lose a cow at its first calf birth and had to pull about half of them.

When the cow was giving birth, the feet came out first and we attached a rope to the calf's legs. When the mother cow had contractions, we pulled. That's why you call it *pulling a calf*. It took strength, but my mother was real good at pulling out the calf. If there were complications, my father took over.

We sold our Herefords for beef, but our Holstein and Guernsey mixes were for milk. They are great cows for rich milk and lots of it. As a kid, I thought all I ever did was milk, milk, milk. The cows were sometimes uncooperative and I got kicked every now and then. If you hurt a cow when you were milking, she kicked you one. Sometimes she kicked you because she felt like it. Sometimes I got it under my knee and she put me down on my butt too many times to count.

It took us a while to wise up before we tied the two back legs of the cows so they couldn't kick us. That didn't stop them from annoying us, though. If they didn't get you with their hooves, they got you with their tail. While we were milking, they swished their tail and if they had a cocklebur caught in the hair, it could cut you.[1] We tried to keep the tail combed out, but we couldn't always see the burrs.

After milking, we took the milk down to the house and my mother ran it through a gauze strainer into pans or buckets to get out the hay and dirt that inevitably fell into the bucket. Then she put the milk in a cooler. If we milked in the morning, by evening the cream came to the top. We skimmed that off and put it in another container. Mom whipped it or let it sour and churned it for butter.

Mom made the best butter, whipped cream, and yogurt and a dish we called *clabber*. To make clabber, she let the milk sit until it soured and jellied. To eat it, we put sugar or honey in it and ate it like pudding. It was a common food in the south during the American Civil War, although some people found it revolting.[2]

Nothing was pasteurized. We drank raw milk and dad tested the cows for bacteria regularly and we never had a problem.

Mom salted the butter as it was considered gross to serve it unsalted. Mom used redwood butter paddles to work all the milk out because milk made the butter go bad and it wouldn't taste right. Then she put it in a little mold or scooped it onto a dish. With the paddle, mom drew pictures on top of the butter of snowmen and trees just for fun. She warmed the bread in the warming oven and we spread butter on the bread and let it soak in. Oh, my gosh, you've never tasted anything as good from the store.

Unless the cows ate a gourd vine. Cows will eat vines, they'll eat citrus fruit. The milk will come out bitter and you'll think you've been poisoned. If you feed the cows well enough with hay and cottonseed cake, they won't eat the gourd vine. Unfortunately, the gourd vines are the first up in the spring, they're green and the cows like them.

And there are other things cows eat that are bad for them. On the Malpais, the monsoon rains made everything grow and that's not always a good thing. As a result, the grass grew so rapidly it lashed our stirrups as we rode through the pasture.

We rode though Johnson grass, Sacaton grass, Gama-grass and lots of weeds. Johnson grass is toxic, and you had to be careful about the weeds, especially locoweed, which is in abundance in the southwest. If a cow eats it, it goes crazy. Same with a horse. Once they eat it, they love it and will hunt it up. They don't always get sick the first time they eat it, its effect is cumulative, but after a while they show symptoms that look like Mad Cow Disease like lethargy, loss of balance, trouble standing and walking and nervousness. They lose weight and fall down a lot.[3] We dug out the locoweed wherever we found it.

Jimsonweed is another plant that affects cattle. It belongs to the nightshade family and has rank-smelling foliage, large white or violet trumpet-shaped flowers, and roundish prickly fruits. Like locoweed, it can kill a cow.[4] It's amazing the cows survived at all with the banquet of benign and poisonous plants laid out before them, and not being able to tell the difference.

In the spring, we rode through fields yellow with bladder pods and saw orange, yellow, and sometimes white, bronze and rose California poppies. Our ranch lands were ablaze with wildflowers, mesquite, paloverde, ocotillo, cholla, prickly pear and purple lupine. The lupine was like locoweed and made cows sick and crazy if they ate it.[5]

The cattle loved wild onions. They're okay for them to eat, the cows won't get sick, but if they're milk cows, you sure don't want them eating them. Their milk will taste oniony and their breath will knock you into the next county.[6]

The cows mouths are so tough, they will eat cactus. Sometimes they'll eat the fruit off the cactus and their mouths will drip with purple saliva.

Besides breeding cattle, we also bred horses. This was a side business of my dad's ranching enterprise. We had a thoroughbred stallion called Tony and we cross-bred him with our wild range mares. When we were ready to round up their colts, we had to find where they were grazing.

Tom and I learned early on how to run horses out of the pasture and bring them into the corral. Dad couldn't run them because a full-grown man on a horse was too slow.

First we had to make sure the wind was blowing from them to us before we sneaked up on them. Otherwise, they could smell us and spook. When we were close enough, Tom, the lightest, walked his horse slowly in front of the herd, mounted up and started to run. Sometimes I was out front, too, but usually I got in the back. Quickly, the horses started to run and we pushed them toward the corral.

We had to run them light, too, because if they ran by you, they sometimes kicked you and could even break your leg.

The other horses followed Tom's horse, and Tom led them through the gate into the big, round corral, rode out the gate and dad shut it behind him. The horses were so winded by the time we got them into the corral, they were seldom trouble.

After we brought in the colts, dad got in the corral with a cowhand and roped the two-year-olds. In the middle of the corral was a big snubbing post set in cement. They roped a colt, tied one of the back feet, pulled it up so the horse couldn't rear up and fall, and tied it to the post to restrain it.[7] Dad petted him, fed him, rubbed a saddle blanket all over him, let him smell it, and then put it up on his back. Most of the colts got gentle right away and didn't need much persuasion.

After that, dad set a light saddle on him, got up on him and rode around the corral. Sometimes the colts bucked outrageously. Soon, they got over the bucking stage and then my brother and I rode them. Once in a while, they bucked with us on, but not too often. A bucking horse always has his head down between his front feet. We learned how to yank their heads up. If a horse can't put his head down, he won't buck.

Tom and I took care of the wild colts after they were halter broken. We fed them and doctored them and one day a month dad shoed all the horses. Then the inevitable happened. They were sold. A California group came out and bought them for polo teams. The horses were also sold as kids' or women's horses because we had trained them so well.

It used to break my heart when my beautiful sorrel mares were sold. We knew when we were riding them that this would happen, but we got very attached. My father thought it was just a business deal. For us kids, it was much more. But selling them was part of ranching.

20. *My Dad Threatens to Shoot*

In our explorations around the ranch, we saw a lot of wildlife. After rains or when it was humid, the hairy tarantulas came out of their hiding spots and strolled around as if in slow motion. At night, the bats dive-bombed the mud tanks looking for a drink and hung out in the barns. The cats went for their babies. To them a bat was a rat with wings. Sometimes we saw bobcats, but they were shy and ran from us.

One afternoon we were over at Betty's house, our parents were in the house doing something, and we were outside playing. All of a sudden we saw three strange creatures the size of big house cats with long skinny tails. They were walking in single file on all fours across a dam on the dirt tank above the house. They were part raccoon, yellowish brown and black with a masked face, but part something else with a longer body and a long snout almost like an anteater.

Betty's dog went crazy. He bayed and charged after them. One of the creatures ripped open the dog's leg and the dog killed it. We rushed into the house screaming.

Dad said, "They have tails straight up?"

I said, "Yeah."

"Oh, that's those monkeys from Mexico," he said.

Everybody ran out of the house and saw them. Dad said they were called *coatis* or *coatimundis* and this was the first time he'd seen one this far north of Sonora. It was a dry year, and apparently they had come up for water. They're agile like monkeys, have long fingernails and they clutch onto things. They can hang in trees by their tails and can climb down a tree headfirst. These guys had rings on their tails (not all of them do), and a white nose.[1]

Uncle Jim, who had spent more time in Mexico than my dad, had never seen one. Our dads kept the carcass of the one the dog killed for ages. Neighbors came to see it because they'd never seen one either.

We doctored the dog and he got well. He stayed away from coatis after that.

Speaking of the dam above the house... In 1931 on the 4th of July, we were at Betty's place. I was eleven. My mom and dad usually took us someplace to watch fireworks, but it was pouring rain and we had spent our allowances on firecrackers anyway. We were lighting our firecrackers in the doorway of the house, throwing them out in the rain and they made a big bang.

The tank above the house where we saw the coatis hadn't been finished long. It backed up water for about a mile and was fed by springs out of Texas Canyon, so it always had water. Uncle Jim and my dad went up there in the rain to inspect it and came down looking mighty serious.

They had noticed that the rain was forcing water over the spillway of the tank and that worried them. Suddenly we heard a big cracking noise, and water that was accumulating in the mountains churned down Texas Canyon and boiled over the spillway with so much force that it ate into the dam and took a chunk of it away.

Lucky for us it didn't come our way, but ran out on the creek bed side and raged down the creek for about 3 to 4 miles, that's how big and powerful it was. It flooded a neighbor's house and they had to get up on their woodpile to avoid being swept away.

We saw so much on the ranch: animals, floods... but what we didn't expect to see were people sneaking around under cover of darkness. When we were quite young, dad told us emphatically that if we saw lights way out on the ranch to stay away from them and never to tell anybody about them. The lights belonged to Mexican smugglers bringing stuff into the United States. During Prohibition, they sneaked in alcohol, until the law was repealed in 1933, and then any contraband was the rule.[2]

Dad said he didn't want us going to court as kids. He knew how long it could take if we got involved with the criminal justice system. We had enough to do without wasting our time. And he was not impressed with our courts and prosecutors after how his brothers were treated following the Bartell shooting.

I think he was just plain scared for us. He didn't want anything bad to happen to anybody. His relationship with the Mexicans was live and let live and everybody got along fine. He didn't want to destroy the trust we had developed over years.

At the same time, dad was no coward. If you got in trouble, you could very well expect to get shot up, and you had to protect yourself, your loved ones and your property.

A case in point... Once when we were driving across the pasture on the way to Highway 80, my dad saw a guy surveying in our meadow. My mother was driving, and dad said to get over to where the guy was fooling with his equipment. I thought, *Oh, this man's in for it.*

Mother drove off the road and out across the meadow. She stopped the car, dad got out, and said, "What are you doing on my property?"

The man said, "We're surveying. We're going to bring a pipe in here for El Paso Natural Gas."

"You did not come to ask me," said my father. "You see that gate up there? If you don't get in that truck and get out that gate, I will put a bullet where your suspenders cross." The man could see my dad's pistol tucked behind his belt.

The man jumped in his truck and left in a considerable hurry. Putting in a gas line really messes up a pasture. If the guy had asked my dad and showed some respect, my dad might have said Yes. You didn't mess with people like my dad.

21. My Famous Cousin

During the Depression years, lots of relatives visited the ranch. One of them was my cousin, John Stewart Williamson. If you're a science fiction fan, you may have heard of him, as he became the preeminent science fiction writer of our age. As a matter of fact, he is credited with creating the term *science fiction*.

When I knew him, he was just Jack and he seemed like a lost soul. Twelve years older than me, he was born in 1908 to Stewart's sister, Lucy Betty Hunt, in Bisbee, Arizona, in an old adobe.

When he was a tiny baby, his family moved to Mexico. They crossed at Agua Prieta, then went by rail and stage, and finally put Jack on a horse for a long day's ride cutting through the wilderness with no roads to Stewart's ranch. Jack's parents went there to work, first on El Rancho la Lobo in Sonora, and then on the El Tapila ranch. This baby lived in the mountains and he had never seen a pane of glass and he was cut off from people.

His parents were teachers with good educations, but for some reason they preferred ranching. Lucy had her college degree and she married a man with his Master's. Before Jack was three, they left Mexico in a Conestoga covered wagon and moved to Portales, New Mexico, where they lived on a small hardscrabble ranch, trying to scratch out an existence. They lived well below the poverty line.

In 1918, a couple of years before I was born, it didn't rain and there was no grass. Cousin Jack's father had a few cattle, and they were starving, so he took Jack, who was then ten, and they drove the cattle around eastern New Mexico and into Texas looking for grass. Jack drove the chuck wagon. At the end of the summer, they shipped the cows to Kansas City.

Jack's father got on the train with the cattle, and Jack remembered waving goodbye and wondering if he'd ever see him again. It was common for a rancher to accompany his cattle to market, but Jack didn't know that. My father always went with the cattle he shipped to the yards in Los Angeles to make sure they were okay and to get paid on the spot.

Like my dad, Jack's father went with the cows, sold them, and sent the money back to the bank. But then he went to work in the copper mines in Bisbee to support his family. Eventually, Jack's father returned, but in the meantime, Jack worried about him.

We went to Portales when I was ten and visited Jack and his family. At twenty-two, Jack was the oldest of four children. My dad called him a dreamer.

We were shocked at how they were living. It was hand-to-mouth, like paupers. They lived in a rough looking homestead that had a small clapboard house with a porch. The house had a couple of bedrooms, a kitchen, no inside bathroom. The chickens were kept in the yard and ran around on the porch so the varmints couldn't get them. They had pigs, a few head of cattle and a steel tank for water. My father was astounded at what he saw because they were college graduates. Compared to them, we lived in exquisite luxury.

Jack lived in even worse conditions than his parents and siblings. He'd built himself a shack away from the house for privacy. It was made of raw pine, about 10-by-12 feet, with a dirt floor and the roof was made out of grass.

Jack viewed himself as an uneducated farm boy with no job, no money and no future. He had a total of six years formal schooling and was mostly home taught.[1]

He later described in magazine and newspaper interviews what his life was like growing up on a ranch a long way from neighbors. For the few years he went to school, he rode horseback to the schoolhouse and that was his only contact with kids. In writing science fiction, he once said, "I didn't know enough about anything else to write it."[2] Since he placed his humans on other planets, he could make them act in ways we might consider bizarre on earth and get away with it. He said that he didn't really understand how real people interacted.

Against his desires, he did a lot of heavy farm work, drove cattle while on horseback, seeded fields, picked corn, and carried out whatever drudgery was needed. Bored and depressed, he started creating epic fictional stories with himself as the main character. I think he hated his life so much that he recreated his life through strange characters. As well as writing, he told stories to his siblings to keep them, and himself, entertained.

I remember him for his far-out stories. But I wasn't into science fiction. I was happy in my life and my passion was history and biographies, real life, not escapism.

To be fair to his parents, they tried to educate Jack. They did their best to teach him at home, and even with little money they subscribed to magazines like the *Saturday Evening Post*, *Harper's* and *Scribner's* to expand his mind. Aunt Lucy read a great deal and had wanted to be a writer herself. She bought a mail-order fiction writing course that Jack made good use of. What got him going was an issue of *Amazing Stories* that he had requested from a free ad. And in 1928, at the age of twenty, he sold them his first story, *The Metal Man*. He visited us at the ranch after he sold it and he was thrilled. He wasn't paid much, about ½ cent a word, but it was the beginning.[3]

I saw Jack every now and then throughout the years when we visited his family or he came to our ranches. He was a big guy, didn't worry about how he looked, and often wore mismatched socks. He was too much into himself to care. During the Great Depression, things were the toughest, and we saw a lot of him and his brother Jim. But the thing Jack wanted to talk about the most was the Paramore Crater on the Malpais Ranch. Every time he visited, he wanted to go over and stare at it.

We talked about other things, too, like life in Mexico when he was a kid, but the crater was his thing. I think it helped him visualize alien environments.

He talked about people from different planets and I was fascinated by him. My father said, "Don't believe everything Jack tells you." I laughed when he said that. I was aware that Jack and I grew up in a different life.

After several years, Jack made a little money at his writing, not enough to quit his day job on the ranch, but he was successful enough to propose marriage to Blanche Slaton Harp, a girl he'd known since he was a boy. They'd gone to school together and she owned a kids' store in Portales.[4]

After getting married, and having Blanche's steady income supporting his writing habit, he joined the Masonic Lodge, the Rotary Club and the Methodist Church. This made him feel like less of an outsider and more like a member of the human race, yet he didn't foresee the drain on his time. The organizations wanted him to participate in events. He was too busy writing. I think his problem was that he loved to be around people, but he was so way-out imagining stuff that he couldn't relate to people.

He decided to immerse himself in psychoanalysis. He said, "I was unhappy in many ways with the way my whole life was progressing."[5] He was in therapy, off and on, for three years, and felt it was worthwhile for finding out who he was inside.

During World War II, he joined the Army as a weather forecaster in the South Pacific.[6] About ten years after the war, still feeling undereducated, he went back to school and earned his BA, MA and Ph.D.[7] He was admired, if not worshipped, by many writers including Isaac Asimov, Frederik Pohl and Ray Bradbury. Isaac Asimov said his greatest moment, after having his first story published, was when he received a congratulatory note from Jack.[8] With his credentials and background, Jack taught college for many years and was known to all as a kind, gentle man.

Throughout his life, Jack had more than fifty novels and many short stories published. He won every science fiction award including Hugo, Nebula and Pilgrim Awards, and was named Grand Master of Science Fiction by the Science Fiction Writers of America. He was the first to write about genetic engineering, antimatter, in vitro fertilization, organ transplantation, and using nuclear rockets to colonize the moon. He invented the word *terraforming*, which means to change an alien environment into one where humans could live and flourish.[9]

Jack continued to write and have his books published almost until his death at age ninety-eight in Portales in November, 2006.

How did my relationship with Jack affect me? Jack's life motivated me. He made me realize that all things are possible. That the mind can accomplish remarkable things, that it can see and dream and invent the impossible. That a poorly educated ranch boy could rise to great heights.

This helped me with my teaching. It inspired me to encourage kids, all kids, no matter their disadvantages or behavioral problems, to succeed.

22. Time to Leave

We knew from an early age that after we finished 8th grade, we were going away to school. Dad told us, "I have to be sure my girls have a good education because their husbands could die or leave them and they have to have a way to make a living."

He was very forward thinking. He thought ladies should do anything they wanted to do. He never told mom she couldn't do something. Even though he was a rancher with a poor education, he had a big vision for us.

First he thought maybe I should go to high school in Douglas. A school bus went there, but the daily trip was too expensive, as well as time consuming.

Mom and dad considered moving to Douglas, like some ranch families did so their kids could go to school, but that was out of the question. Mom didn't want to live there, and Douglas was an hour and a half away. You couldn't run a ranch from long distance.

Dad decided to check out California. I had aunts and uncles there, and although I'd never met them, they would look out for me. He shipped a load of cattle to

California and stayed with his sister, the one I'm named after, Dorothy Valerie Haines.

My aunt had a huge home in Pasadena in the Los Angeles area that she'd turned into a boarding house for kids going to school. The downstairs had two baths, the upstairs had three, and there were little rooms all around. Next door was one of the best high schools.

When dad came home, he said, "That is the place that I want my kids to go to school."

He said that first I was required to attend grade 9 in a junior high, which was a couple of blocks away from my aunt's place. I'd never heard of a junior high before. Junior high was a California idea for grades 7 to 9. My aunt insisted that I live with her, and Nell would join me the following year. Dad told Uncle Jim who thought it was a great idea for Cousin Betty and he planned on sending her there, too.

I was excited and eager to go, but at the same time apprehensive. I'd never been away from home by myself and this was a new adventure. I was scared, too. I didn't know any of the kids I'd go to school with.

Thank goodness there was still the summer on the ranch. Besides the usual chores, it was time for dances and fun. At the dances, I didn't sit on the benches like a lot of the girls, I danced with the boys. But I didn't date much. There weren't many boys my age and what few there were lived on ranches far away.

There was one boy I had a problem with. We were playing Anti-Over at school, chose teams and got on either side of the schoolhouse. We threw a tennis ball over the roof to the other side, and if the other team caught it, they shouted "Anti-Over..." and one of us had to join the other team.

In one of the volleys, the ball flew over the roof toward me, and I got ready to catch it. This boy shoved me out of the way because he wanted to catch it. I poked him in the gut, jumped on him and beat him up a little.

The teacher came out, pulled me off and said, "That's not a very ladylike thing to do."

"You tell him he shouldn't be shoving and pushing and calling me names," I replied.

The guy was on my own team, and that was the one and only time he pulled that on me.

Maybe that was the reason I didn't date much. Word may have gotten around that I was a hellion. Then again, maybe I didn't date much because I read magazines like *The New Yorker* and *The Saturday Evening Post* and was more sophisticated than I realized. Yet my fear was that once I got to junior high school, the California kids would think I was a hick and laugh at me.

To get ready for school, I had to make my uniforms. I'd learned how to sew from my mother, but I was never as good as her. She learned how to sew when there were only a few basic patterns available. Mom had taught me on real cheap material so I could make mistakes on the old treadle machine. She helped us cut and taught us how to pin the pattern on the cut.

Oh, man, were they touchy at school. The skirt had to have two pleats in the front and two in the back and the blouse had to be a plain, cotton, white midi-blouse.

Just Plain Dorothy

In August of 1934, at the age of fourteen, I packed my stuff in a trunk and my mom and dad loaded it in the car. We got up early in the morning to go to California because it was summer and hot as blazes. We wanted to get going while it was cooler. It was a big car and Tom, Nell and Bess came with us. First we drove to Tucson and had lunch. Then on to Yuma where we spent the night. It would take us two days because we only went 35 to 40 miles an hour and that was fast then.

The car didn't have air conditioning. It had vents that let in hot air. My mother was inventive and put a 25-pound block of ice in a tub on the floor in front of the passenger seat. The air flowing through the vents over the ice created a cooling effect.

To give you an idea how hot it got, the second year my parents took me to LA, my dad had bought a new Ford car and had it Simonized to preserve it. As we drove along, the Simonize ran off the car in trickles.

From Yuma, we went to Indio, from Indio to Blythe. We were familiar with Blythe because that was where the trains came from to get our cattle. From Blythe, we went to Los Angeles and arrived late in the afternoon.

The first day in Los Angeles is not something I have ever forgotten. And I don't mean that in a good way.

My Uncle Frank, who was married to Aunt Dorothy, thought that since we were all here, he should show us the town before the rest of my family headed back to the ranch. The Rose Bowl stadium, built ten years before for football games, was the big thing to see, and all of us hopped in his car. We'd been driving for two days, but I was energized. This was all new to me.

On the way, Uncle Frank decided to show us the famous Colorado Street Bridge on Route 66, which connects Pasadena with the Eagle Rock neighborhood of Los Angeles. He wanted us to see it because the bridge was an amazing engineering feat.

It actually curved across the Arroyo Seco gorge, a deep, treacherous canyon with a flowing river below. When it was finished in 1913, it was the first curvilinear bridge ever made and the tallest concrete bridge, spanning nearly 1,500 feet over the gorge. It was a 150 foot drop to the bottom, and I'm not telling you this so you will go sightseeing in Pasadena.[1]

We stopped and my uncle told us how wonderful it was to come down to watch the Tournament of Roses Parade on New Year's Day just before the football game. Then he warned us that the Colorado Street Bridge had another name: *Suicide Bridge.*

More than 100 people had leaped to their deaths, and the bridge was said to be haunted with their spirits. Uncle Frank recounted strange tales of ghosts wandering the bridge, unaccounted for weeping and shouting sounds from the canyon below, and of a woman in a long flowing robe standing on the railing, who then jumps and vanishes into the mist below.[2]

As we were leaving, we saw a man wearing a jacket walking on the bridge. We went off to the Rose Bowl stadium, had a good look, and then headed back the way we had come. At the bridge, my uncle stopped at a spot underneath. "Be sure to look up and you can see how high that bridge is," he said.

We looked up and suddenly heard people screaming. I looked out through the back window and the man we saw walking on the bridge a little earlier jumped, and as he hit the ground, missing our car by only a few feet, I saw his jacket flap over his head.

I was very upset. I don't know if I was sobbing, but my mother tried to calm me down. She said, "He didn't want to live. We don't dwell on that."

My father wanted to see if he was all right.

"No," my uncle said, "let's get out of here."

Uncle Frank revved the car and we left. That was my introduction to California.

As my mother advised, I tried to put it behind me, but I had nightmares about what I saw and have never forgotten the terrible image of the man's dark jacket fluttering over his head.

We had arrived two days before classes began and I went down to register and attend an orientation at South Pasadena-San Marino Junior High. The building was huge, a gigantic, sprawling campus. Coming from a two-room schoolhouse, I felt intimidated. So far, I was having a terrible time.

"I can't do this," I said to my mom and dad. "I'll be dumb. All the kids are smarter and they know each other. I don't know anybody."

My parents kissed me goodbye, got in the car, and headed back to the ranch. My mother never revealed if she cried when she left me, but she always said we were not to be blubbering on about things. I told people I felt fine about going off to school. Being here was a different story. When they drove off, I felt alone.

A-L-O-N-E.

23. Alone and Scared

On Monday, my first day of classes, I was too nervous to eat breakfast. I walked to school and all the way I told myself I didn't want to go. And when I got there, I was scared...

God, was I scared.

I was supposed to check in at my homeroom, but I didn't know about homerooms. I went to the office and they sent a kid who knew the school to take me there.

At Apache, the largest number of pupils in an entire grade was four. Here I walked into a class of about 25 kids and I didn't know a soul. Happily, my homeroom teacher was the art teacher and I loved art. That took away some of my anxiety.

The teachers at the school were strict and meticulous. Every morning our uniforms were inspected to make sure they were fresh and clean, our skirts had the right number of pleats and the blouses pressed. If you were found with a mark on them, you were in trouble.

At noon on my first day there, kids filed out of the classroom and I followed them to lunch in a cafeteria.

I'd never seen food served where I could pick what I wanted to eat. That was the first time I drank milk from a tiny carton. It wasn't like getting a glass of frothy milk right from the cow. Even so, I thought it was pretty neat. I liked the hot lunch, but a lot of kids didn't. Many left most of their lunch on the plate. That surprised me. We were taught that when you sit at a table, you eat what's put in front of you.

The best food was after school let out. At first, I didn't know what was going on. I saw a colorful truck drive up in front of the school and a man inside rang a bell. The kids flocked to his wagon, gave him a nickel and came away with this thing on a stick. It took me a moment to realize it was ice cream. I took to this newfangled invention right away.

The ice cream was great. The weather wasn't. A lot of people believe the sun always shines in southern California. Maybe it does in some parts, but not where I went to school in South Pasadena. That first year I think I saw the sun ten days. The fog rolled in at night and all day we walked around in pea soup.

And it rained. It rains a lot in California in the winter. I had never owned in my whole life a raincoat. But I had to wear a raincoat and darned old galoshes. The campus was built with separate buildings university-style, and we slogged through the puddles between buildings to get to our classes. We wore wool skirts and wool pants and while we sat in class, we saw steam radiating from our clothes. The dank smell was awful.

Though I was uncertain about how I'd do on the academics and might make a fool of myself, I knew I could do the art. For our first project, the school brought in a famous Mexican artist to teach us fresco-making. His name was José Clemente Orozco, "regarded as one of the foremost mural painters in the western hemisphere."[1] With only one arm, he had painted frescoes throughout Mexico and the United States.[2] And he was *my* teacher.

At the time I met him, he was already well-known, but like so many artists, he worked for next to nothing. He was supposed to receive a healthy commission for painting a mural at Pomona College, but when the professor who hired him said they had little money to pay him, he replied, "Never mind about that. Have you got a wall?"[3]

I don't know what the junior high paid him for teaching us how to make a fresco, but we had a big wall in the patio area. The building was built in the Mexican style with massive arches and the patio and the wall we were to paint on were protected from the rain, which meant our fresco, away from the elements, would last forever.

The theme for the fresco was early history in California, and first we had to draw our picture on a piece of paper. I drew Indian wives sitting around a fire, something I had observed at home. Then the teacher gathered our drawings and organized them into a collage for the wall.

He had somebody assemble scaffolding, and then showed us how to mix the slaked limestone plaster to a certain consistency and mix the powdered earthen paints.[4] Then he showed us how to use the brushes. The traditional brush for fresco painting contains no metal and has long, soft bristles bound by string to a wooden handle.[5] The teacher instructed us on when to use big brushes for grasslands and sky and how to use small brushes for the fine work.

Making a fresco is hard on you physically. The teacher had the students trowel three coats of wet plaster onto the walls and that was difficult because each coat had to be completely smooth. While the last coat was drying, we punctured our drawings with small holes along the shape of the images we had drawn.

Then we pressed our papers up against the moist wall, dipped our hands into small bags of charcoal and dusted it over the perforated holes in the paper. Upon pulling the paper off, we saw our image with a dotted line of charcoal dust.[6]

Then we dipped our brushes and painted the picture, allowing the paint to dry before starting the next color.[7] It was painstaking work and took several weeks to complete the whole process.

The fresco stayed on the wall for many years after I'd left, but when the building was eventually restored, our glorious mural was covered over with cement. What were they thinking?

Making the fresco is the most cherished memory of my time away at school. But I wasn't there to become an artist. I was there to study serious academic subjects and make something of myself.

My greatest fear on going to California was that the teachers and the other kids would think I was as dumb as a bag of nails. After two weeks, I realized how wrong I'd been. The kids brought up in the California educational system had the benefits of a big institution with lots of money to hire the best teachers. They had a huge library where you could look up anything in the world, yet junior high could not compete with my two-room country schooling. They were not as well educated as I was.

The students didn't know their history. They hadn't studied the U.S. Constitution. They didn't even know the constitution for their own state.

I was behind in algebra, but in math basics they were way behind. The teacher put a bunch of facts in division on the board and we had to do them in a minute. I saw those kids counting on their fingers and they couldn't finish them in time. When we started the basics of English, the kids didn't know how to diagram a sentence. That's when I quit feeling inferior. In 9th grade, they didn't know the fundamentals that I'd already learned.

I felt better about myself and my academics, but at the beginning of my schooling in California, I was lonesome and friendless. I had to live in California for 10 months to validate getting a free tuition and my father wouldn't cut corners. I was only allowed to go home for the summer and summer was a long ways away.

My uncle, Edgar Ryder, who was married to my youngest aunt, Nellie Sue Hunt, who my sister was named after, took pity on me. He lived in Glendale and was chief engineer for the Los Angeles Water Department. On weekends, he sometimes took me to the aqueduct and we went into the tunnels. That was fun.

My aunt took me to art galleries and museums. We went to the La Brea tar pits and museum to see dinosaurs, mammoths, dire wolves, and even a saber-toothed tiger they had wrestled out of the tar. As my Uncle Sam now owned a ranch in La Brea Canyon, when we went to the tar pits we visited him.

Uncle Sam had about 100 head of cattle. To me that was not a ranch, more a hobby farm. He built a big swing on a hillside on posts embedded in cement. I got in that swing and flew out over a ravine like I had wings.

24. No Dogies in the Car

To lessen the pain from feeling homesick, my mother and I wrote letters every week. I told everybody about what I did during the week and mom told me about the activities on the ranch. Now and then, my dad wrote, but it was mostly my mom. At school I had access to a phone except I couldn't call my parents because they didn't have a phone on the Malpais.

Writing letters improved my writing skills. I had to answer all of mom's questions from the previous letter and I wasn't allowed to give one word answers. My father said, "If it's gonna be *Yes*, then you'd better explain."

Even though I liked getting letters from home, nothing substituted for being with my family on the ranch. Uncle Frank and Aunt Dorothy were kind, but they were not my parents. Who do you go to when you're feeling bad?

Sometimes I told my aunts and new friends at school what I was feeling, but most of the time I kept things to myself or told my mom in a letter. With the letters I didn't feel like I'd been abandoned. And my mom baked cookies and cakes and sent them.

A lot of snooty kids attended school. They usually lived in Flintridge, an exclusive area of mansions and big cars. One annoying kid named Pat tried to hassle me. Her family had made its fortune in soap and I guess she felt cleaner than the rest of us.

The soap kid had her chauffeur transport her to school and it was strange seeing him rush around and open the car door for this irritating child.

One day she said in a demeaning way, "You're from Texas. I can tell by the way you talk."

"No, I'm not from Texas," I said in my best hillbilly drawl that meant *Don't mess with me.* That was the only thing she said in a derogatory fashion that I recall, ever.

I shared an English class with the soap girl, and the teacher told us to write an essay. Pat replied, "Why, I don't write. I'll have my father's secretary do this."

"No, you won't," said the teacher. "You'll write it like everybody else."

Pat was a type of person I'd never encountered before. I wonder if this was who my father had in mind when he said I should go to California and experience the elite.

On my own without my family monitoring me, I felt independent and grown-up. To make sure I didn't go hog wild, my aunt took me, and later Nell and Betty, to her church most Sundays. She was Christian Science and I wasn't too keen on what they believed and paid as much attention as I'd paid to the itinerant preachers.

Unfortunately, Nell stayed with it. Years later, she married a guy from Davis-Monthan Air Force base in

Tucson and they moved to Japan. It was against her religion to have her heart checked and she died from a heart attack.

My uncle the water engineer, another Christian Science believer, was heavily involved in the church. They believed we could cure everything with our minds. I think your mind has something to do with whether you heal or not, but to cure an illness, a heart condition or to stop your throat from closing up after a scorpion sting? I'm lucky I never got sick in California.

Leaving home created a void in my life, but, although it frightened me to death, the experience made me resourceful and self-reliant.

After finishing 9th grade in junior high, I was planning on going home for the summer by taking the train for the first time. It was mid-June and my uncle, aunt and I set out for what should have been a brief car ride to the station, but there was so much fog, we had a hard time getting there and I nearly missed my train.

During the race to the station, my aunt warned me the trip would be hot. The diner cars were sometimes air conditioned, but not the passenger cars. My aunt said I should get a wet towel from the restroom and sponge myself off to keep cool. Her idea worked for ten minutes, then I had to wet the towel again and again.

I traveled all night, all the next day, and the day after that. The train stopped at every darn mail stop along the way until it got to Douglas. I got off the train and mom and dad threw their arms around me and hugged me. We walked out to the car, and there was a shiny new four-door Ford sedan.

Oh, it was a beautiful thing. My Uncle Jim preferred Chevrolets. The Chevys had solid wheels, they got stuck in the mud, and the rear axles went out on them. Fords had spoked wheels and seldom got stuck.

My father wouldn't be caught dead driving a Chevy. And my Uncle Jim hated Fords. *Brothers.* I think they had to have something to disagree on.

On the ride back to the ranch, mom said to dad, "There's no putting dogies in this car." A dogie is a motherless calf (pronounced *doh-ge*). Dogies have no respect for new cars and poop where they please. But this was mom's car. Dad always had a Ford pickup.

"Well, how do you think I paid for this car? With those calves and cattle," said dad.

A few days later, mom and dad were out, the new car smell wasn't even out of the car, and they came upon a dogie a few days old lying in the dirt. Dad picked up the little calf, got a feed sack from the trunk, wrapped the baby in it, and put it in the car between the front and back seats. My mother said, "Can you believe it? Already carrying dogies."

My brother and sisters and I took care of the dogies. We bottle-fed them by hand four times a day and didn't overfeed them. They could get scours, severe diarrhea that could kill a calf. We isolated them in a corral or in the barn to keep warm and mucked out their stalls. It was a lot of work.

I thought we should be compensated for all the time we spent getting them ready to sell. Well, that was a joke. When you worked on the ranch, you just worked. If someone came and stayed, they worked too. Nobody got paid, except for all you could eat.

25. Getting Out the Hayseeds

In mid-August, 1935, I returned for the 10th grade to South Pasadena-San Marino Union High School. This time, I was accompanied by my sister Nell and my cousin Betty. They were a year behind me and I advised them about surviving junior high. Most important for Betty was that I showed her how to iron her uniforms properly to keep those darn pleats straight. We stayed with Aunt Dorothy and didn't feel lonely. We had each other.

For the first year of high school, I was required to pick a major and chose both art and history. Every student had to take music, which I didn't like much, but after my experience with Señor Orozco, how could I not love art?

In junior high, I worked in the library at lunchtime or after school and I continued working there in high school. I didn't care whether I had to shelve books, stamp them in or fill out index cards. I loved books and would do any menial chore to be around them. The bonus was I got to read the new histories and novels before anybody else did.

Going to a big-time California high school exposed me to culture that wasn't available on the ranch or in the nearby towns. On the Malpais, we thought the height of sophistication was going to the movies. I never thought I'd actually see something as spectacular as an opera.

The teachers took us to the Mason Opera House in downtown Los Angeles.[1] Instead of our uniforms, we wore white gloves, cute little hats, nice dresses and a wrap. We sat in the balcony and at the appropriate moments held opera glasses to our eyes to capture the action up close.

The first opera I saw was *Aida* and the libretto or text was stunning. And the staging... it was magnificent and heartbreaking. It's a love story that takes place in ancient Egypt about an enslaved Ethiopian princess named Aida who everybody adores. Like the ending of many operas, she ends up dying in her lover's arms.

The story has pageantry and a cast of hundreds of characters including soldiers, priests, slaves, and prisoners. At times, animals ambled onto the stage, and I mean big animals from the local zoo like elephants, camels, horses and a lion. We paid for our own tickets, and everybody was expected to go.[2]

The school sent us to the theater, too. We caught the streetcar at Fair Oaks and Banks and went up to the Pasadena Community Playhouse to see performances such as Shakespeare.[3] And we went downtown to hear the Los Angeles Philharmonic. Dressed like debutantes, we sat in the balcony, gazed at the orchestra through our little opera glasses and marveled at the music of Igor Stravinsky and Arnold Schoenberg.[4]

We went to high school to get the hayseeds out of our hair and we achieved it brilliantly. Besides attending the opera, theater and the philharmonic, we learned ballroom dancing, clog dancing and modern dance.

I knew how to dance when I got to school. We did the Texas two-step and a waltz you did to country western music. But everybody at school was expected to take ballroom dance classes as an extra but mandatory activity outside of school. We learned the foxtrot, the rumba, and the tango... *Oh yes, oh, Lord...* Now that was a dance, with abrupt movements and head snaps. While the music played, our teacher held a drum and pounded it to keep time.[5]

The ballroom dancing included the Quickstep, the Charleston, the Black Bottom, and the Shimmy, a dance that got the infamous Mae West thrown in the slammer. We didn't do that one. We did the Viennese Waltz, an elegant, stylized dance, unlike our countrified waltz.[6]

To make sure we did things right, we were taught *the etiquette of ballroom dancing*, things like: Don't wear heavy perfumes, Wear a loose enough dress, Accept graciously an invitation to dance, Let the boy lead, and Don't hang off your partner like a dead weight he has to drag across the floor.[7]

When boys asked us to dance, we gave them our dance cards to sign. The classes emphasized how to become a well-bred young woman who could follow and a man who could lead.

We were taught clog dancing, not the Irish River Dance we see on television, but a tap dance with its roots in traditional Appalachian clogging. We wore black patent leather shoes with a green bow and you didn't dare let your tap get loose. It would rattle and throw everybody off their rhythm.[8]

Besides dancing and all the cultural events, my big thing was sports. We did Physical Education every day and intramural sports after school. I belonged to the Girls Athletic Association (GAA), and played every sport I could. We played a lot of softball. Back home, we used a hardball and our bare hands. In high school, we used gloves. Hitting a softball with a bat was like smacking a mattress and I hated it. The ball wouldn't go anywhere, not like when you hit a hardball over the bleachers.

I liked all the sports, but basketball was relatively new to me. The only time I'd played it before was in the 8th grade at Apache. We had one basket and argued over who shot baskets next. I was not very good at it because I have a depth perception problem I didn't realize at the time.

California was big on tennis. The first time I played was at junior high and then high school, and, as you might expect, I was a washout. But softball... I was great at it, which made no sense. If I had trouble judging the distance of objects and their spatial relationships and was a disaster playing basketball and tennis, the problem should carry over into softball. It didn't.

I couldn't get enough of sports. Until high school, I'd never been to a basketball or football game. On weekends, we had women's sports and field days. However, lots of weekends we just went on picnics.

Our social life was completely different than at the Apache school. We had social hours at high school dedicated to getting to know other kids. A high point for me was going on a movie set during Hollywood's heyday. A group of us from school went to Glendale to watch them shoot a Ginger Rogers and Fred Astaire film. Ginger was dressed in white, the most gorgeous thing I'd ever seen.[9]

Another high point for me was my first earthquake. I was fixing breakfast peeling an orange and heard a low rumble. I looked out the window and the telephone poles were swaying. I screamed. We were on the second floor and I was afraid the house would collapse. Then it rumbled again and I ran into the other room where somebody said, "Oh, that's nothing." I sure didn't want to see *something*.

In high school, Dad wouldn't allow us to date, so sometimes we partied at each other's houses or went out Friday nights to school dances.

To help with our expenses like shows, dance classes and admissions to events, we got allowances. We never got them at the ranch, but this was culture and had to be subsidized. Mom sent us our $5 allowance every month, which went a long way when you consider the streetcar only cost 5 cents.

With all our cultural events, you may wonder when I had time for my studies. I admit that I wasn't a leader in high school, either academically or socially, but I did okay. It helped that the school didn't grade us. They didn't want to ruin our chances for a college education.

26. The Honeymoon Ranch

While I was a senior in high school, my family decided that the Malpais ranch was too small. By then three families were living there: Uncle Jim's, Uncle Joe's and mine. We were still using both the Malpais and the Slaughter Ranch to run cattle; yet the two of them were not big enough to run enough cattle for all of us to earn a decent living.

My dad and Uncle Joe looked around and in October 1937 found a couple of ranches in Arizona's White Mountains in Greenlee County. Dad got the 4 Drag and Uncle Joe got the Flying U Drag, which was below the 4 Drag, but the ranches did not connect. They were about 10 miles apart and it took about 45 minutes to drive between them.

The Hunt brothers didn't sell the Malpais. Jim, Charlie and Sam hung onto it. Since Uncle Charlie was a doctor and Uncle Sam had a job in California, Uncle Jim kept things going.

Because the 4 Drag was on Eagle Creek, it was also known as the Eagle Creek Ranch. Its most popular name, though, was the *Honeymoon Ranch,* and it had a beautiful log house that became the headquarters for the cattle operation.

As the story goes, the forest ranger that first lived there married his sweetheart and brought her back to the ranch. She was not impressed and only agreed to stay if he got her a piano. To make the marriage work, he had one shipped in pieces, probably on pack mules, and reassembled it in the cabin. Without the piano, there would have been no honeymoon.

Before leaving the Malpais, dad sold off our cattle, then bought about 2,000 head from the previous owners of the 4 Drag for a startup herd. The Flying U Drag, where Uncle Joe and Aunt Edith lived, was mostly for farming and pasture land.

The Honeymoon was 42 miles from the small town of Clifton. From Eagle Valley 10 miles down to the head of Eagle Creek was a stretch where a lot of people lived in big cattle ranches replete with orchards. The Honeymoon had an orchard, too, full of apples and other fruit.

The head of Eagle Creek was above the Honeymoon about 4 or 5 miles and was fed by warm water springs. In winter, Eagle Creek got a little ice along the edges but it never froze over. There was a huge campground park about a quarter mile from the Honeymoon and we went through the park to get to the ranch.

On the way down to the Honeymoon, we rode through wildflowers, tiny violets, yellow flowers, and Columbines. In the fall, wild grapes grew everywhere up on the pines and the sumac and the grape vines turned red. After the first frost came, it looked like the trees had been decorated for Christmas. Unfortunately, the grapes were sour.

Honeymoon Ranch

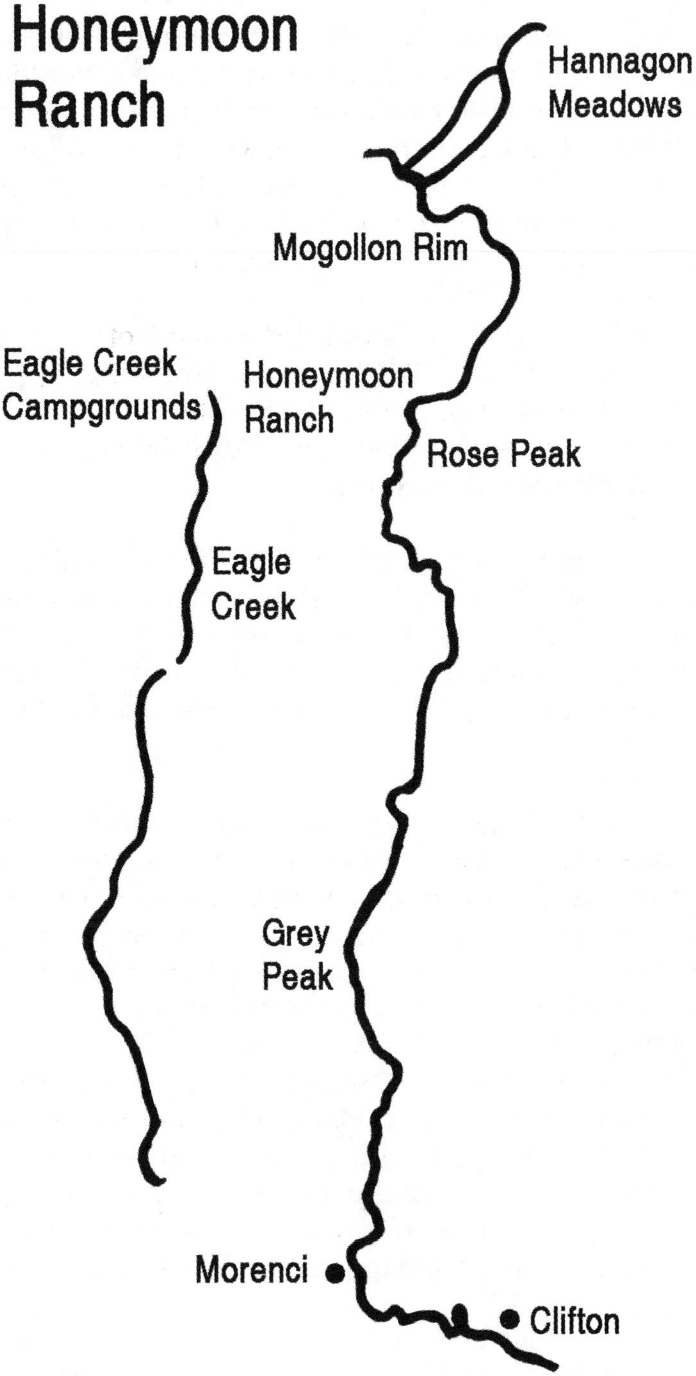

Virginia Creeper was all over our front porch on a trellis. Brought in from the east coast, it has large leaves and will grow anywhere. It turned red, too, died in the winter and sprung back in the summer as soon as it got warm.

The first time I saw the house, Betty was with me. We went inside and one of my parents' visitors was an old lady named Ma Castro. She was sitting about 6 feet from the fireplace and chewing tobacco enthusiastically. We sat down in the living room and Ma Castro said, "Honey, move over..." and she fired a spitball of brown tobacco-laced saliva directly into the fireplace. I wondered how she was with a pistol.

After finishing high school, I decided to take a year off before college and live on the new ranch. Finally, we had a telephone that was on a party line and our call had four long rings, although half the time the phone didn't work. We needed a phone to report if a fire broke out.

Like on any ranch, I had chores, but I spent most of my time reading. I had a favorite spot on the big porch where I sat, flipped pages and lost myself in a story.

The Honeymoon was not at all like the Malpais. The Malpais was in a desert climate, hot and barren. The Honeymoon was lush with forests of pine, aspen, spruce, fir and ponderosa pine trees, and we grazed our livestock in high meadow grasslands like Hannigan Meadow at 9,000 feet. Temperatures during the summer rarely got above 80 degrees and we had no trouble with water because the winter snows and summer rains created many streams and lakes.[1]

Our house was at about 7,000 feet. During the winter, icicles stretched from the eave of the house down to the ground. And it was cold, well below freezing. We heated the house with a large fireplace, and in the evening, dad slipped a big pine knot into the fire and let it burn. After that, he banked the fire with ashes and the embers stayed hot all night. In the morning when he got up, he raked out the ashes and the coals came to life. With a little kindling, he built up the fire and put on another big pine knot.

Pine knots deposited a lot of soot in the chimney and we cleaned it regularly. We attached brushes to a long pole and shoved it up the chimney, but it was a bad job because we were showered with soot and our skin turned black. If we didn't do it, we could end up with a chimney fire and burn the house down.

Dad tended the fireplace, mom's domain was the woodstove. She was good at stuffing in kindling and getting a fire going quickly. She made our food on it, heated water for our baths in the stove's water tank and warmed up the kitchen. In the bedrooms, we had kerosene stoves, but never did light them much because my father figured they weren't safe.

Even so, I didn't freeze. My bed was covered with a *sugan*, a thick quilt ranch workers used when sleeping out on the range. There were two parts, the top and the backing. For the top cover, mom cut up old jeans and sewed them together with yarn into a patchwork. She stretched the covering on a frame, or sometimes she made the cover on the floor with a bedding needle and ran red, orange or blue thread up and down and tied a knot. She sewed the top cover onto an old Army blanket for the backing. Then she added fill in between the top and the blanket.[2]

Along with the sugan to keep us warm, we wore heavy pajamas and slipped into bed under flannel sheets.

When it got really cold, we stuffed a hot water bottle under the covers and shoved it to the bottom of the bed for a foot warmer. Sometimes mom or dad heated a brick in the fireplace, wrapped it in an Army blanket or newspaper and put it at the foot under the covers. Our cats got in bed with us and went down to our feet to sleep.

My mom and dad's room was off the living room and got heat from the fireplace. My room, shared with my sisters, had been added on later and it was big, built with thick logs and chinked with mud, but it was a distance from the fireplace. My brother's room was off the kitchen and got the heat radiating from the woodstove.

In the White Mountains, it first snowed in October and then we had snow on the ground for the rest of the winter. Often it snowed all day and all night and lay in banks. We had to use chains on our car or truck to avoid skidding off the road. On occasion, a snowplow ran up and down the Coronado Trail. We stayed home in front of the fire during the snowstorms because when it's snowing heavily, you get snow-blind in a car pretty fast. If it was snowing lightly, sometimes we rode our horses through the white fog. We couldn't see more than a few feet in front of us and didn't even hear the horse's footfalls because they were muffled.

As winter approached, we drove the cattle under the Mogollon Rim for protection. About the latter part of April or May, if the weather was good, we herded them back up to their pastures in the mountains and they stayed for the summer. As fall came on, most of them lumbered down by themselves to the ranch, although we had to go up there to round up a few laggers.

As you can appreciate, the Hunt brothers did not have the best reputation after the Bartell killing and subsequent trials. My dad and Uncle Joe hoped that moving to the Honeymoon would change things. It didn't.

Before they bought the 4 Drag and Flying U Drag, there was a lot of cattle rustling in the area. As a matter of fact, years earlier, rustling was so out of control that in 1928 the Texas and Southwestern Cattle Raisers Association sent brand inspector-cattle detective Graves Peeler to Clifton, Arizona, to shut down the rustling operations around Eagle Creek, right near the Honeymoon Ranch. An expert tracker and fearless lawman, Peeler stayed for two years and sent a lot of thieves to jail. Despite those efforts, when the Hunts took over the Honeymoon seven years after Peeler had left, cattle rustling was nearly as bad as it was before.[3]

My dad had a solution. To some it may appear drastic, but after everything my dad and Uncle Joe had gone through, it was the best anybody could come up with. He hired a gunslinger.

This was, after all, still the wild and wooly west.

In Mexico, Stewart Hunt had a cow boss called Jess Simpson. As well as being a hired gun, Jess helped out moving cattle, repairing fence and setting traplines. In Stewart's early days, as family legend goes, he and Jess didn't have much cash for food and ate mustang colts "to save the beef that could be sold for money."[4]

Nevertheless, Jess's main duty for Stewart was to prevent cattle rustling. Laws, if they had any, were nearly unenforceable in Mexico, and in order to control cattle thieving, many cattle ranchers and mining companies hired *range detectives*. That was a charitable title for someone who specialized in intimidating people and, on occasion, perhaps committing murder.

According to family stories, Jess killed a man in Sonora and Stewart sent him to Chihuahua to get him out of sight. A short time later, he had to bring Jess back because he killed two men where he was hiding out.[5] Stewart wanted Jess out of the country, the sooner the better.

When Uncle Joe and my dad bought the Honeymoon, the ranchers neighboring on the north end had been stealing cattle for years. There was also word that the neighbor to the south had taken down some fence and was using the 4 Drag land for grazing. After Jess arrived and started riding fence, the thieving stopped. My dad always said, "Don't mess with my fence."

Cousin Ken calls Jess an "old reprobate and enforcer." He says that Jess carried a .30-30 Winchester rifle in a scabbard underneath his right leg and pulled it out on the slightest provocation. Jess was known as the orneriest human being the west had ever seen. He was a renegade and I would not meet Jess Simpson in the middle of the night anyplace.

On the other hand, my brother Tom shatters the myth that has grown up around Jess. He says that Jess didn't shoot anybody. "He was all right. He was a raunchy old goat, not fit for civilized people. He wouldn't bother anybody who wouldn't bother him."

I remember one time when Tom was a teenager, he was out with Jess and they were on their way back from somewhere driving to the 4 Drag and Jess was drunk. Tom pushed him out of the car.

Tom says that's not what happened. He says they were driving back from town in the ranch pickup, it was late, and they got stuck in the mud. Jess had new chaps on and didn't want to get them dirty, so they backed out and drove to Clifton where Jess had more to drink. Jess went to the local jail to sleep it off and Tom took a hotel room.

My dad had a slightly different take on this incident. He said that Jess was supposed to bring the truck and my brother to the ranch. They got into Clifton and Jess went out and got drunk. My brother went to the sheriff's department and the sheriff called dad and told him old Jess was spending the night in the hoosegow until he sobered up, Tom was staying in a hotel, and not to worry. Next morning, Tom stuffed Jess in the truck and drove him to the ranch. You do have to ask: would my dad have let my fourteen-year-old brother go off with a vicious murderer as Jess was purported to be?

There isn't real proof that Jess killed anybody, but his reputation certainly had the desired effect. If his job was to scare the *bejesus* out of cattle rustlers, he was good at it and saved my family a lot of money.

Getting smashed out of his mind was typical Jess. He and my dad sometimes drove cattle for seven or eight days. When they got close to Springerville or McNary, Jess lit out for town and got stone drunk. Dad bailed him out of jail again and again.

According to Ken, if Jess wasn't in jail or laying somewhere dead drunk, on occasion he and dad drove cattle from the 4 Drag across the San Carlos reservation, then across Turtle Mountain, and went north to the train tracks at McNary. I recall another route they used to drive cattle. They ran them over the Black

River to the town of Bylas, an open area on the Natanes Plateau on the west side of Point of Pines, from where they shipped the cattle by train. I drove the truck north of Safford to meet the cattle drive and then we all went on to Bylas.

No question that Jess Simpson was a piece of work, but he was always gentle and nice to the kids. And he could do anything. He fixed fence better than anybody I'd ever seen. An elk will tear a fence down for miles. They put their heads down and get their horns under the fence, pull it and lay that fence on the ground. Fixing that mess was Jess's real job, to ride fence and cut trail. Cutting trail is when you come across a trail that shouldn't be there and then follow it. Jess was looking for would-be rustlers, so if he saw a fresh trail, he followed it. I never heard that he found anybody.

Without question, life on the Honeymoon Ranch was a lot better than life on the Malpais or in the Animas Valley. In addition to the ideal location up in the mountains with lots of pasture and water, it was big enough that my dad and Uncle Joe didn't have to move cattle around to better pastures or water sources. We used 50 sections or 50 square miles above the Mogollon Rim and 50 square miles below the rim. (With 640 acres to a square mile, we ranched 64,000 acres.) It saved them time and effort they could spend elsewhere.

A big portion of land around the Honeymoon was Bureau of Land Management (BLM) forest land. We leased BLM property and bought up as much as possible around it in order to expand our grazing area.

During the summers on the Honeymoon, my dad was up in the cow camps with a bunch of cowpokes rounding up cattle, branding and doctoring. I went up there to be with him and my brother. Otherwise, I wouldn't see them all summer.

The cows were up in mountain meadows such as Hannigan Meadow, Boy Scout Cienega, Gobbler Point and Point of Pines, site of ancient Indian burials.[6] We brought everything we needed in saddle bags. For washing, we jumped in the river and went for a swim. It wasn't too cold. We drew drinking water from running streams and didn't boil it. It was good, clean water.

At the Hannigan Meadow camp, we slept in a wood frame building with a dirt floor. The Boy Scout Cienega had cabins with dirt floors. Otherwise, we slept outside. We picked off the rocks, raked pine needles into a bundle and slept on that. The great thing about the Boy Scout camp was they had a stove range that made our stay much easier.

In the other camps, we didn't have a range and cooked instead in the Dutch oven, a heavy cast-iron pot with a lid. One of its best features was a lip around the lid for holding coals.[7] We dug out a pit in the dirt for the oven, and when we got up in the morning, we built a fire under it.

While at the cow camps, I learned to make upside-down cakes and jerky gravy. Dad got up in the morning and made big batches of hot biscuits and white gravy in the Dutch Oven and then bacon or fry steaks with a little touch of lard or oil.

I went up to the cow camp about three times every summer, each occasion for two to three weeks. Maybe it was for the company, maybe for my dad's pancakes.

To assist with the cattle, we brought along our cowdogs that we hand-raised to watch and herd because it was rough country. They went into places overgrown with brush or filled with boulders where we couldn't go.

Sometimes the cowdogs didn't find the cattle they were searching for. Cows up in the mountains for a long time can turn wild and find places to hide. If we came across one, they were not easy to rope or corral. To deal with this, dad built wild cow traps. A cow trap was like a corral made out of posts and fencing with a V-shaped gate that opened in but not out. Dad put salt in the cow trap and the wild cows pushed the gate to get at that salt and it shut behind them. Sometimes an elk barged his way in and then you had yourself an elk, unless he tore up the fence trying to get out of the trap.

One day, my dad went up to check on a wild cow trap and he found in the middle of it some city idiot sitting around a big campfire. My father questioned the guy's intelligence, as only he could do, and ran him off. The guy was lucky he didn't get a bullet where his suspenders met.

27. A Far-Out School

After my year off school, I planned on going to university in the fall of 1938. Dad expected me to attend college in Arizona, but I'd made a lot of friends in California and wanted to go to Stanford with my friends.

"*NO*, uh-uh," said my dad.

"Uncle Charlie went to Stanford," I said. My dad's brother had graduated from Stanford as a doctor.

"It's a far-out school and you are going to school at the university in Arizona," he said.

To him, *far-out* meant too many avant-garde concepts. He liked traditional programs and ways of teaching.

I told him that the University of Arizona was not known for strong academics or for offering the best courses and was considered a party school.

"This is our university and if it's not good enough for you, then we have to make it good enough," he said.

My dad was like that: *if it's not good enough, make it good enough*. He and mom said we had to support and protect what we had in Arizona and make it better. We were protecting the ability to have a continuous education, starting in first grade and going all the way through high school and college until we finished.

When I went down to register, the university required us to choose a major and minor and I chose history as my major and English and Physical Education as minors. After a while, I switched my major to Speech Arts and Dramatics. I was not yet thinking of teaching as a career.

When I was ready to begin college, my sister Nell was home after graduating from high school in California. My brother, Tom, who had been living with a family in Morenci and going to Morenci High, was home, too. My youngest sister, Bess, was still going to Eagle Creek School, a grade school south of the Honeymoon Ranch.

Since dad wanted all of us to go to the University of Arizona, he decided the best thing was to buy a house in Tucson "so all the kids could be under one roof for school." In 1939, he bought 1024 E. 7th Street, off Park, and moved us in. Nell and I went to the university, Tom went to Tucson High, Bess went to Miles Elementary in Tucson and then to Mansfeld Junior High. Mom stayed with us for a time, but I was eventually crowned "head of household." And everybody had to do what I told them to. If only...

As it happened, our place became a magnet for friends and orphans. One was Faye Dunseth. Faye's parents were killed in an automobile accident and she was forced to live with her cranky aunt. As things were not working out, Faye came to live with us. She became a close friend and felt it was her duty to cook and do laundry. We didn't say no.

My mother said, "You dragged home every stray dog, cat and kid." We always had lots of people at the ranch and I was merely continuing that custom. Sorority girls lived with us, as did the Darnell girls from Apache. We fought but we got along.

We had three bedrooms, a living room and dining room, kitchen, big pantry, but only one bathroom for a bunch of girls and one boy. On Saturdays and Sundays, we cleaned and ironed and washed, and the rest of the week we were slobs. We were too busy studying to clean.

Date night was a mad house. I had more than a few boyfriends. No serious romances, but I made it my business to have a date every Saturday night.

Just as I was beginning my third year at the university, an event interrupted my frivolity. It was an incident that reminds us how fragile we are.

28. Uncle Joe

After enduring years of trials and appeals following the killing of Chester Bartell, in 1924 Uncle Joe left the Animas Valley and found a job in the Bisbee copper mines. He was still under indictment and didn't know if he would go to jail.

He left the mines and for a short time worked with my father on the John Slaughter Ranch. In December, he was finally acquitted and could think of the future again.

He took a job with the Bisbee YMCA as director of boys' activities, stayed for four years, met Edith, his wife to be, and married in 1928. For several years, they lived on the Slaughter Ranch, which was still under lease by the Hunts.

In 1934, Uncle Joe ran for the state senate, just ten years after being acquitted of murder, and was elected an Arizona State Senator representing Cochise County. People were smart enough to know that the charges against Uncle Joe were bogus from the beginning and had more to do with politics than anything else. Everybody liked Uncle Joe, and after his run-in with the law and its inequities, people felt he could make a difference for the citizens of Arizona.

A popular legislator, he was reelected in 1936. Uncle Joe continued his interest in cattle during his time in the senate and became an officer in the Arizona Cattle Growers' Association. The following year, he and my dad bought the Honeymoon Ranch.[1]

Realizing he couldn't do both jobs well, he decided to focus his energies on cattle and left the senate. However, his political friends had other ideas, and in the summer of 1940 they visited the ranch to talk him into running for governor, something he thought was worthwhile.

A few months later, on October 6, 1940, while I was away at university in Tucson, the phone rang in the middle of the night. As the semester had just begun, our mom was staying with us to get us settled. She answered and one of the hands on the 4 Drag told her that my father got killed. My mother said, "It can't be, it can't be..."

The phone at the 4 Drag was on the porch and had poor reception. "Oh, I can't believe this..." my mother said and came in the bedroom and told us, "Your father's been killed by a horse."

We were in shock. She went back to the phone and the reception must have improved because the hand told her it was *not* my father. It was my Uncle Joe.

Apparently, my dad, Jess Simpson, Uncle Joe and a bunch of the hands were herding cattle on the ranch. Uncle Joe was chasing a calf when his saddle girth broke. He became tangled in the saddle straps, fell backwards, was dragged onto rocks and broke his neck.

He was forty-five years old and left his wife and two boys, Phillip, and my cousin Ken, who was six at the time. It was a terrible tragedy for my family. After enduring so much heartache as a result of the Bartell trial and working hard to make the ranch prosperous, my uncle was dead.

Joe was my favorite uncle. He's the one that gave me the clove of garlic and told me to bite on it. He teased me... and he played with us. I remember one Christmas he gave us a makeup set. My father had a fit. We were too young to put on lipstick, but my uncle thought it was funny. That was him, always having fun with us.

We went to the funeral a few days later at the Presbyterian Church in Bisbee and he was buried in Douglas. In an obituary in the October 8, 1940, edition of the Arizona Republic the reporter made no mention of the Bartell killing and trials. It would have been bad taste to bring up such a terrible thing about a man who helped a lot of people and lived an exemplary life.[2]

Uncle Joe left behind a successful cattle operation, but the Honeymoon Ranch was so huge, over very rough terrain, that my dad, who was then almost sixty, found it too difficult to manage by himself. Heartbroken over his brother's death, within a year he sold the ranch and moved to Tucson.

Uncle Joe's death represented something I hadn't faced before. I was a young woman, untouched by death in my family. I realized that at anytime, no matter how smart I thought I was or how cultured I had become, life could end before my dreams were fulfilled.

In my sadness, I became determined to make every minute of my life meaningful.

CP Hunt and Susan Mary Harris

Stewart Hunt

The brothers, L-R: Charles, Jim, Jack, Sam, Joe

Sallie Stewart as young girl

Jack Hunt as young man

Shetland pony, Prince: L-R: Dorothy, Nell, Tom, Bess

Dorothy, age one or two

Dorothy and baby Nell

Mrs. Keeling, Dorothy's Grade 4
teacher, Apache School, 1930

Chevy school car. L-R: Nell, Tom, Bess, Dorothy, around 1930

Johnny Stride pole, 1927

Dorothy in Jr. high school uniform, 1935

L-R: Ken, Phil, Uncle Jim branding cow using running iron, circa 1930

Jack Hunt and Tony, Malpais Ranch, 1931

Jack Williamson as young man

Jack Williamson, 2002

Jack and Sallie Hunt, circa 1935

Picnic at Honeymoon Ranch, Ma Castro in apron, circa 1938

Honeymoon Ranch. L-R: Nell, Betty, Dorothy, Ken, 1938

L-R: Faye Dunseth, Nell, Dorothy, Bessie, circa 1940. College years.

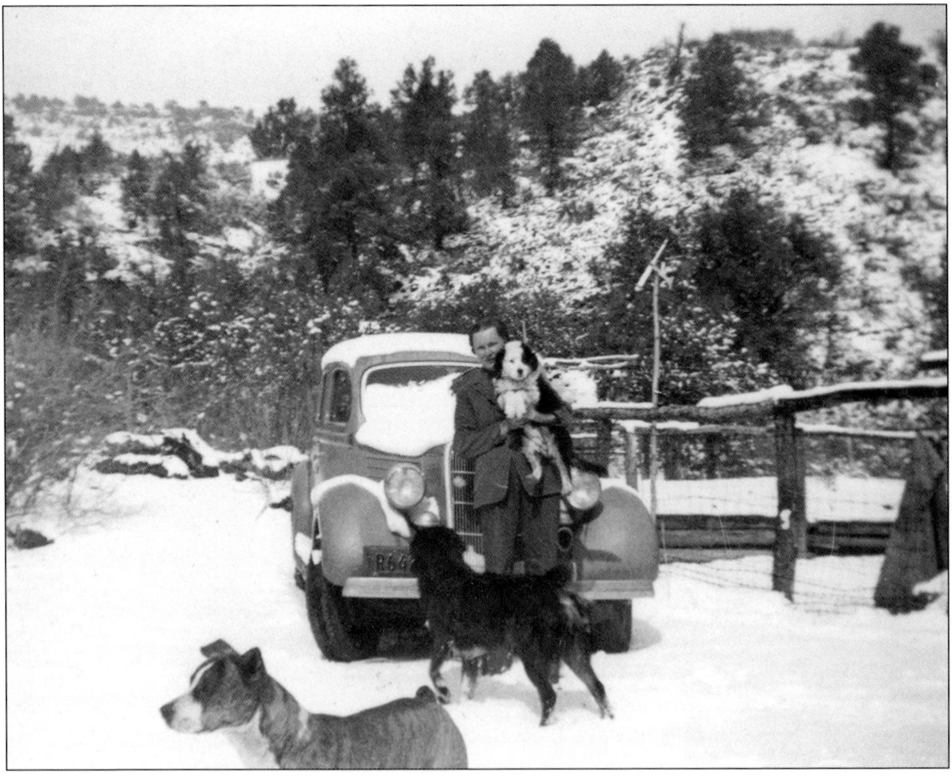

Dorothy and dogs, Honeymoon Ranch, around 1938

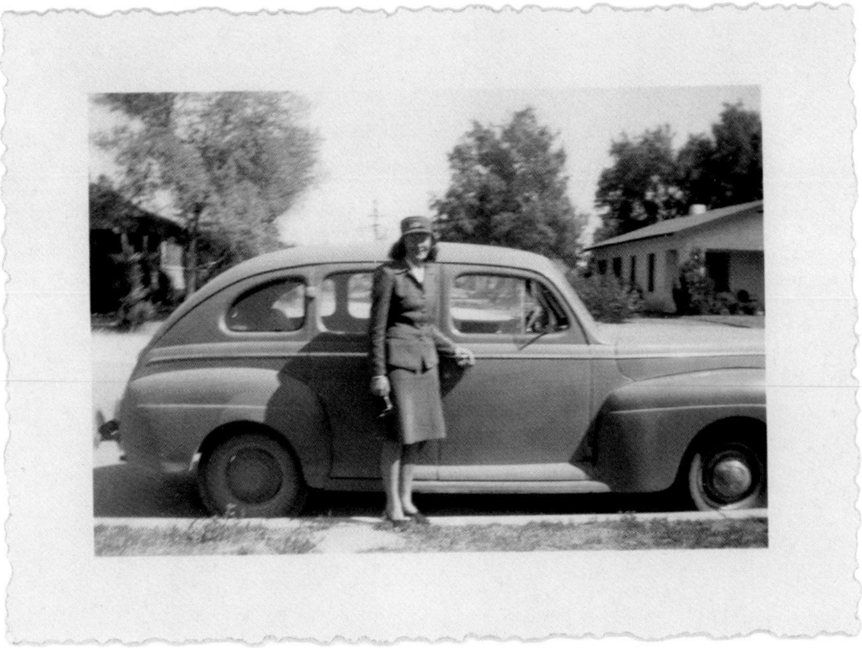

Dorothy in Red Cross uniform, 1942

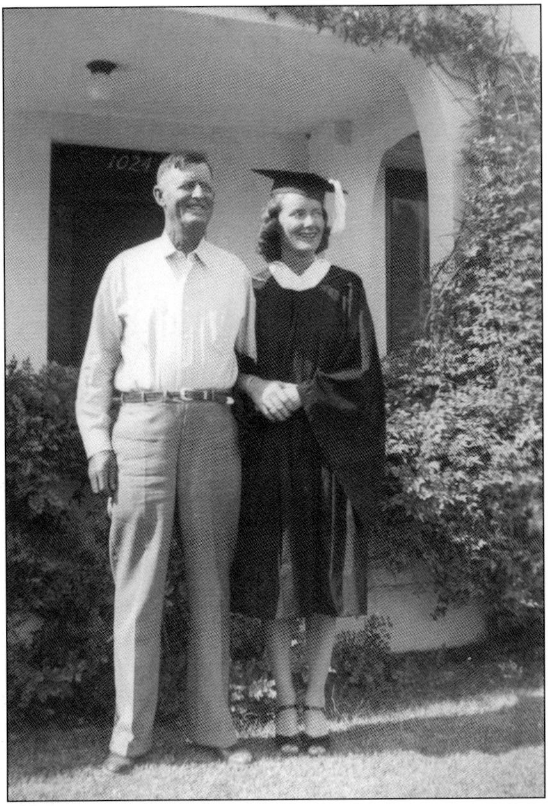

Dorothy, Jack Hunt. Graduation from University of Arizona, 1943

Harold's grandmother,
temperance worker

Harold Finley when Dorothy
met him, 1945

Harold Finley, Air Force photo, 1944

Dorothy, Harold Finley, wedding day, June 19, 1946

Dorothy's wedding, 1946, L-R: Isabelle Finley, Nell, Dorothy, Harold, Bess, Faye Dunseth

Ford stake truck. Harold with baby John, nephew John Raasveld, 1948

Sallie Hunt, John Finley

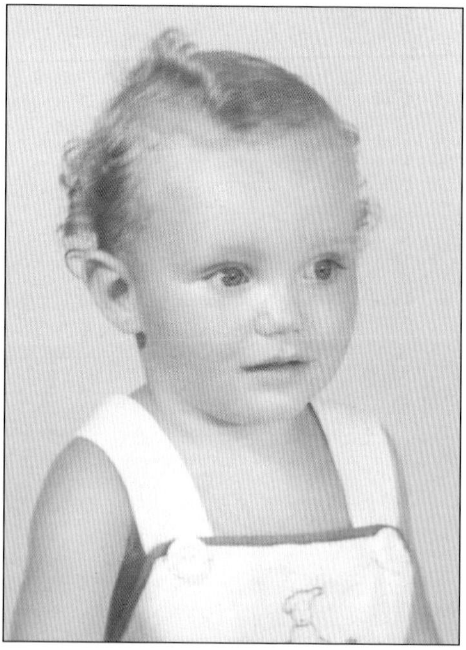

John Finley as toddler

Bill Corcoran, 1990

Dorothy, Glennalee Foulk, 1994

Dorothy, The Honorable Jim Kolbe, (R-Ariz.), U.S. House of Representatives, 1990

The Honorable Jon Kyl, Senator (R-Ariz.), Dorothy, Dick Cheney, former Vice-President of the United States of America, 1993

Richard Leakey, Dorothy, Kenya, 1988

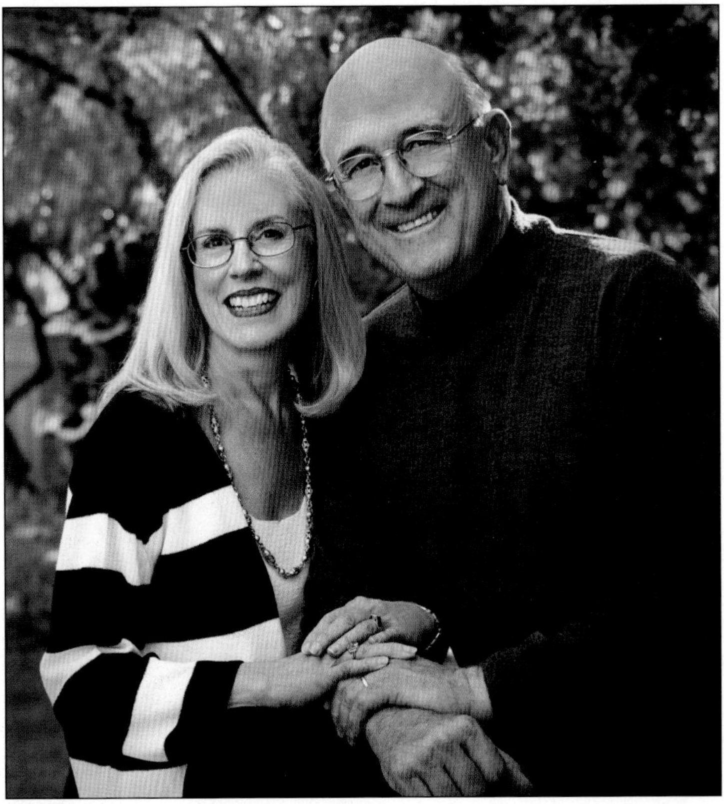

The Honorable Mayor Robert E. Walkup, City of Tucson, AZ. His wife, Beth.

Grandchildren: Jessica, Alex

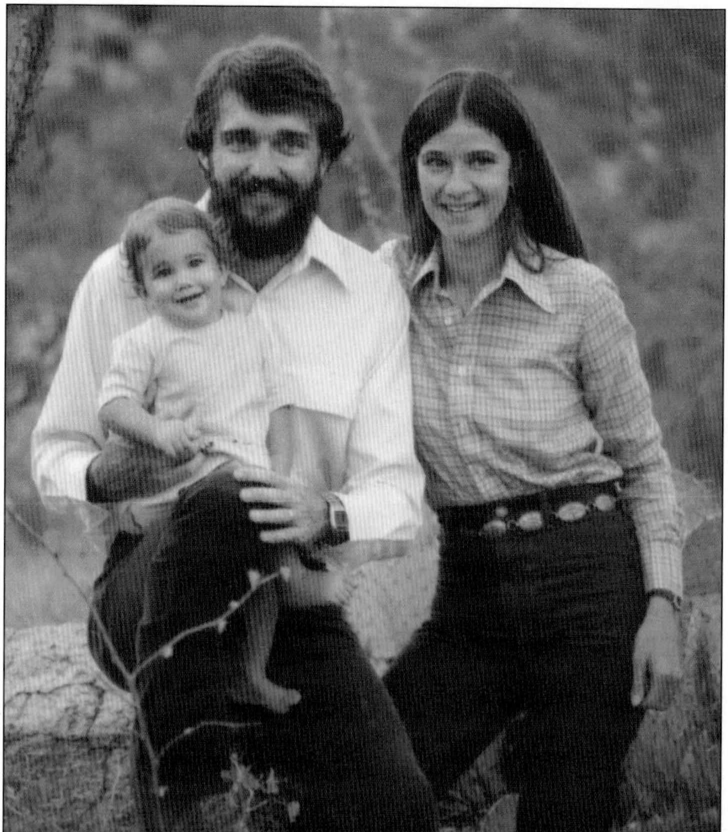

John, Audrey and baby Jessica, circa 1979

29. War Comes Again

During my first two years of university, I spent the summers working on the Honeymoon Ranch. By the third summer, Uncle Joe was gone and my father sold the ranch.

My days riding fence and herding cattle were over. Now I was a city girl and set out to find a job to help pay for college and landed one in the old court house filling in taxpayers' names and their property in big ledgers. Being used to the outdoor life, it was not as much fun as riding the range.

Before going to the city, my only other paying job was during fire season in the White Mountains. The ranchers that used federal forest land had to send their cowboys to fight the fires and I helped out by wrangling the firefighters' horses. They paid a meager amount. I would have done it for free.

My first fire was way up on top of the rim and our riding horses were down at the Honeymoon. My job was to ride out into our pasture, round up the horses, and herd them down to the house and into the corral. To get them ready, I bridled them, and when I ran out of bridles, I used hackamores or lead ropes. Then one of the fire rangers trailed them to where the firefighters needed them. Trucks were useless. The ground was so rough that only horses could get through.

I only worked two fires, both at Rose Peak. The second one was the biggest fire we ever saw in the White Mountains. My father brought all his men and it took about a week to put it out.

My father didn't fight the fires. He cooked for about 25 firefighters. When they came for meals, he expected them to wash up and eat like gentlemen, but as soon as they got off the fire line and smelled my dad's cooking, they ran in and shoved each other and slopped food onto their plates.

To socialize the young men, my dad hammered pegs around the eating area and tied them together with rope. He told the firefighters that anybody who came in without being invited... well, his pistol hung out of his belt.

I can understand the fuss. He was a good cook. In the morning, he made them coffee, bacon, ham and eggs. He fixed a big lunch with beans and meat. In the evening, he made another big meal. He didn't have a chuck wagon, he cooked out on the ground using Dutch ovens and skillets over an open fire.

The firefighters were mostly young cowboys. They used shovels and lit backfires. It was backbreaking work and I'm happy my job was only wrangling horses.

After working at the courthouse, I returned to school. A few months later, on December 7th, 1941, the Japanese, with no warning, attacked our naval base at Pearl Harbor, killing thousands of our sailors and civilians and sank most of our Pacific fleet. In response, on December 11th President Roosevelt declared war on the Japanese. The Germans then declared war on us and we were plunged into World War II.[1]

I watched the boys I grew up with and many fellow students enlist and head out to basic training in preparation for going overseas. With the men leaving, there was more opportunity for women, and in 1942 I got a part-time job teaching swimming at the YWCA. And there seems to be a family dispute about how the devil I was able to get the job if I couldn't swim.

My brother Tom and Cousin Ken say this is an example of my overpowering self-confidence and take charge kind of personality. Tom says that the university needed somebody to teach swimming to the children, and I went down and applied and got the job, even though I didn't know how to swim. "Sounds like something Dorothy would have done," he said, "growing up in pretty tough straights and living through pretty hard periods."

Come on now. Do you think I would have lied about my swimming ability when young lives were at stake? Despite that, the myth persists in my family and I don't know why. Perhaps it's because it's such a good story.

I hate to ruin everybody's fun, but I knew how to swim. At the University of Arizona, everybody was required to earn a swimming certificate or we couldn't graduate. To get the certificate, I had to do a sidestroke and the fast Australian crawl from one end of the pool to the other. Then I had to backstroke while saving a drowning person, holding him under the chin. If that isn't swimming, I don't know what is.

Maybe I wasn't the strongest swimmer in the world, but I was fully qualified to teach swimming. Don't listen to my brother Tom who to this day still says I can't swim.

And there's another reason I had to know how to swim. *Boys*.

During my university days, swimming was an important part of our summer social life. While in college, there were no country clubs in Tucson but for $25 you could belong to the Arizona Inn and swim in their pool. We lay out under the cabana, and on Sundays, for a few bucks, we ate a brunch of crab cakes and home-baked bread served around the pool while the few boys who hadn't gone to war ogled us.

Sometimes my sister Nell joined me at poolside. She attended university as a freshman the same year I did and she was a genius when it came to math. I was gifted in verbal communication, more interested in people than in numbers, and took psychology courses to find out why people do the things they do.

Cousin Betty joined us at the University of Arizona for her first year. Instead of living at the house, she lived in a university dormitory. Betty wanted to be an actress. She said, "If I told my father, we would have had to shoot him to make him let me go to a drama school."

Betty attended the U of A for a year after which her dad told her she was wasting her time and to go to business school. She did as she was told and ended up sharing an apartment in Phoenix with another rancher's daughter. She didn't dare bring up drama school. She said that once Uncle Jim had made up his mind, "that was the end of that."

Besides hanging out at the pool, I loved to dance, and before Betty left the university, she joined me in dance excursions with servicemen. "You did your part," she said. I don't think she did it out of a sense of duty.

A friend of mine who was a Chi Omega told me that my sister and I must be sure to join the sorority when we arrived at university. I went to the first tea to find out about pledging and saw that they only talked to Anglos and that bothered me so I didn't go back.

However, I was chosen by Zeta Phi Eta, an honorary sorority for women in dramatics.[2] The honoraries were different than regular sororities. They seemed more concerned about good grades than the color of your skin or your ancestry. Boy, was I naïve. I knew a neat gal in dramatics and we attended the same makeup class and practiced on each other. As I was the treasurer of the sorority and an officer, I nominated her.

About two weeks later, a national officer of the sorority asked to see me. She said we had a problem because our new member was Jewish.

"You know, we don't take people of this faith in the sorority," she said.

I said, "So?"

"They have a tendency..."

"Don't tell me that," I said. "I will leave."

"No, no, we don't want you to drop out."

"This is ridiculous," I said. "Would you like us to go to the newspapers and tell them why we can't have Jewish girls?"

"Oh my, oh my, oh dear, no."

They must have had that rule all along. The girls told me I'd have problems because I went up against a national officer, but I didn't care. The injustice made me mad.

My mom and dad never judged people. They taught me that everybody was a human being and you treated them the way you wanted to be treated. I am not biased. It's what's inside, not what's outside that matters. I never heard from that national officer again.

Unfortunately, at that time, most of the sororities discriminated against anybody who wasn't white, well-off and well-connected. I had a friend from Flagstaff, a real smart person, but we weren't supposed to bring him to our sorority parties because he was Jewish. Well, baloney. I brought who I pleased.

The dramatic sorority was not the only one I was involved in. I was also a member of the Alpha chapter of Pi Lambda Theta, which focused on high scholastic achievement and leadership and is for people wanting a teaching career.[3] I belonged to Delta Sigma Rho, which was an honorary debate fraternity for both men and women.[4] That one helped me hone my negotiation skills. (After college, I was elected into Delta Kappa Gamma, an honorary sorority for educators. I became chair of the M U chapter in Tucson.)[5]

Maybe I was Miss Socialite hanging around the pool with sorority girls, but I wasn't empty-headed. I hated bullies and stood up for those who were discriminated against.

Belonging to sororities during the war years was no big help anyway in finding fine young men. The college men were enlisting or being drafted into the service and pickings were sparse.

That didn't stop us. What we lacked in college men we made up in servicemen. I was particularly attracted to flyboys. They were everywhere. Pilots trained at Ryan Airfield in southwest Tucson, at the airport in Avra Valley and at Davis-Monthan Air Force Base (DM).[6] I thought, *Now, how am I going to meet the men from the base?*

Here's how I did it. For PE at college, we played golf at Randolph Park (now called Reid Park) and the cavalry was stationed nearby. Opposite one end of the golf course the guys curried their horses in the late afternoon about the time we were playing golf. And the boys were anxious to meet university girls.

The teacher sat up in the clubhouse at the starting point and couldn't see us when we were on the course. We teed off at the first tee and played the second one. Then we strolled down the hill to the fence, well out of sight, and talked with the boys. After a while, we picked up our ball, moseyed on up the hill and played the last hole. We filled in our scorecards and the teacher thought we were doing what we were supposed to do. We thought we had the wool pulled over her eyes.

One day, all of a sudden, the teacher called us in, and had a big *Coming-To-Jesus* party. Somebody had ratted us out and she told us we were not to fake the game anymore. So we quit meeting the boys at the bottom of the hill, but by then I had met two men, both attorneys conscripted into the service.

Getting busted did not end our scheming. The engineers rebuilding DM were billeted south of Randolph Park, but they weren't allowed to leave the base except to play ball at the park. We made arrangements to watch the baseball games and a whole carload of us went out and cheered at the games. We were unstoppable.

Soon the construction of DM was finished and the engineers went elsewhere. What were we gals to do?

I was fond of a boy at the university. He was a 4-F, and did anyone want to be seen with a 4-Fer? I mean, if a 4-Fer was physically unfit to fight during wartime when the country was taking anybody on two legs, then the girls didn't want them either. Very small-minded of us, but that was the thinking at the time. That budding romance never got off the ground. But I didn't have to pine for long. The Air Force took over the base and the ball games resumed.

Around that time the YWCA on 5th Street began holding dances and I went every Saturday and Wednesday night. At first, the military people didn't have bands and we danced to scratchy records. Many of the boys had never danced before and they stepped all over our feet. The DM recreation people asked me if I would teach ballroom dancing to the recruits for 50 cents an hour. I figured anybody could learn how to dance. I was sure wrong about that. Some of those boys were hopeless.

We quickly outgrew the space at the YWCA, which was only one big room. The Bates home on Stone Avenue, which later became the Mountain Oyster Club, let the Y use its facilities. So we danced Saturday night at the Bates, and one Saturday a month the Pioneer Hotel let us have dances in their ballroom. Sometimes we met the servicemen at night for dances at the armory. On Sunday afternoon we went to tea dances. That was the only time the kids from Ryan Field were allowed out. We danced at the Santa Rita Hotel, too, in a room called *the Passion Pit.* I'll leave that to your imagination.

Monday night, we had a YWCA meeting. Tuesday night we usually went out. Wednesday night we danced at Davis-Monthan, where they replaced the record player with a live band. Sometimes we gals were loaded into the back of GI trucks, given blankets for the cold, and driven out to Marana where the U.S. Army Air Force, as it was known then, had moved the intermediate flight training. We danced for several hours and then endured the bumpy trip back home.

In school, I took the necessary classes, but there was a class every freshman had to take called *Social Fundamentals.* I hated it, but now I think it was one of the most useful classes in college. It was really an etiquette course and taught proper behavior for young ladies and gentlemen in social situations. It coached us on where to wear gloves, when men should wear their ties, what '*formal*' and '*informal*' meant. '*Protocol*' was the best part of the class, how to set a table for important people, that sort of knowledge.

I still do a lot with the military and they're big on protocol: the proper seating arrangements for dignitaries, the proper respect for rank. Once for an important dinner, I put the place cards out according to seating protocol. Then someone who was helping me changed the seating chart. When the guests got there, they picked up their place cards and we had superiors sitting with subordinates... It was too late to move them back and it was embarrassing.

As well as proper dinners, the military had proper dances, and you had to know how to dress and conduct yourself. Most important for the girls were good dancing shoes. Mine were *I. Miller's.*[7] They were very comfortable brown alligator leather with high heels. I bought them at Jacome's Department Store at Scott and Congress Streets for around $60.[8] That was expensive and I saved up my ration coupons to buy them, but, jeez, you had them forever.

Besides all the fun, I actively supported the war effort by driving an ambulance for the Red Cross. I took a six-week training course with Monte Mansfeld who owned the Ford dealership. Monte is said to have played the greatest role in Tucson's growth and is known as "the man who returned from Washington with Davis-Monthan in his pocket."[9] He sold the equipment to the Red Cross and his men taught us how to drive the ambulance. It was easy for me because the ambulance had to be double-clutched just like our ranch trucks.

One day there was an accident near the base and a woman was badly burned. I took off in the ambulance, picked up the patient and delivered her to Davis-Monthan, but they did not have a burn center. I had to speed her over to St. Mary's Hospital.

We didn't have paramedics then and I was the only person with the patient. I had Red Cross training for emergencies such as stopping someone from bleeding, putting on a bandage and attaching a splint. I was not trained to handle severe burns and injuries. I heard that after I brought her to the hospital she lived.

Transporting the injured wasn't my only job with the ambulance. The Air Force had built a little airstrip on the far south side of town where Raytheon is now. It was an important refueling stopover for planes when they were being ferried from one base to another. The airstrip's terminal was one old lonely shack with a refrigerator, and it was the duty of the Red Cross to stock it with fresh water and sandwiches. I drove the ambulance loaded with food supplies and restocked the fridge. Maybe it seems like nothing, but every bit helped.

Back at school, I was training to become a speech therapist, but nobody hired speech therapists. It seemed like a dead-end endeavor. Then, when I became a senior in the fall of 1942, a marvelous thing happened. The Speech Arts and Dramatics Department called and offered me a job helping people with speech problems.

To record people's voices, the department used a Wire Recorder Machine, an invention dating from the 1890s that used wire instead of today's magnetic tape. Its sound quality was almost as good as a crackly 78-rpm record. Then it was state of the art.[10]

This was no little handheld gizmo. As the prototype, it was a big, heavy machine that stood from the floor up to my waist. Today we record for hours, but then you could only record for 15 to 30 minutes. That was a big deal. The Wire Recorder broke down all the time. But I learned to fix the machine by myself and finally had a job at the university.

School children and university students with severe speech problems came to me for help. Although bright, they were devastated because they could not carry a thought through or express themselves clearly. I worked with children who lisped, who were stutterers and children with autism type symptoms who didn't talk at all.

To control stuttering, I taught the children how to form their message. In the olden days, they put a stone in the mouth. That didn't work. It was better to teach them breathing control and other techniques. In lisping, it's usually the Rs and where they are made in the mouth. I taught them how to put their tongue a certain place. Little kids have trouble with Rs and Ss, and once you teach them, they don't forget.

For that job, I was paid 35 cents an hour and thought that was pretty good. At the same time as I was working, I was taking a full load of 21 semester hours, including 6 hours of apprentice teaching. Although more focused on speech therapy as an occupation, I was becoming enamored with the idea of teaching as a career. My stint as an apprentice teacher convinced me of that... in spite of what happened next.

I was sent to do my apprentice teaching with a *critic teacher*, Frederica (Freddie) Wilder, at Safford Middle School. Critic teachers were the same as supervising teachers now. Even though I was supposed to do my practice teaching in English, Freddie was teaching Speech Arts and Dramatics. I wasn't about to let this opportunity slip away and decided to do my apprentice teaching in dramatics. The problem was I didn't tell anybody what I was up to.

At the end of my apprentice teaching, we put on a school play. I was the director, and on the day of the performance I looked up and saw my teacher from the university, Dr. Oliver Kelleam Garretson, who we called "OK" Garretson,[11] with Dr. Robert Morrow, the Superintendent of Schools for the Tucson Unified School District (TUSD).[12]

Freddie thought my work was good and gave me an A for the six credits. Dr. Garretson changed my grade to a B. Perplexed, I went to see him.

"You're supposed to be doing your apprenticing in English," he said.

"Oh, no..." I said. "My major's Speech Arts and Dramatics." This did not help my case, as they didn't have apprentice teaching for dramatics.

"Do you know why I gave you a B?" he said. "Because you defied me."

I said, "I didn't think switching over was very important."

What do they say about digging a deep hole that's filling with water? Stop digging. I didn't and argued with him further. I guess OK Garretson was not okay with what I did. He stopped me and said, "If that was your decision, *my* decision is to give you a B for not following instructions."

Instead of six units of As, I had six units of Bs. When I saw him standing in the back of the room, I knew I was in trouble. But if I could go back in time, I wouldn't change a thing.

In early 1943, a group came from Globe, Arizona, where they were short of teachers and tried to persuade some of us to quit school and go up there to teach. Globe was a small town near the Apache reservation with a violent history of robberies, shootouts and murders. Its population was mostly made up of mining and cattle people. I told them I'd let them know.[13]

I thought about it and decided I was up for an adventure. I went downtown to the telegraph office to send a confirmation and ran into a gal I knew. I told her about the job in Globe.

She reminded me I was graduating in May and asked why I was throwing away my hard-earned degree for a job in a small town. She said I had a hole in my head and listed the reasons why it was a bad move: I might not come back; teaching there would only get me a temporary teaching certificate; and did I really want to teach in Globe?

She was right. I contacted the school and told them I didn't want to get a temporary certificate. Even though they were upset with me, I'm so grateful my friend talked me out of doing something I'd regret my whole life.

30. My First School

Soon after the Globe fiasco, I was offered a contract to teach at Wakefield Junior High in Tucson.[1] And in the fall of 1943, I started my first job, teaching English and Phys Ed. Maybe I should have done my apprentice teaching in English after all.

We had the best principal, Noble Hiser,[2] also known as Old Ironsides because he was a stickler for rules. I got to school in the morning, taught English class, then pulled off my skirt and put on my uniform. I rushed down and taught PE. Then I quickly got my skirt back on and ran upstairs and taught English again. Then I made an unspeakable error. One cold, windy day, I put warm-up pants over my shorts and went outside for PE.

After I finished, Old Ironsides called me to his office. He reminded me that I was required to wear my white PE uniform with shorts everyday no matter the weather. I think maybe he liked to see my legs. That's what my fellow teacher and friend Bill Corcoran says.

I'm not fishing for compliments, but apparently my legs were a topic of conversation even among the students. Bill Valenzuela, a former student at Wakefield, reminded me of an incident at school. He and a few other students saw me in the hall and frequently whispered comments behind my back.

"We used to talk about you all the time in Spanish," Bill told me. "Later on we learned you were from Mexico. God, did you hear us?"

"Yes, I did," I said.

"Did you hear us when we said in Spanish, 'Look at her legs... *whew*.'"

"Of course."

Apart from showing off my legs and teaching English and PE, I had other responsibilities like lunch duty. The boys' physical education teacher, Mr. White, and I hightailed it over to Hollinger Elementary School (called Government Heights School then) while it was serving lunch to their kids. They made good soup and a sandwich for a quarter.

We ate and got back to Wakefield in time for playground duty at our kids' lunch time. We organized about 300 kids into soccer or volleyball teams to keep them busy. If there was an altercation, I took care of it. There was no running to the principal. It was our job to control the kids.

Then someone decided that in addition to keeping an eye on the kids, the PE teachers should sell donuts for about a nickel each. One of us did the selling and one of us watched the playground. Our donuts were a hit and we had to get the shop teacher out to help us wrangle the crowd. The money went to the student activity fund to buy musical instruments and uniforms for the kids that didn't have money to buy those things.

The second year I taught at Wakefield we had so many students attending school we had to keep 60 to 70 kids on the playground at all times in order to make room for the rest of them in the classrooms. Many teachers and parents felt that PE was a dumping ground for kids. I suppose it was. For our efforts as professional babysitters, we earned a meager $1,700 a year, comparable to about $20,000 today.[3]

For my gym class, the girls dressed on the stage of the auditorium with the curtains closed. I called that the Iron Curtain, and that was their only dressing room. They had to wear fresh gym suits every week with their names embroidered on them just so. I had a desk at the back of the stage where I kept my books and records.

If it rained and we couldn't go outside, we went into the multi-purpose room. We used it to eat lunch, play games, do arts and crafts and teach. For the rest of the time, the boys and girls hung out on one huge playground. We had a volleyball net, one set of baskets and softball equipment. The playground was primitive, and having gone to a small schoolhouse, I know primitive. Under these conditions, I taught PE and coached the after-school sports.

Sometimes unexpected things occurred and it was hard to put a positive spin on them. A bridge and a ditch were behind the school. On a Sunday night, the bridge washed out and a car went off the bridge and ran into the concrete embankment.

A woman was propelled out of the car and nobody could find her. The next day, a kid on the playground saw her body in the wash and screamed. The police came right away, but the children were upset. We talked with the kids to give them a chance to vent their feelings and they asked questions like, "Why didn't they warn these people," and so on.

Awhile after we answered their questions as best we could, the kids calmed down. I'm not sure they had a grasp on what death meant and soon put the incident out of their minds.

I had some outstanding students at Wakefield. One was Tommy Price, my homeroom president for the three years I was there. Bill Valenzuela says that Tommy was my pet. "Anything we wanted to know, we had to go to Tommy Price," says Bill. "He could get away with anything." That's not accurate. I stepped on Tommy, too.

All kids have a tendency to be naughty, and one time at noon I was walking across the schoolyard in my gym shorts carrying my clipboard and crossed into the back alley. There I discovered Tommy and some of the boys smoking cigarettes. I'd never seen anybody swallow a lighted cigarette before.

Some years later, in 1950, Bill, Tommy and a bunch of the boys signed up for the Marine Corps to go to the Korean War. Some were only seventeen. Bill was sixteen.

He says that his mother didn't know what she was signing. He had just finished 10th grade when he headed off to boot camp in San Diego. When he got back from training, Bill says people asked him:

"So, how was boot camp?"

He replied, "Oh, it was a piece of cake. I had Miss Hunt as a teacher at Wakefield."

Bill says, "the shop teacher was very strict, but didn't scare us. We could twist him around our little finger. But we were afraid of Miss Hunt. She was strict and meant it."

I don't know what to say about that except *guilty as charged.*

"We all need somebody to guide us," says Bill, "and when we became young men, we understood that she had faith in us. We wanted to make her proud of us."

I was proud of them, but I was distressed when they went off to war. Because I was afraid they might not come home. Those were my kids. Every one of them returned.

A lot of the kids I taught were poor and the military was one of the few occupational avenues open to them. They lived in the barrio, around 44th Street and South 6th across from the VA Hospital. One of the girls was especially poor and couldn't afford tap shoes for a dance competition. I'll let Bill continue the story...

"The girl came to school one morning, opened her locker and there was a pair of tap shoes," says Bill. "That bad, bad Miss Hunt was not about to take credit for it and it took us years to put it together. We didn't know she had a soft side until we came out of the Marine Corps and then it was too late to take advantage of her."

All I can say is I did love my kids.

31. War Torn Sweethearts

While I was teaching at Wakefield, I fell for a pilot from Davis-Monthan. I'm sure that doesn't surprise anybody considering the constant exposure I had to flyboys. It was more than a fleeting romance. We became engaged to be married.

My fiancé's name was Norm. He flew a B-24 bomber and was shot down. He said it was no big deal. They put him on R and R for a few weeks and sent him back to active duty.

The second time he was shot down turned our lives around. In 1945 while flying out of Italy, his plane was hit over Germany and crashed in a field. A German farmer's wife found him and dragged him to her house. She knew a doctor who had been trained in the United States and got him to examine Norm. With no anesthetic, the doctor amputated Norman's leg on the dining room table.

They eventually took him to a German military hospital for treatment. He said they kept putting white powder on his leg and he found out later it was sulfa to keep down infection. In the hospital, he found his bombardier and a few of his crew. The others had been killed when the plane went down. It was remarkable that any of them survived with the B-24's tendency to catch fire.[1]

Before long, he heard battle sounds and knew the American front line was getting closer and closer. He told me that the intensity of the blast noise from the rapid fire anti-aircraft guns was horrific.

Then down the street came our tanks. The nurses ran behind his bed and begged him to tell the soldiers not to rape them. All of a sudden, the doors flew open and in tramped a sergeant. He was a big man and Norm was glad to see him. The sergeant ripped off his emblem, gave it to him and said, "I am here to get our people out."

They transported our wounded to an American hospital and Norm was ill for a long time. They finally brought him back to the United States and sent him to the Percy Jones Army Hospital in Battle Creek, Michigan. It was set up as a military hospital in 1943 for wounded World War II soldiers.[2] They did everything from neurosurgery, plastic surgery and amputations to rehabilitation, so he was in the best of hands.

On May 8th, 1945, the Germans surrendered and the European part of the war was over. The Japanese war still raged until early August when we dropped atom bombs on Hiroshima and Nagasaki.[3] Around that time, I went to see him and almost didn't recognize him, he'd lost so much weight. He told me he probably would never get the use of the other leg and was not sure what he wanted to do or what he'd be able to do and said we should not get married right away.

With things undecided about my future with Norm, I headed back to Tucson. I kept writing and calling and in September 1945, he went back in for surgery. Then, after being engaged for a year and a half, he called and said, "I don't think I am going to be married." I was brokenhearted, but understood what he was doing. I said *Fine* and we broke up.

After Norm was injured, he had a hard time adjusting to civilian life. I would have stuck by him. His selflessness in letting me go saved my future happiness.

32. When Dorothy Met Harold

My dad was going crazy hanging around the house in Tucson. He was used to being outside, feeling the sun on his back and the wind in his face. In 1945, he chucked city living and bought the Double A Ranch just outside of Fairbank, Arizona, near Tombstone.

I was teaching my second year at Wakefield Junior High and visited my family for the Thanksgiving holiday. While mom and dad went to the train station to get my brother who was returning from military service, Nell and I decided to go to the Fairbank country store to get the mail. As well as selling food and sundries, the store, run by the Finley family, was the community's hub to the world, providing post boxes, newspapers and a telephone.

I was in my jeans, my hair was long and I had braids down both sides.

"Aren't you going to fix up?" said Nell. "The Finley boy, Harold, is home from the war and mom is a good friend of Mrs. Finley." Nell knew Harold from when the family went to get the mail, but I had never met him.

"I don't care," I said. "I don't go with boys who are my mother's friends' sons. And if you think I'm going to marry one, ha, ha...” Nell laughed until the day she died about that.

At the store, Harold Finley asked what we were doing. I told him we were going to feed the cattle up at the windmill on the ranch.

“I’ll be glad to help,” he said.

“I don’t need help,” I said. I was perfectly capable of doing it myself.

We said goodbye and Nell and I drove off to the windmill. I was getting the cottonseed cake out of the back of the truck, and the next thing I know here was Harold. He was gonna help us feed.

You have to admire him for not taking no for an answer. He lifted sacks out of the back and asked all sorts of questions.

The next day, we were at the ranch, it was a long weekend, and dad said, “Oh my gosh, here comes that Finley kid, Harold.”

“He’s come to ask me for a date,” I said.

“I don’t think so,” said dad. “He’s probably coming to borrow something.”

Harold drove in, got out of his car and greeted us. He told my father that his dad wanted to borrow our logging chain. Dad gave me that *I-told-ya-so* look and went out to the barn to get it.

Harold sat on the porch and I thought it strange he didn’t go along with my dad. “How about going out tonight?” he said. “To the movies.”

I thought that was a good idea and said okay.

My dad got him the chain and Harold left. My dad turned to me and said, "See, he didn't come to ask you for a date."

I smiled. Dads didn't know everything about guys.

Harold picked me up that evening and we went to a movie in Fry, later renamed Sierra Vista. In the theater, he was a gentleman. If he had tried to hold my hand, I might have smacked him.

As we were driving home, it snowed, and he told me that his sister had arrived and they were going to Nogales tomorrow.

"Do you want to go?" he said.

"No, I don't think I'd better."

He didn't know the reputation girls got if they went to Nogales with the boys. Then he said his sister and her husband were going. I told him I would think about it and he said he'd come by in the morning.

My mother said she'd met Harold's sister Isabelle and her husband Dave, they were nice people and I'd have a good time. They were farmers from California north of Fresno. I figured with his sister there it was safe, and next morning I got in the car with them. The whole way to Nogales was dirt road so it took a long time to get there, even though we rode in his sister's Lincoln Zephyr.

In Nogales, we went across the line to Mexico. Harold bought tequila and we all bought knickknacks. We had lunch at the Caves because we loved their green turtle soup. It was owned by a Greek guy featured in *Life Magazine* because he said we could seed clouds and make it rain.

That evening, we went up to Nicksville, halfway between Sierra Vista and Bisbee. We called it the crossroads. It had a store, a dance hall and bar and we had dinner and danced. Afterwards, they took me home. We said goodnight and the whole day was rather sweet.

I didn't know what to make of Harold right then. I was feeling bitter about Norm. We had only broken up a couple of months before. I was grieving for what would never be and not sure I was ready to let anybody else into my heart.

After a short time, Harold's charm won out and we started dating. I lived in Tucson during the week and then rushed down to Fairbank on the weekend to go out with him.

I had a boyfriend in Tucson, too, and my brother Tom got wind of him. I think my sister Bess tattled on me because she liked Harold. Tom and Harold were friends and said that they were going to go to Tucson on Wednesday nights.

Oh shoot... They must have thought we were honky-tonkin.' I asked Tom why they were coming on Wednesdays. He said that he thought we were seeing other boys.

Well, that put a crimp in my style. Wednesday was one of my big dance nights. Anyhow, when they came, we fixed meals and then went dancing.

After we'd been going together a little while, Harold told my brother confidentially that after that first date he'd decided he was going to marry me. Tom said, "Good luck." Tom felt sorry for him and didn't have the heart to tell him he was wasting his time.

I think Tom thought I was at the stage where I dated everybody and didn't want to get serious. My brother knew I'd gone out with a lot of educated guys and preferred the intellectual type. Harold had a couple years of college before he was drafted, but didn't go back to finish. My other boyfriend was an attorney.

The competition didn't bother Harold. Without telling me, he went ahead and talked to my dad about us getting married. Dad said, "If that is what Dorothy wants to do."

Harold asked me to marry him and I said, "Let me think about it."

What I was thinking about was not whether I loved him or whether he could make a good living. I asked myself, *Did I want to be married to a bald man?* He didn't have a lot of hair. The most important thing, though, was I didn't know if I wanted to be married ever. I was still feeling fragile over Norm.

I knew my dad liked Harold, and while we were out working the cattle, I asked him what he thought I should do. He said, "I worry about you marrying that Finley kid because how are you going to make a living?"

"Don't worry," I said.

My father's reaction was, "Humph... He doesn't have an education, you do. You won't have a job. He doesn't have a job."

"I'll have a job," I said.

"Married teachers can't teach in Tucson," he said, and he was right. The school district didn't hire married teachers. I could work other places, just not in Tucson for TUSD.

Tom feels there were other reasons dad was wary about me marrying Harold. Dad believed in a few absolutes in life: The first was Ford automobiles, the second was the Democratic Party and the third was cattle ranching. If you didn't know anything about cattle ranching, you were a dummy and he had no reason to talk to you.

Another of dad's concerns was that Harold was a disabled vet. Before the service, he'd been working for Kresses, a big ice cream plant in Los Angeles, but as soon as the war started, he rushed down and enlisted in the Air Force. Because he had a bad back, they didn't let him go overseas and instead assigned him to a photography unit. Then they shipped him off to Officer Candidate School (OCS) in Colorado. There they had him exercise to strengthen his back, which only made it worst.

The doctor finally said, "We are going to let you go on medical leave and see if this will heal up." It didn't and he went home and met me.

He had a small pension of $25 a week, but he wasn't totally disabled as the Air Force doctor had thought. He could work, as long as the labor wasn't too hard and he didn't pick up heavy objects. I still shudder when I think that he lifted heavy bags of cottonseed cake from the back of my truck to feed the cows. What men won't do to impress a lady.

Despite Harold's faults (the biggest one was that he didn't know diddly-squat about cattle), my father liked his eagerness and positive attitude. My dad liked Harold's family, too, for their work ethic and entrepreneurial spirit. When Harold was born, his parents farmed wheat in Washington. They sold the farm, bought a car dealership, sold that, and then moved to California where his father bought a chicken farm and his mother worked in a hospital. Harold's father was a good carpenter, builder and cement man.

They sold the chicken farm, and during the war moved to Arizona where they bought a mobile home park and cabins. With the bases nearby, they were busy renting out to soldiers and their families. After the war, they moved to Fairbank and leased the store. My dad must have figured that go-for-it attitude had rubbed off on Harold.

Whatever Harold's good points and shortcomings, I had to ask myself, *Why would I want to change my life around for Harold?*

I decided he was a person I could identify with. He was honorable, truthful, strong in character and I loved him. I didn't have to think any longer about whether I'd marry him. I said *Yes.*

Harold called me his child bride. I was twenty and Harold was six years older. Everybody I told about the upcoming marriage said they liked Harold and we made a good team. Where I was volatile about things, he was quiet. He calmly smoked his pipe or cigar and never got worked up. He was sincere, honest and a fun person to be with. Harold was down-to-earth and never felt he was better than anybody else or that other people were better than him.

Just before we were to be married, he sat me down and told me he had something terrible to tell me about himself. I knew he was too good to be true. My heart was pounding. He said that he'd been married before. What a relief... Thank God that's all it was.

When he was working for the ice cream company in Los Angeles, he met this gal and married her. After that, it was pure warfare. Seeing that the situation was hopeless, his father told him, "What you ought to do is get to the tallest building and jump off." Harold didn't see that as an appropriate way to handle things and instead, after six months of marriage, got divorced.

Years later when my son John was drinking beer with one of his aunts real late one night, she told him about his father's big mistake. John was surprised nobody had told him. He didn't know what the big deal was. I think Harold felt you should marry for life; to do otherwise reflected badly on your character.

Harold's big secret did not give me cold feet and we got married on June 19th, 1946.

33. John Wayne Comes To Town

After we returned from our honeymoon in the Grand Canyon, we moved to Fairbank. Despite policy, the TUSD school district offered me a job in Tucson. They let up on married people because there was a severe shortage of teachers. The idea of driving back and forth from Fairbank was daunting, it was too darn far, and I said no. I was a married woman and had other priorities.

At the time, Fairbank was a *real going jesse*, which is an old southern term for very active or in an uproar.[1] Surrounded by groves of mesquite trees near the banks of the San Pedro River, it was a satellite town to Tombstone and had a lot going on.

Fairbank was originally an important depot for shipping cattle and ore. After the mines in Tombstone played out around 1901, the Boquillas Land & Cattle Company claimed Fairbank's land and evicted the homesteaders. The company allowed most town residents to stay.[2]

Among other buildings, the town had a hotel for weary travelers, a jail for obnoxious travelers, and the Fairbank Commercial Store, an adobe building leased by the Finleys. It housed the post office, the general store and a saloon. What would a western town be without a saloon?[3]

When I moved to Fairbank, maybe a few hundred folks lived there. And on any given day, you saw hundreds of people from town and elsewhere working at their jobs. They included railroad gangs, sections gangs and telegraph crews. A crew of four worked around the clock to keep the telegraph operating 24-hours a day. We had bridge gangs on call day and night inspecting every railroad bridge. Since all the residences and rentals were full up, the railroad converted box cars into comfortable living quarters for them.

A signal crew inspected train signals for 10 miles in either direction every week, mine crews hauling tailings from the mine passed through town and a pump station crew maintained the town well and supplied water for the steam engines and town residents. The comings and goings and doings were dizzying and endless... A real going jesse.

A few days after I got settled, my new mother-in-law said the president of the board of trustees from the Tombstone school district had called and wanted to speak to me urgently. I called back and she said here it was already middle of July and they didn't have a PE and English teacher at the high school for the fall. Would I be interested?

"Okay I'll take it," I said. See, dad, I told you I'd get work.

Even better, Tombstone was only 10 miles away to the east and I could ride the school bus to school in the morning and home at night. But I never made such a bad salary.

Six months later, Harold, his dad and his friend, Lloyd Stewart, won a government contract to demolish surplus barracks at Fort Huachuca. They bought an old Army GI 6 by 6 truck with a trailer and headed out for the job.

Before they began the demolition, they emptied out the buildings and were told whatever they found they could keep. They found dozens of new Army blankets and Harold paid the government a quarter for each one. Budding entrepreneur that he was, he later sold the blankets at the general store for a profit.

Harold and Tom tore down the barracks and it was hard work, but they made good money on the deal. Then they hauled some of the used lumber to Phoenix where it was in demand. They sold it to Del Webb the builder who used it for cement forms and footings. With the remainder of the lumber, Harold and his father built two duplexes in Tombstone as well as a house for Lloyd Stewart.

Harold had plans for the money he was making from tearing down the barracks. Before we got married, he said that someday he wanted to be a beer wholesaler. When he worked at the ice cream factory in California, he had a friend who was a wholesale beer distributor and Harold thought that sounded like a fine occupation.

While Harold was organizing his business, from September 1946 to June 1947, I commuted every weekday on the school bus to Tombstone. In the evenings, we often went back to see a movie, have dinner out or went dancing. Sometimes we went to Douglas or to Bisbee for events like the 4th of July. We joined our first country club, the Naco Country Club, and it had dances, dinners and entertainment. We went square dancing, we did two steps, we did it all.

In Bisbee there was a big Episcopal Church and one in Tombstone, the oldest adobe church in Arizona, and that's where we went to socialize and keep our foot in heaven's gate.

I belonged to social and charitable organizations like the Order of the Eastern Star (my husband was a Mason), and the Rebekahs, which is the female auxiliary of the Independent Order of Odd Fellows. I went to meetings in Tombstone for the Arizona Business and Professional Women. The Veterans group in Tombstone had dances once a week and everybody went whether they were veterans or not.

The Fairbank store came with three apartments, and during this time we lived in one of them. Harold built a washhouse and installed a washing machine. One day we went out to put the laundry in and there was a rattlesnake in the corner of the washhouse. Harold hated snakes and lizards and ran into the house and got his .22 rifle. When he came back, I said, "Give me that gun."

He wasn't much of a shot and I knew he would miss. I was a crack shot ever since I can remember. I took Harold's gun and *bingoed* the snake in the head. Harold was impressed.

Speaking of crack shots... In the spring of 1947, we were visited by the actor who was to become the most well-known cowboy in the world—John Wayne.

One day producers from the MGM movie company knocked on the door of the Fairbank general store and said they needed water. Harold thought they meant a glass of water. No, they wanted lots of water, tons of water. They were shooting a movie near Elgin and had to make the San Pedro River look like it was flooding.

Unfortunately, the San Pedro was nearly dry. Could Harold help them, they wondered?

A friend of Harold's told the producers we had the water rights in Fairbank. We didn't, and didn't think to tell them otherwise. What we did have was a real deep well that belonged to the railroad and a Briggs and Stratton motor that Harold used to pump the water for all the people around Fairbank. The producers made a contract with Harold for a lot of money to provide the water they needed.

The movie company constructed a makeshift dam on the San Pedro, just a big tarp they laid over a framework they'd built on the riverbed. They drove a truck with a water tank on the back over to the store and Harold pumped it full of water. Then they went back and dumped it into the pool they had created. In the movie, the river had to flood as the cowboys were driving the cattle across. There was even a scene where John Wayne and an Indian tumbled into the deep water, wrestled around underwater with a knife, but only Wayne emerged in one piece.

For fun, they invited us to Elgin every night to watch the film rushes or raw footage, and we listened to them comment on what was good or bad and what to cut.

I'm keeping the best part for last. The name of the movie was *The River Is Red*, soon renamed *Red River*, the movie that critics call one of the best westerns ever made. It also became the movie that launched John Wayne's career.[4] Up to this point, he was not too well-known.

When we met him, he was just a guy wearing a ten-gallon hat. As our store was the only source of beer for miles, Wayne and the crew hung out in the backroom knocking back cold ones. They sat for hours and the more they drank, the more they spent and the louder they got.

People from the railroad and the town crammed themselves into the store to have a look at him. He was a big man, dressed very casual in jeans, a cowboy shirt and a Stetson. He could have blended in with anybody in town. He and his boys kept asking for more beer and I obliged them. I had never waited on tables, but they tipped me handsomely each time I got them their suds.

While they told stories, we were like flies on the wall. The place was never so busy with all the townspeople hanging out. To add to the noise, the movie people played the jukebox while they drank and chin-wagged. Oh, my gosh, they drank beer after beer after beer of Miller High Life and Pabst Blue Ribbon.

There are a couple of lines in the movie that are especially meaningful to me because we lived that life. John Wayne says:

"I'll have that brand on enough beef to feed the whole country. Good beef for hungry people. Beef to make them strong, to make them grow."[5]

I didn't know John Wayne's proclivity for either Ford automobiles or the Democratic Party, but he was unquestionably a man my dad could talk cattle to.

34. Starting Our Business

Harold's family thought it funny that he wanted to go into the beer business. Harold's grandmother belonged to the Women's Christian Temperance Union and was a teetotaler. She marched up and down the streets of downtown Coeur d'Alene, Idaho, waving signs that condemned the use of alcohol. They had a lot of money, but she spent a lot on her campaign to rid the world of boozehounds.

Harold's father, Walter, liked to go out and get a real snootful and kept whiskey in the cellar. Tom says, "You can't hold that against a man."

When Harold's grandparents died, which was soon after we got married, they left a will and cut Harold's dad out of it. They left everything to Emma, Harold's mother, so the family fortune stayed in the family and was not given directly to Walter to fritter away on drink.

When we went into the beer distribution business, Harold's family said, "What about Grandma Finley?" The family joke was that Walter heartily approved of what we were doing. He even asked Harold if he could join him in the business. Harold said *No*, thank goodness.

By the time I finished teaching at Tombstone High in June 1947, I was pregnant. The doctor told me I might never get pregnant because of endometriosis, but I fooled him. However, I was sick, vomiting and carrying on. Not in the morning but by the afternoon. I don't know why they call it morning sickness. The school year was over, and being pregnant, I would not be allowed to return in the fall.

If you think a policy against married female teachers is onerous, how about pregnant teachers? In Arizona, there was no way they were going to let me teach. Now they beg anybody to teach, but then you were an embarrassment.

My son John was born on March, 1, 1948, and I stayed in hospital for ten days because of hemorrhaging. At the age of twenty-eight, I was a mother.

A short time after I got home with the baby, my mother-in-law said she didn't want to run the Fairbank post office anymore and asked me to take over. I studied her books and took a civil service test that showed I knew numbers and could write a money order. Then I became the postmistress for nearly the next two years. Running the post office was a good job because I walked to work each day and brought John with me.

In a bustling place like Fairbank, the postmistress was an important and harried person. The mail arrived on a mail hack from Nogales and the driver and I separated the mail. We sorted it into sacks for free rural delivery for every town between Fairbank and Nogales including Elgin, Patagonia, Sonoita, and Lochiel. Then away he went on his deliveries. After that, I stuffed the mail slots with letters and parcels for the townsfolk.

At the same time as I was working at the post office, Harold was barreling ahead with his beer distributorship. Harold, Lloyd and I pooled every cent we had. I had saved a little money from teaching in Tucson. We had money from the water used to make the Red River flood and from tips after serving John Wayne and his pals.

In January 1948, we applied for a #4 wholesaler's liquor license, and we got it in March or April, around the same time John was born. You might say we had a double birth, my son and our business.

We already had the old GI truck to make deliveries, but we needed the product. So we made an agreement with a guy named Foster from Tucson Distributing to let us *sub-job* for him in Cochise County. That meant he subcontracted us to sell certain brands of beer on his behalf.

We had our license, a deal for the beer, and next we had to get a warehouse to store it. We found an old barn that had been used to stack hay near the Fairbank store. Harold, his dad, Lloyd, and my brother dug down under the barn and poured a cement floor. Using a backhoe, they dug a trench so we could roll the truck down and have the truck bed level to the floor. That was our loading dock. They put on a new roof and we had ourselves a warehouse.

Then we realized that the old GI truck would no longer do. It wasn't dependable enough or built properly for our needs and we ordered a Ford flatbed truck with stakes on the side. That's what all the beer companies were using for deliveries. After it arrived, there was no money to pay cash for it and we made payments.

At first the beer came in by rail. They sided it down at the railroad station and we hauled it up to the warehouse. Then the railroad decided to take the tracks up. We pleaded our case before the railroad commission, but it didn't do any good. As a result, Harold had to drive the truck to Tucson to pick up the cases of beer.

Then the real work began: *selling.* Harold drove from town to town delivering beer to the bars. We sub-jobbed Falstaff and Miller. Miller was a small line for us then. But we got Hamm's. Then we got Moscow beer and it was popular for quite a while. Brands were popular for a time, and then for reasons unknown fell out of favor with beer drinkers.

Soon Harold's back acted up from all the lifting and he had to spend time in the Veterans Hospital having physiotherapy. That seemed to help and he went back at it full steam.

Harold's partner Lloyd Stewart decided to move back to Georgia and we were relieved to buy him out since Harold did most of the work anyway. We were happy the day we signed the papers for the purchase, but then things got tougher.

The next day, Harold was moving things in the back of the truck and a stack of beer gave way. He fell off the truck and broke his elbow. With Harold's arm in a cast, he couldn't do the heavy work, so on weekends I enlisted Harold's fifteen-year-old nephew, John Raasveld, Harold's oldest sister's son, and we loaded the truck with beer. That's when the cases were made of wood, not cardboard like today, and I built up muscles in places they should not have been.

I put six-month-old John in his bassinet on the front seat, squeezed him between the two of us, and we drove to Bisbee selling beer to the bars up and down Brewery Gulch, my dad's old haunt. After Bisbee, we hit some of the smaller towns.

I don't know how I did it all. I grew up ranching where there was no whining or complaining and you got on with things. Making deliveries and selling beer off the back of the truck seems like such a long time ago. After we got our license in 1948, we sold about 120 cases of beer a day. In 2002, we sold about 15,000 cases everyday.

What a difference a few short years make.

35. On the Move

When John was two, we moved to Tombstone, at one time the most lawless silver mining camp in the country. It still looked the way it did in the 1800s. It had good restaurants, bars and meeting places and people from all over the world visited for a taste of the Old West and to escape angry wives, debt collectors and the law.[1]

We moved into one of the duplexes Harold and his dad had built and eventually took over Lloyd's old house. I gave up my job at the Fairbank post office, but got a job teaching 6th grade at Tombstone's elementary school. Having no experience in elementary, I taught the way I had learned in school and for three years, 1950 to 1953, taught every subject.

At the same time, I kept the books for the business and ran the office, which was in our home. At first I didn't know where to put the numbers in the ledgers and took a correspondence course in accounting and bookkeeping.

At the beginning, the business didn't generate much revenue because there were so many expenses. Tom says I went back to teaching to put groceries in the pantry and he's not wrong. However, the reason we didn't have much money is because we put whatever money we made back into the business and kept trying to expand it.

To increase business, we sponsored events like Tombstone's Helldorado Days, three days of notorious shootouts, dancehall girls, a cowboy parade and even a beard contest.[2] We sponsored parties at the VFW (Veterans of Foreign Wars) lodge, giving them money or buying a table and putting people at it. If they had a special event license, we gave them beer. We gave away a lot of beer. Since this took lots of money, we were always broke.

One day a reporter for the *Tucson Citizen* called, said he was sick and would I like to take over his job? I told him I had no experience at reporting. He said I was the English teacher and that's all the background I needed. As I'd never let lack of experience hold me back before, I agreed. I've always believed that you should just get out there, learn it and do it.

Since Tombstone was a hotbed of dissent on most issues, I had a lot to write about. One of the big concerns was the fight over who owned the water meters and who had to pay for water. In the evenings, I went to meetings, wrote about what happened and sent the stories to Tucson for editing. Sometimes they were printed without editing.

One day a Tucson reporter called me up and congratulated me. I said, "For what?" He said, "Don't you know you got an AP byline?"

Getting named as the reporter in an Associated Press story was usually reserved for the most experienced and distinguished writers. Some of the reporters had been writing for decades and never got a byline.

The pay for my articles was by the inch of copy. The more I wrote, the more I made. When you're in business for yourself, the most important thing was getting known. What do they say? Just spell the name right.

At this point, we were still sub-jobbing for Foster who had the beer distribution for all of Cochise County. We paid him wholesale prices and then sold his beer to the bars. However, very shortly we became the only distributor for Miller, Hamm and Falstaff. Then Foster offered us the entire distributorship for Cochise County and we jumped at the opportunity.

Our hay barn warehouse in Fairbank was now way too small and we decided to move to the Bisbee area to expand the business. But where were we going to get the money? We sold the duplex to help finance our move to Bakerville, near Bisbee, and rented a house.

A warehouse was hard to find and our friend Jim Brophy eventually built us a new one in Bakerville on the railroad line. The most memorable part of the warehouse was a community of Slavic goat herders living nearby. They grazed their goats on the grass near the warehouse and during the hot afternoon, the goats slept under our loading dock because it was cool.

Nearly four, John went with me to the warehouse everyday and attended a pre-school close by, but his greatest joy was talking with the goat herders, mostly old men, and playing with the goats.

The business continued to expand. We added more brands of beer and hired a person to help in the warehouse. I stopped teaching, quit writing for the *Tucson Citizen* (as they already had a reporter in Bisbee), and devoted myself to keeping the books for the business.

Two years later, a friend of ours changed our lives. Frank Kalil had a soda pop franchise in Tucson, and when he found out we were in the distributing business, he asked us to sub-job his soda pop. Harold hauled down a load and sold them, but pop was not up our alley. Then Kalil bought out Foster and took over the big Pima County beer franchise. Afterwards, he told us he didn't know why because he didn't even like the beer business and asked us to buy him out.

Once again, we didn't know how we were going to get the money, but agreed and in the spring of 1953 packed up, moved to Tucson and rented a house. Jim Brophy fronted us the money for the expansion, but it was hard to find a warehouse that suited our needs. After a lot of looking, we rented the old Standard Oil bulk station at Main and 4th across from the railroad tracks. Having a spur to our warehouse, we were set.

We stayed about one and a half years before we ran out of space and moved to Toole Avenue and rented from Tucson Warehouse and Transfer. It had the advantage of a cold cellar where we kept the kegs. We hired two drivers who also acted as salesmen along with Harold.

My relatives like to joke that when Harold started out and frequented every little bar, he sold the barkeeps a case of beer during the day and then returned that night and drank it to show he was real interested in them. The next day he went back and sold them another case.

There's probably more truth in that story than I care to admit. I'll tell you why they ordered from Harold. They liked him. He was the most honest man they'd ever met. That honesty was one of the things that attracted me to him.

People used to say that if they wanted to find us, they knew where to look—the nearest bar. Bar hopping was our business and our entertainment and we especially liked bars that had bands like the Bay Horse and the Maverick.

We were at Toole about three years and thrived. We had salesmen, we had delivery men. And, yet again, we ran out of space for our trucks to load and unload and had to expand. The business was making money, but our next expansion needed a lot of capital. We took on a partner, Milton Straus, and Harold used Milton's contribution to buy out Jim Brophy. We bought a lot over on 36th Street and had a prefabricated, barn-shaped Butler building put up and it had lots of room.[3]

As the new partner, Milton took over the book-keeping and left me without a job. We had reinvested everything in the business and needed a second income to help keep us afloat.

36. Pueblo Gardens

Early in the morning on the Friday before Labor Day in 1955, I went down to 1010 East Tenth Street, the offices of the Tucson Unified School District (TUSD), and lay in wait for Dr. Robert Morrow.

My family had known Dr. Morrow since he had been the Superintendent of the Arizona State Schools for the Deaf and the Blind. He was now head of TUSD.

When he came in the door, he saw me and said, "Dorothy, what are you doing here?"

"Dr. Morrow, I've got to have a job," I said. It was just before the school year was to begin and teachers were usually hired long before then.

He said he'd have to find a place to put me. "How about Pueblo Gardens?" he enquired. Pueblo Gardens on 33rd Street needed a 6th grade teacher.[1] It was a job not too many teachers wanted as the school was located in a rough neighborhood and had a reputation for unruly kids.

I took it, but I didn't know how elementary school was currently being taught. Dr. Morrow sent me to see Dr. Dorothy Talbert, who was the Intermediate Grades

Supervisor,[2] and she scurried around and collected a huge stack of papers and manuals, all the courses of study for elementary teaching, and loaded me down.

I had four days until school began to get ready. I went home and stayed up half the night reading.

On Tuesday morning I reported for work and was assigned a class of forty kids. I had the dubious honor of being the new kid on the block and the other teachers shuttled the troublemakers to my class before I knew enough to protest.

To say it was a challenge is an understatement. When I started, we didn't have books, we didn't even have enough desks. I had never taught the way they did here with group lessons. I didn't know their techniques and methods.

I needed help and called Dorothy Talbert. She sent me a helping teacher from her supervisory staff who taught me how to put my plans on the board. For example, using my lesson plan, I wrote the vocabulary on the board that I wanted them to learn that day and the page we were going to do in math. We knew when to go to lunch or to an assembly. We wrote down what we would do in the morning, what we'd do in the afternoon. At the end of the day, I reviewed what we had done in the plan and what we were going to do tomorrow. I give all the credit to the helping teacher. Without her, I wouldn't have known where to begin.

Being new, I started out being strict. After that, I was able to be more lenient as I went along. To keep them out of mischief, I thought the kids ought to have a lot to interest them and came up with some novel ideas.

My first brainchild was a school newspaper that I produced with the 4th grade teacher, Betty Treadwell. Every month, students from the 4th, 5th and 6th grades submitted articles and we gave each child a byline like a top *Associated Press* reporter. The kids took the paper home and showed their parents what they had written about the events at school. The paper got so big by the end of the second year that we had four sheets and opened it up to the other grades so the little kids could write, too.

Once the newspaper was well underway, I sprung my next idea on the unsuspecting student body. I proposed an after-school science club. The response was overwhelming.

For our first science project, I thought we should hatch some eggs and went to a farm and got some fertile eggs. As there was no money to buy an incubator, I made one. I sealed over a cardboard box, put in a light-bulb and a little dish of water so the air wouldn't get too dry and put in the eggs. A hen will turn her eggs everyday so we had to do it for her.

I told the kids they had to be very careful they didn't have even a speck of grease on their hands. Otherwise, the grease would go through the shell and the egg wouldn't hatch. The kids washed up like doctors about to perform an operation.

To tell if an egg had a little chicken inside, I told the kids to put the egg in warm water and observe it. If it bobbed up and down, it had a chick. Pretty soon, three eggs hatched and out popped baby chicks chirping and squeaking. Some of the kids had never seen a little chicken, much less held one.

As time went on, the chicks got bigger and we needed chicken coops that my husband helped me build. As long as the kids were in the room, the chickens were quiet. But after a couple of months, if the kids went outside for recess, the chickens raised such a fuss the teachers in other classrooms complained about the squawking.

So we took the chickens out for their own recess on the playground and they scratched and messed around in the dirt looking for bugs to eat. When we were ready to go back in, they followed us and got into their cages on their own.

When the end of the school year arrived, the kids were so attached to the chickens that they brought letters from their parents asking if they could take the chickens home for the summer. I agreed and sent the chickens off for vacation.

I thought the chicken thing worked out pretty well and was open to bringing in more critters when one of the kids brought a salamander to school. We put it in a big green glass battery jar, washed the rocks and put them in there for the salamander to hide under. The salamander got so friendly we could reach down into the terrarium with a piece of fresh ground beef between our fingers and the salamander ate it right from our hand.

One little girl couldn't stand touching the creature and her mother came to school to complain that her kid shouldn't have to do that. "Nobody's pressuring her," I told the child's mother. "Whoever wants to feed the salamander can." That seemed to satisfy the mother, but it wasn't three months before the little girl was feeding the salamander by hand and she became petulant if the other children got a turn and she didn't.

She was the first one through the door in the morning to feed the salamander.

For our next science club project, I thought it might be fun if we raised hooded rats. They are white with a black "hood" marking on the head and shoulders. We got a pair and before long we had a litter of babies.

Then I was called down to the office. The principal said, "Dorothy, it is unsanitary to have rats."

It wasn't unsanitary, but the principal was reacting to an incident in the lunchroom. One of my boys put a baby rat in his shirt pocket and went to lunch. The rat climbed up, peeked out of his pocket and a kid from another class screamed.

"What in the world were you doing?" I said to the boy.

"Well," he said, "I didn't want to leave him inside so I took him for a ride and he peeked out of my pocket."

"We won't be having anymore rats peeking out of pockets," I said firmly.

I told the kids we would not be able to have rats anymore if they took them out. That stopped the problem. The kids loved to be in my science club and I ended up with 42 kids. If a kid was naughty, though, they were banned from the club or from being on the newspaper staff. For them, that was the end of the world.

School was for the kids to learn the basics. But besides that, they had to do fun things. We were studying the Middle Ages and we made a church with stained glass. The kids helped put the colors on the stained glass and we mounted the project on the bulletin board. Fun is how they learn and that's what they remember for the rest of their lives.

On Thursdays, we listened to Standard Oil's half hour radio show for music appreciation. They played mostly symphonies and music from different countries like Africa, Mexico and Poland. Before we tuned in, the kids and I read the teaching manual that came with the program. I didn't consider myself good at teaching music, but got by. When it was over, I asked the kids what instruments we heard and where we heard them.

As my students took band and orchestra, after each broadcast kids demonstrated instruments that were played like violins, cellos, trombones, trumpets, oboes, clarinets and the English horn. If kids couldn't afford their instruments, I rented them for them. My plan was to make my room so interesting that the kids didn't have time to get into trouble.

I discovered that nearly all the kids in my classes didn't get newspapers at home or read them. To improve their current affairs knowledge, once a month we read aloud Scholastic Magazine, a publication for children.

I loved standing in front of the class teaching and interacting with the kids, but I noticed after I got home that my feet were swollen. One day I said to the kids, "Golly, my feet burn in this building. This floor seems hot."

"Mrs. Finley, they're all hot," one of them said." That's the way the building is built." I went to see the principal and she said, "They put hot water in the pipes in the floor and that's supposed to heat the rooms."

You know what that did? It made everybody's feet swell. Any dumb kid knows better than to put heat in the floor. Somebody had the big idea because heat rises.

When the second semester rolled around, the principal assigned me an apprentice teacher who was going to watch and learn from me. I explained that I didn't feel ready for an apprentice yet, but they said not to worry. I guess I did all right because I was given an apprentice teacher for every semester after that.

When I first started teaching, they sent me to observe teachers in their classrooms and that was quite helpful. In my third year, they asked me to do demonstration teaching. Administrators and new teachers flocked to my room to see how I taught classes and handled discipline. They didn't simply sit quietly. They asked questions and it was very trying.

As if that wasn't hard enough, after a while I was told to demonstration teach in front of a camera for everybody for all time to see. Oh my gosh, I hated it. It was too stressful. You see, demonstration teaching put a damper on my fun-loving nature. I had a reputation at Pueblo Gardens for being a practical joker. I admit it. Sometimes I was naughty.

I taught with a gal named Myrna Hilliard and one day when my kids were cleaning under the sink in my room a kid came to me and said, "Oh, Mrs. Finley, look."

In his hand he had a big old dead cockroach about two inches long.

"I'll tell you what I want you to do," I said. "You cup it in your hand like this and you go tell Mrs. Hilliard I am sending her something."

He went into her classroom and said, "Mrs. Hilliard, excuse me, but Mrs. Finley sent this to you." And he raised his closed hand.

She held out her hand, he dropped the cockroach into her palm and she shrieked something awful.

The kids just hooted and hollered.

Pretty soon I heard heels coming down the hall. Click, click, click... It was the principal. She stormed into Mrs. Hilliard's room.

"What's going on down here?" she asked.

One of the kids said, "Mrs. Finley sent Mrs. Hilliard something."

The principal clomped into my room and said "What did you send Mrs. Hilliard?"

"Oh, a little dead bug for biology," I said.

She was mad. "Let's keep things a bit more professional in here," she said.

The kids found the incident really funny. News of what happened spread quickly and I believe I am famous across Tucson for the cockroach episode. My friend Glennalee Foulk, who taught school for years, heard about the practical joke and believes that it's important to laugh with the kids.

"Teachers have to learn that the teaching is really important," she said, "but the enjoying is also important. When they do funny things, you laugh and you recognize them. And when you do funny things, they laugh. And they recognize that it goes both ways."

Sharing humor shows your human side. And it's equally important to show you support a child when they do good work. I had a student whose father was the principal at another school. She was always willing to help and got good grades. Her father called and said that his daughter was not good enough to graduate.

I assured him that his daughter had truly earned her good grades and invited him to school to go over them. He said it wasn't necessary but I said yes it was. He came in and I showed him her permanent record.

He said, "You know, my daughter adores you. I figured that's why you gave her good grades."

This lovely, smart girl eventually got her Master's degree and became a teacher. Her principal said they never had a better teacher. One day years later I saw her father and I asked him about his daughter.

"Dorothy, if it hadn't been for you, she never would have gotten through," he said.

"Yes, that's because you didn't believe in her," I said.

I wasn't an easy person to have on staff because I spoke out. Whether it was a parent, another teacher or an administrator, I said what I thought. That's the only way you can own where you work. I was very protective of Pueblo Gardens. If anybody said unkind things about the school, I stood up for it. That's what I mean when I say you own it. It must be important in your life.

37. Helping Teacher

One day a TUSD supervisor asked me if I wanted to join the supervisory staff. I couldn't believe it. I hadn't taught 6th grade for even three years in the district, and with all my projects like the science club and the newspaper, how could I leave?

It was a great honor and recognition for the hard work I'd done. At that time, they only chose one teacher as a 6th grade helping teacher. They asked my principal to let me go at the end of the third year and she became very upset that I was leaving.

To get ready, as I only had my K-12 certificate, I took supervision courses at the University of Arizona, and before long moved downtown to the administration building at 1010. My role was that of a helping teacher. The helping teacher who assisted me when I started at Pueblo Gardens was instrumental in making me a good teacher and I wanted to be just as useful. When I asked for direction on how to do it, I was told to help teachers teach like me.

For the next two years, from September 1958 to June 1960, I was required to visit a certain number of schools and observe a certain number of teachers everyday. After each encounter, I wrote a critique. I showed teachers things I had done such as how to organize and how to keep control of the class. I showed them useful textbooks, got them materials and furnished them with whatever they needed to make their experience better.

As a helping teacher, I traveled all over town throughout the school district, especially to classes run by new teachers. One thing that really worked: When I found teachers who taught the way I did, I asked them to demonstration teach. Then I brought other teachers to their classrooms.

How can you tell if teachers need help? If you walk into the room and they don't have plans on the board. I taught teachers about the organizational pattern of their room, how to write their lesson plans and how to operate groups simultaneously. When I was a student, my elementary school had three or four classes in different grades running at the same time in the same room. From experience, I knew what worked.

I told teachers that kids are more alert in the morning so start with reading, math was second and then go to sciences. In the late afternoon do art because it's relaxing.

At the end of the school day, I told them to leave about fifteen minutes to go over the plan for the next day. When I taught, I often finished by saying, "We had a good day today. When you go home, you tell your parents what we did."

The next day, I asked, "Did we finish our reading yesterday?" Did we do this, did we do that. Then we wrote on the board what we were going to do today. My students knew what they were going to do every minute of every day.

Even if we were going out to recess, I asked them, "What are we going to do?"

"We don't know what to do," I recall one of them saying.

"Then run around the fence."

Just like the teachers, kids have to learn to plan at school and know what they did and where they are going. When my students went home, their parents asked them, "What did you learn in school today?"

One of mine did not dare say, "Nothing."

38. White Elementary

At the end of my second year on supervisory staff as a helping teacher, Irene Erickson, the Assistant Superintendent in charge of Elementary Education for TUSD,[1] called me down to her office. She asked me to become a principal at a newly built school called John E. White Elementary.[2]

It was a shock. Not because I didn't expect to be a principal one day. It was where it was located.

She told me right off that White Elementary was our southernmost school and the boundaries went out to the Indian reservation. Since the reservation was not an organized district, the Native American children could go to White or any school they chose. The challenging part was that the people who lived out there had been to many different schools and had no continuity in their schooling.

"You're out there by yourself," said Miss Erickson, "but I think you can handle it." She made it sound like I was heading west on a wagon train.

I mentioned that I didn't have a Master's degree, a requirement for being a principal. She said I could go back to school and get my degree. In the meantime, they'd give me temporary certification, and in the fall of 1960, I became the first principal of White Elementary, a spanking new school with six rooms.

I was at first a *teaching* principal, which meant you have all the same administrative duties as a principal and are additionally responsible for teaching one grade of students.

From the beginning, I knew it was not going to work. I didn't have enough time to spend with my kids and do lesson plans. I didn't have time for the extra-curricular. There were six grades and six teachers, counting me, and I didn't have time for the other teachers. If parents came to see me in the morning, I couldn't take time away from the class. They'd have to come back after school or early the next morning before class began.

You cannot do two full-time jobs and do them well, although I sure tried. I was very disciplined and well-organized. In the morning, I taught the 6th grade. In the afternoon, I did administration and my assistant put telephone calls through to my room. I did the mail at noon. But no matter how efficient I was, there weren't enough hours to give everybody the time they needed.

Then things changed. As my second year of school was about to begin, an overwhelming number of new children arrived to pre-register for classes, especially kindergarten. And we only had six classrooms and no multi-purpose room.

Dr. Morrow visited my school on the first day and saw that my classrooms were so full I had students sitting on the floor. He asked why and I said, "I don't have enough desks."

The problem was the administration didn't realize how fast the subdivisions were going up. When TUSD decided to build White Elementary, a subdivision called Manzanita Manor was on the drawing board. Nobody expected it to be built for some time.

However, the mines were going full blast and people needed a place to live. People from the barrio wanted to move to escape the high crime rates in their area and buy new, affordable homes. With a huge demand, the houses seemed to spring up overnight.

As a result, we were besieged by loads of little ones coming through our doors. Somebody concluded that the best proposal was to bus all the Manzanita Manor kids downtown. Well, those families were really annoyed. They attended a raucous public meeting and said they'd just moved out of downtown, had worked too hard to get their kids into a brand new school and "you are not taking our kids back there."

Fortunately, Mary Lynn School, which is now the Lynn-Urquides Elementary School, was not far away. It had room and the extra kids were sent there. Seeing this problem was only going to get worse, the administration immediately ordered more classrooms for White.

With so many new kids, I became a full-time principal and didn't have to teach as well as do everything else. In a short time, we had six new classrooms down on the annex and a new multi-purpose room. They also built an auditorium with excellent acoustics for the orchestra and chorus. However, when you put up new buildings that quickly, sometimes you are asking for trouble.

The stage floor buckled in the multi-purpose room and they couldn't figure out why. We got a hydrologist out and he said that water coming off the roof was going underneath the building. They installed a breathing apparatus so the air could get in and then redid the floor.

Then they decided to build a freestanding library. White was shaped like a U and the library was to go in the center. The engineers and the builders did up a design and I knew they were going to have problems because the water table was at ground level. I told them to build it on the other end of the building. The engineers and builders looked at me like I didn't know what I was talking about and proceeded to put the library exactly where I told them it should not go.

After they dug down about 30 inches to pour the footings, the trenches filled up with water. They used pumps to get the water out and then poured the footings anyway. After they installed the floor, it buckled and they had to start over and float the floor. Even so, it was hard getting it to dry and it cost a whole lot to get that library in.

A parent donated a rowboat to the librarian and she sat in it and held story time for the kids. Instead of getting bent out of shape, we laughed. You change what you can and what you can't you learn to live with. In the end, we had a beautiful library and new classrooms.

But guess what didn't change? We still didn't have enough room. We kept growing and had to move in six portables. I didn't like portables. They were not attached to the school and the kids usually had to leave them to go to the bathroom. Trying to cool or heat a portable is very difficult. They're either overheated or freezing. But portables were there to stay, and by the end of the fourth year, the school had more than 1,000 kids.

During the time the construction was going on and the school was enduring growing pains, I was studying for my Master's degree. By September of 1962, after attending evening and summer classes, I was awarded a Master of Science with a major in Educational Administration. I was finally legitimate.

At some point, a deal had been made for the kids from the Tohono O'Odham reservation (known as the Papago then), San Xavier district, to go to the Sunnyside School District. The Indians abruptly stopped going because they were mad at the school administrators.

The first thing we knew about the bad feelings was when it was time for back-to-school registration. Trucks started arriving with kids sitting in the back with their grandmothers. One of the reasons they didn't want to go to Sunnyside was that the school checked the children's heads for lice and they felt they were being singled out. I let them know that at White we checked everybody's heads for lice, whites, Native Americans, Hispanics, every kid that walked in the door.

The Tohono O'Odham seemed to like the school and this may have encouraged other Native Americans to attend. Later on in 1964 when the federal government established a new Yaqui reservation of 202 acres, I got a call from 1010 and they wanted to know why I hadn't registered the Yaqui kids who had moved from Old Pascua Village around Oracle and Grant to New Pascua, west of the airport and I-19.[3] They said that the tribe's chairman called to complain that "Mrs. Finley doesn't want us."

I said, "Yes, I do."

My teacher Glennalee Foulk and I went over to the reservation, which was really poor, to find out what was going on. We walked around and met the people and the kids and became quiet friendly.

I knocked on the door of the tribe's chairman and asked him, "Why are you getting me in trouble downtown? Why didn't the children show up for school?"

"You didn't ask us," he said. He wanted to know why I hadn't been out in person to invite them to school.

"I am asking you now and I want you up at the school."

That did the trick and he piled the little kids from the village in his truck, roared up to the school and enrolled them.

39. *Kids Make Me Laugh*

As I was at White fourteen years, you can imagine the things that I saw. The trouble kids got into...

I knew one little boy was going to end up in prison. He was red-headed with freckles and was always late for school. One day he came to the counter in the office and had a big old rattlesnake stretched around his neck, one hand behind its head and the other at the rattles.

"Mrs. Finley, look what I brought you. I found this rattlesnake and killed it," he said.

Why, that snake was wiggling and rattling so I knew it wasn't dead. I said, "You hold that snake as tight as you can and let's walk down the hall."

I told the secretary to find the custodian. We marched down to the end of the hall and out the door. After the custodian arrived, I told the boy, "Throw that snake as far as you can." He did and the custodian cut the rattler's head off with a shovel.

The next morning when I got to school, a doily sat in the middle of my desk and on it was about eight rattles.

The teachers thought that was funny and the story ended up in the newspaper.

Eight or nine years after the boy left school, I received a call from a prison in Texas. My student was incarcerated and the boy had given them my name. The caseworker thought the boy's childhood played a part in his bad behavior. I can believe that. He never had anyone to care for him except us. They wouldn't say if what he was in for had anything to do with snakes.

In my first year as a teaching principal, I had a little kid in my class who couldn't stand it if I threw away mail. After my assistant put the mail on my desk, I threw the junk mail in the trash can first thing. This kid became upset and said, "Anything that comes in the mail is important." Then he dug it out and put it back on my desk. Sometimes he opened the envelopes just to make sure there was something inside.

As well as the mail police, I had kids who liked to clean. If the custodian was sick, the kids got the broom out and swept the floors. I said, "Wait a minute. We don't have to sweep the floors." "Oh, yes we do," they said. It was their school and they felt it was important to keep it clean.

One of the best stories from White is about the mother and father who came to see me because they felt I was too hard on their little boy.

"Mrs. Finley, you are being far too strict with my kid," the father said.

"Oh, tell me why?" I replied.

They said the kid felt I jumped on him for no reason. "Well, if he told you that, I don't blame you. Let's call your boy down."

He came in and I said, "Tell your mother about the chewing tobacco."

"Chewing tobacco?" the mother said. "What were you doing with chewing tobacco?"

"I found it out in the bushes, but I didn't *do* anything, I was just chewing," the boy said.

I asked the boy if he wanted to tell his parents about the magazines he had on the playground.

"No," he said.

The teacher on playground duty had seen him showing around magazines that "would cause a playboy to pale."

"I think they want to know. Tell them where you found them," I said.

"Oh, Mrs. Finley, I don't want to."

"You went home and told some story about me jumping on you for no reason. Let's be honest."

"Found them in the garage," the little boy said.

"Who do you think they belong to?" I asked.

At this point, the kid was sniveling and his father was turning purple. I opened the bottom drawer of my desk, pulled out the magazines and plopped them on the desk. The covers said everything you needed to know.

The father grabbed the kid by the arm and ran for his life.

The boy's mother said, "I want to die."

After that episode, he was the best kid in school.

I've had parents come to my office for outlandish reasons. A father came in and asked to see his kid. The kid entered and the father pulled a paddle from behind his back and whomped him.

I said, "This is not the place to do that. You can discipline him at home."

Apparently, the kid had done something wrong at home and the father wasn't going to let him get away with it. I was horrified and sent the man packing.

I usually took the parents' side of an issue, but sometimes the parents went too far. A mother who was an active volunteer brought in her little girl, the cutest tomboy. "Mrs. Finley, my daughter is not to go outside and play without her jacket on," she said. "She plays so hard, she ends up with a respiratory infection. It is always bad and we have to go to the doctor."

The mother said, "I don't expect you to watch her every minute, but she knows she has to wear her jacket."

"I can't," I said. "I have all these kids."

I told her I'd talk to the child's teacher, but the girl was in 5th grade and wearing her jacket was up to her.

Three or four days went by. Then kids ran into the office and said, "Mrs. Finley, there is a woman out there beating a kid."

I went tearing outside. It was the mother and she was paddling the girl's bottom. She said, "I drove by here and I saw her without her jacket."

I explained that her daughter had a substitute and I was sorry the teacher had not gotten the word. "She better not do it again," she said.

I thought, *Oh shoot.* That was the last time the child went out without her jacket. Nowadays, the mother would be arrested for what she did.

It was common then for a parent to come on school property and interact with her child. That was before we had a slew of divorces and didn't know which parent had custody. We passed a rule and put up signs that said nobody could come on school grounds or enter a classroom without going through the main office and identifying themselves.

There were other reasons we didn't want parents wandering around the hallways. A woman called and said, "My husband did not come home last night and I know he is drunk. I don't want him picking up the kids. Is there anything you can do?"

I rounded up her kids and put them on the early bus, but before long, the father arrived and sat himself down in my office with his Stetson hat in his hand between his knees. His drinking buddy was stone drunk out in his truck.

"I love my kids..." he said, and started to cry. "And now they are not here. I know you sent them home."

"Your wife called and wanted them home," I said.

"My wife is mad at me," he said.

"I don't want to see you drinking again, is that clear?" I said.

"I didn't have that much. You know that I really like you, but I don't want you sending my kids home when I'm gonna pick 'em up."

Drinking was a real problem. Another man, an attorney, sometimes showed up at school soused and wanted to go to the classroom to see his kids.

"Let's get this over with," I said. "Then I want you to leave."

He saw his kids, embarrassed the heck out of them and himself, and then went out to the parking lot and stumbled along the cars. He came down often enough that the teachers referred to my encounters with him as "Mrs. Finley and her boyfriend."

There's more to the story. Once he showed up very drunk, patted me on the behind and told me I was his extracurricular activity. A number of the teachers, including Glennalee, stood outside my glass office and laughed. Afterwards, I said, "Not a one of you came to help me." Glenna said, "I knew you could handle it."

The things I put up with. But I'm not sure who made me laugh the most, the parents or the kids. If I had to take a vote, it would probably be the kids. Somebody came into my office one day and said, "You know, there's a wedding going on in the playground."

"Now what?" I said. You think you had heard everything.

I went outside and saw a bunch of kids in a sandbox acting out a wedding. One boy was the priest, and a little boy and girl were getting ready to say their I-dos. I told them that we did not practice weddings at school.

After the Vietnam War, some Vietnamese boat kids attended White. Their father was an airman and their mother Vietnamese. The first time we had a big rain, I looked out the window and saw two little kids hunched over around the flagpole. They weren't wearing raincoats or hats and this was during the winter. It can get quite cold during a storm.

The lightning was streaking across the sky and it was thundering. Nobody here spoke their language, but I said, "No, no, no." And brought them inside to get dry. I called the father who was at Davis-Monthan. He said, "You know, they love the rain."

The next day, it rained again, and darned if they weren't out there sitting around the flagpole. Maybe the rain reminded them of the winter monsoons in Vietnam when it rains from November to March.[1] We went to the Vietnamese woman's house to talk about her children, which was hard when she didn't understand English that well. She got out Cokes, 7-Ups and a whiskey bottle.

We tried to explain we couldn't drink on the job, but she didn't understand. We called the father and he said, "She thinks she's being hospitable."

Many families came from other countries, spoke different languages and had unfamiliar customs. In some cases, their hygiene was not up to the standards we were used to. Some kids did not have clean clothes. One little seven-year-old boy was so dirty (*how to put this delicately*) he smelled. We took him to the nurse's office and he cleaned himself up. I took his clothes home and washed them.

The mother and father stormed down to the school and carried on about the horrible thing we had done. "I am sorry," I said, "but we have a shower here and I know it is difficult for you to get water."

The father said he was going to see the County Attorney about us bathing his child and washing his clothes without their permission. The kid loved to come to school, but they couldn't understand why since we "were mean and embarrassed him." I thought, *We will see about this.*

A bunch of us got new clothes for the boy and left them by the shower every morning. When he arrived at school, he went to the nurse's office, looked around to make sure nobody was watching and took a shower. He toweled himself off and put on his clean clothes. About the time school was getting out, he went back and put on his dirty clothes to go home. We took the new clothes and towel home and washed them and the next morning we left them by the shower.

He did this all the way through 2nd, 3rd and 4th grades and never told anybody. If the kid wanted to shower on his own, that was his business. We never heard a whisper from the County Attorney.

40. Integration

When I was the principal at White, I performed many functions, but one in particular I felt was essential. To make the school a pleasant place for the teachers to practice what they had learned.

To achieve that, I created an intermediate teacher council, a primary teacher council and an overall council. The intermediate council of 4th, 5th and 6th grade teachers chose a teacher to represent them and the primary council of kindergarten through 3rd grade teachers chose who they wanted to speak for them. All the teachers were in the overall teacher council.

Here's how it worked. When we were getting ready for our Christmas program, for example, the representatives of the grade councils discussed their plans and then sent their delegates to tell me what they had in mind.

With the overall council, every teacher in the building met with me at the same time. We discussed their ideas in an open forum and they had a lot of feedback. As well as creating a wonderful work environment where everybody got heard, it prevented gossip and rumors from forming.

As a result, we had happy teachers at White that enjoyed teaching. And if they enjoyed their experience, the kids would enjoy learning. I felt that it was most important to let the teachers have their freedom to teach however they wanted as long as the kids came out knowing.

I had excellent teachers and the teachers and students came from all races. But it wasn't always so. When I started teaching in 1943 at Wakefield, the schools were officially segregated. It had been that way since 1909, when Arizona, still a territory, passed legislation that segregated children of the African race from pupils of the white race.

In 1913, the district rented a building that was designated an all "Colored School." As reprehensible as that may sound now, it was something the black community requested in order to instill pride in their children. By 1918, a two-room school called Dunbar Junior High was built exclusively for black kids.[1]

When I taught at Wakefield, my principal, Noble Hiser, was good friends with the principal of Dunbar, Morgan Maxwell, Sr., and I took my kids to Dunbar for sports. Blacks, whites, Hispanics... everybody played together. I don't know if anyone knew we were mixing the races in athletic competition and having fun. We never heard a complaint.

Dr. Morrow was always offended by segregation and he talked about it often. In 1949, he demanded that segregation of Negroes end. Two years later, his wish was granted, and the State Legislature repealed the segregation law, almost thirty years ahead of the federal court-ordered desegregation order of 1978. Tucson School District 1 (later called TUSD) was the first school district in Arizona to desegregate. Dunbar Junior High's name was then changed to John A. Spring Junior High.[2]

The idea of desegregation was a good thing, but it created its own problems, namely busing. In order to maintain a balance of African-Americans to whites, students were bused out of their area to schools they didn't have a connection with. Busing was an enormous cost that should have gone to paying for textbooks, fixing deteriorating school buildings and teacher salaries.

I think kids are better off going to neighborhood schools. If you want to up the standards, that's fine. But kids need to be at school with their friends.

White Elementary was known as a balanced school. We had black kids, white kids, Mexican and Chinese. At one time, seventeen different Indian tribes went to White. Then one day the U.S. Department of Education sent somebody down to see if we really were integrated. It was around Thanksgiving Day because the children had created a beautiful exhibit in a display case in the front hall. In the scene, Pilgrims and Native Americans were represented by dolls.

The man from the Department took a look and said we should have more Indians. I said, "Where do you get more Native American dolls? I got all we could find." Doll companies rarely manufactured them.

Then he said he wanted to visit the classrooms. We went to a 4th grade room and stood in the back. The man turned to me and said he wanted me to point out Native Americans.

I was appalled and said, "We make no difference with children. I am not going to stand here and point my finger at kids."

My response displeased him. Then we went to another classroom and he turned his back on me and asked the teacher how many Native Americans she had and she told him.

"I don't see any Indians in here," he said.

Either his eyesight was poor or he was looking for war paint and feathers in their hair. A blond-haired, blue-eyed boy in the back row overheard him and said, "You didn't count me."

I said, "Are you Native American?"

"Yes I am."

The guy from the Department of Education said, "Not with that coloring." It seems he was not immune to racial profiling.

"You want to see my monthly check?" the boy said.

No, he guessed he didn't.

To press his point, the little boy said, "My mom is Anglo and my dad is from the tribe in Oklahoma and he gets a check from the tribe every month."

We went to the main office and the man said, "I've only seen two rooms."

"Do you really want to go back and ask the kids in every room what they are?" I said.

After the bruising he had received from the blue-eyed nine-year-old, he'd had enough and left.

Sometime later, I got a call from TUSD saying that a supervisor complained that I didn't give Hispanics the same privileges as whites. Flabbergasted, I said that was not true.

Well, they sent out a young guy from home office at 1010 and he started in on me. He said I should be more sensitive to Hispanics. I asked him where he came from. He said Guadalajara. I said, "You came up here when you were a kid. Heck, I have lived with Hispanic people more than you have. I'm probably more sensitive than you."

I had always had rules that every child was to be treated alike. You don't look down on any kid. For him to even suggest that I wasn't treating Hispanics equally was outrageous.

"My sisters and brother and I were the only blue eyes in school at Chiricahua," I said to him. "Part of my family is Mexican. Why do you think I was sent to White in the first place?"

Like the other guy, he scurried out of there as quickly as he could, but the issues just seemed to grow. Soon the administration insisted that I have a teacher to whom the kids with poor English language skills could go.

I understood the department's concerns. When I was at White, less than 50 percent of the kids that started with me in kindergarten graduated out of 6th grade. But I didn't think the language problem was the cause for the dropouts. In any case, I called Hispanic parents and asked them if they wanted their kids to join the special class. Most were insulted. They said, "Not our kids." They all spoke English well.

Then I talked to a family that had recently arrived from Mexico. If anybody needed help, their kids did. The father worked for a radio station and the mom spoke poor English. "You are not putting my kids in there," said the father.

Then another family moved in from Mexico. They had lived down on the farms and I thought their kids were the perfect candidates for the special class. I was out on the playground with their children and a paper was blowing around. I said to the oldest little boy, *papelito.* I wanted him to put it in the trash, but I could not think of the Spanish word for wastebasket. I said, "Put it in the..." And he said, "In the wastebasket?"

"Do you speak English?" I said.

"Ha, ha," he replied.

Without enough students, we lost the special teacher and the English as a second language class.

After many years of desegregation, a federal judge said in 2007 that he would release TUSD from the desegregation order if it could prove that it followed the order and had a plan to give students equal opportunities in the future.[3]

Then in April of 2008, a judge said TUSD no longer had to follow the desegregation order, despite not having proved that its programs achieved racial balance to an acceptable degree.[4]

I wonder what Dr. Morrow would have thought of this decision.

41. Community School

If you want a good school, you must get the parents involved. I didn't want them saying we weren't doing a good job with their kids if they were not participating. I sent notes home to parents and asked if they wanted to help. I encouraged them to attend school meetings where I solicited their comments and told them our plans.

Parents' participation in school activities was not a new concept. When I was a kid, everybody in the community had to do something at school because we just didn't have resources.

A community school to me meant that parents provided assistance in any capacity. One mother said, "I'd like to help in the library. I don't know anything about putting books on a shelf. Do you do it by size or what?" We taught her how to shelve books and run the library. Later on she got a job because of what she had learned from us.

A woman named Maria made gorgeous baskets. She said, "I don't know how to teach anything, but I'll help." I put her to work teaching teachers and kids how to make baskets. Another parent played guitar and sang. She made up songs with the kids.

There are so many things parents can do to make it fun and help the kids, but sometimes only cash helped. To raise money, we sold ice cream. The kids actually did the selling and filled the student activity fund. That was essential for funding projects like buying autograph books for every 6th grade kid who was graduating. After the concluding morning assembly, they sat down under the ramada and kids and teachers signed their books and wrote a little something. Former students tell me they still have their books.

I was dumbfounded that many principals thought it was an achievement if they saved money in their budget and gave it back to the school district at the end of the year. Whatever was turned back was money not spent on the kids. Me? I spent every penny on those kids.

When I found out that other principals had returned money from their budget, I went down to 1010 and asked if we could have some of it. We needed things like electric typewriters for the secretaries. I made a big plea and we got money other principals turned back.

On my tombstone they are not going to inscribe: *Here lies Dorothy, Saved money.*

42. Schumaker Elementary

In 1974, the principal at Schumaker Elementary was retiring and the district asked me to take over. After spending fourteen years at White, I wasn't sure I wanted to leave, but felt the change would be good for me.

I was allowed to take one teacher with me and I chose Glennalee Foulk, a good teacher with a positive attitude.

Before my arrival on Tucson's eastside, Beulah Lavin, the former principal, told everyone that I was upbeat with a lot of different ideas. I sure had those. I was concerned whether the teachers were ready for change. As it turned out, I did not have to worry.

I began the new school year by placing myself at the front entrance on registration day. I greeted parents and kids and before long knew everyone by name. "We're ready to go with a new year," I said. The invariable response from mothers was, "Thank goodness. They're yours now."

Like White, I made Schumaker into a community school. I set up meetings with the parents and outlined our plans. With nineteen classrooms, we had lots of room for adult education in the evenings. To get the parents involved, we asked them to volunteer at sports and music events, and along with many teachers, they were raring to help out. And if they had a specialty, I asked them to tutor kids.

A retired CPA, an executive from the Ford Corporation, said he wanted to help with math, and he came down during class to work with kids. He was leaving school one day around Valentine's Day and he said, "I got the most precious gift." It was all he could do to keep from crying. He pulled out a Valentine from the 4th grade kid he'd been coaching. The kid had cut out a heart and written *I Love You* on it.

I wanted to get kids engaged in the arts. We attended dress rehearsals of plays, and took 200 kids (of 500 students) at a time to the symphony at the University of Arizona. Before we went, I visited every class and warned, "If I see one person talking when the symphony is performing, we will leave. I don't want to hear about what students from other schools are doing. Do we have to be awful because somebody else is awful?" They answered, "Noooo..."

The kids were well prepared for the experience. In class they read information about the music, listened to tapes, and the teachers talked to them about what they would see and hear. Once there, the kids were enthralled. I stood in the back of the auditorium so I could see every student and I never had a problem.

I brought lots of new ideas to Schumaker. They weren't new to me because we had put them in motion at White: the student council, teacher councils, concessions to raise money for student activities, a student newspaper, lots of clubs for kids like the drama club and the science club.

And, boy, did we raise money. We set up an ice cream concession in the back hall and the 6th graders ran it. Funny how I never heard a complaint. Soon we had quite a bit of money in the concession fund for special projects.

On that success, I scrounged around and bought a big second-hand commercial popcorn popper that had been in a movie theater. We bought oil and corn in 100-pound sacks cheaply and taught the kids how to make popcorn.

After a bit, we asked the parent-teacher group to help and one of the mothers sold popcorn occasionally, but Glenna was the supreme popcorn maker. As she says, "One of my few skills is I could run a popcorn machine." She's being humble, but I have to say she did excel at popcorn popping.

The money kept rolling in and before long Downtown called and chastised me. You know what they say: no good deed goes unpunished.

"Dorothy you can't do that."

And I said, "Who said?"

Well, *they* said.

I pointed out it wasn't *my* concession, it was the Student Council's concession, but the folks at 1010 didn't want kids selling stuff in the lunchroom. I finally wore them down and they said, "Okay, anyplace but the lunchroom. Because kids won't eat their lunch."

I moved the popcorn popper out on the porch under the overhang and you could smell the freshly popped corn up and down the street. Parents in the neighborhood flocked to the school to buy some. As soon as the kids finished lunch, they were allowed popcorn, and because of the move, we sold even more. *It was a real going jesse.*

Soon Downtown found out we had $8,000 in the student activity account. An administrator called and said, "Dorothy, we have got to see you." I thought, *Here we go again.* Down I trudged to the Administration offices.

The administrators said I had several thousand dollars and the rest of the schools didn't and it was because Schumaker was an affluent school. I didn't know where they got that idea. We raised the money because we worked hard to make it for the school.

"You have to spend your budget within one year and run the student activity account through the bookstore," said a supervisor.

"The children will have to vote to change it," I said. It was their money and they would lose control of it.

"You have to turn it over to us."

"What about the PTA?" I said. "I could give it to them. They always need money."

"Next time you can give it to the PTA. This time it goes to the bookstore."

"Okay, whatever I have left. First I have to pay all the outstanding bills and then we'll turn over the balance."

There was no way I was turning over eight grand of the students' money without them benefiting from it. The kids voted that I should go on a shopping spree and I went out and bought everything for the school I could think of. We bought books and equipment, tissue and construction paper, arts and crafts materials. Even so, we ended up turning over several thousand dollars to the bookstore.

People say "poor schools." But I say, *Poor schools, my foot. Lazy principals.* You can get the things you need for your school if you dream up how to get them and work for it. Of course, you have to figure out a way to avoid handing over your loot to the bookstore.

Among other things, Schumaker became known as a haven for kids with special needs. Many "Failed to Progress Appropriately" children were sent to Schumaker from all over the city and we knew these four-years-olds would not be ready for school.

The failure to thrive program was an experimental Adaptive Education problem where we didn't try to fit the children into a program, but designed a program around their specific physical and mental needs, skills and behavior. Adaptive Ed covers visually and hearing impaired kids, those with dyslexia or with learning disabilities or difficulties, retarded children, kids with limited cognitive skills and kids with physical disabilities.[1]

No matter the obstacle, we taught them that everybody took part and had responsibilities in the classroom. We taught them their colors, word sounds, appropriate conversation for kids their age and how to work together. When it was time to go to kindergarten, those kids were ready. They had goals and a desire to learn.

The only problem I had with the program was not the kids, it was parents. When parents found out what we were doing, everybody wanted their kid in there. I told them, "We can't take every kid. The program is for kids that are not making appropriate progress."

The parents admitted their kids didn't fall under the guidelines, but they wanted them in there anyway. They felt that the children were getting special attention and were learning to read. Sometimes I had to say no and no again.

We had truly needy children who deserved to be in the programs. I had three classes of hearing impaired with two speech clinicians to help them, as well as some kids from the Arizona State Schools for the Deaf and the Blind. I had a class of gifted students and a class of children that had failed to mature the way they should have. We provided remedial teaching to correct faulty study habits and to make kids more competent in their subjects before they entered school. It was a highly successful program and our test scores for District 1 were at the top.

Around Christmas time, kids from the Arizona State Schools for the Deaf and the Blind asked to be in the Christmas pageant. One little girl said she'd never been in a Christmas program. I said, "You can be this year." During the show, they hummed along with the music because they could feel the vibrations through the floor.

In the last song, Silent Night, the chorus sang and the hearing impaired kids hummed. The deaf kids stepped out of the line and signed the words to the song. By the end, there were tears in people's eyes and the audience stood up and clapped for a long time.

The little girl that I mentioned a moment ago was profoundly deaf, and the deaf kids were asked to put on a talent show. She didn't know what she could do.

Her teacher said they would make a hat for her and she could be Mary of Hearts and tell a story through pantomime.

While the girl performed, she passed out cookies she had made. Her parents were thrilled, for the child had never had any recognition. See, you have to know your kids. They can do more than they think they can.

We sometimes had problems with hearing impaired children. One child hated wearing his hearing aid and pulled them out of his ears, as a lot of hearing impaired kids did. Then he hid them and said he couldn't find them. Eventually, we found them in his desk and I gave him heck for that.

He said, "I don't want to wear them. I want to be like the other kids."

"I wear glasses," I said. "You don't have to wear glasses."

He said, "It's different with you."

"What's the difference?" I said.

As punishment, I made him clean the tables in the cafeteria. Hearing aids picked up a lot of extra noise. The biggest reason they didn't like wearing them, however, is that other kids made fun of them.

If I caught a student making fun of somebody's hearing aids, he was in big trouble. I said, "We don't make fun of your hair color, we don't make fun of somebody's hearing aid." I didn't tolerate them making fun of anybody's handicaps.

My husband Harold and I set up a bank account and bought batteries and other components for hearing aids so no kid that needed a hearing aid would be without one.

43. After The Strike

Everything was going beautifully at Schumaker. The special programs were working, the teachers and students seemed happy, but on October 2nd, 1978, barely a month into my fifth year, the Tucson Education Association, which represented teachers, called a citywide strike.

I didn't think my teachers would go out on me. My teachers were involved in running the school through their teacher councils and had as much say as I did in what happened. Why ruin a good thing?

As it happened, teachers from Saguaro High School came down and heckled my teachers when they crossed the picket lines. We were the only school that carried on through the strike with all its own teachers.

On the first day of the strike some of the parents didn't send their kids to school because they were afraid they might get distressed. By noon, the kids were back in school as we had everything in hand.

The reason for the strike was about the number of hours teachers spent in the classroom, the number of students and the pay. But my teachers felt they were fairly treated. A principal from one of the other schools said to me, "If you didn't molly-coddle your teachers, they would be out too."

"If you treated yours like human beings, they would be in," I replied.

I treated everybody who worked for me with respect. I expected them to work, but they had families, too. If anything went wrong in their families, I told them to go home and I'd take their classroom. In my first speech to new teachers, I told them, "You will treat everybody in this building with respect, you will treat the janitor the same way you treat me."

I also had a rule that you could not skip break. It was important that the teachers bonded and socialized with each other. We had a strong feeling of family and that's so good for children to see teachers being friendly to each other.

The teachers' strike lasted a week, and 2,300 of the 3,000 teachers had walked out. The teachers got some benefits as a result, but it soured some relationships between teachers and administrators and between teachers and teachers. I think the strike could have been avoided.[1]

After that tense week, things went, more or less, back to normal. We had dances once a month and teachers took turns chaperoning. You know why I had the dances? I noticed when I taught junior high school that kids had no idea about socializing.

We called our dances *hops*, and the 4th, 5th and 6th grade boys and girls attended. The student council supplied the 78 and 45 records and we had big bowls of popcorn and bottles of Coke and 7-Up.

Kids are ingenious and imitative in revealing ways. I was down at one of the hops and watched them take turns serving soda to other students. They poured a little bit of 7-UP and then filled the rest of the cup with Coke. I said "What are you doing?" One said, "Mixing the drinks."

I thought, *Wait until that gets home. Mama, we mixed drinks at the dance...* But home is probably where they saw it being done.

I went to the teacher and said, "You know what they are doing there?" She said, "They're pouring the drinks." I said, "Sure they are." We put an end to that real fast. 7-Up and Coke... I laughed so much.

The kids weren't bad. I don't think I've ever known a really bad kid. One day, I got back from a principals' meeting and four boys were sitting at the table in front of my office.

"Okay, what are you here for?" I said.

"Mrs. Finley, have you had any coffee yet?"

"I certainly have. What are you doing in here?"

"We got to tell you something."

"You better get it straight," I said.

They told me how they'd been naughty and wouldn't keep quiet in class, and the teacher kicked them out and told them they couldn't come back until they had seen me. I said that if I ever, EVER, saw them in my office again, they knew what was going to happen.

"Oh, Mrs. Finley..."

I said, "If you can't behave, I am going to call your fathers."

"Mrs. Finley, please don't do that." They sounded so sweet when they were in the doghouse.

"I don't make deals with kids," I said.

I called my assistant and said, "Mrs. Janson, would you bring me so and so's card. I want to see where his dad works." That was all I had to do. Never saw those boys in my office again.

In some cases, the naughty children didn't have fathers and needed a male role model. One day Mabel told me there was a woman waiting to see me in my office. She had recently lost her husband and was having a hard time. I had changed her son's room assignment to a class with a male teacher and that upset her. The boy wanted to be with his friends.

"I'll tell you why I put your kid in that class," I said. "Because your husband is now deceased and your kid needs a male teacher." I felt her child needed a positive male image or father figure and I had to match the kid up with the teacher that would be best for him. She said, "He sure does." She left the office satisfied with the decision.

Not all the parents were as agreeable as the woman whose son's class was changed. Sometimes angry parents stormed into my office. My first objective was to disarm them by saying, "You know, I don't blame you for being angry. Let's get your kid down here and talk about this."

That usually worked and parents calmed down and allowed me to get to the bottom of the family's situation.

I enjoyed seeing people become successful and encouraged staff and even parents to excel. A student's mother went to see Glennalee and told her she hated everybody with a college education. She and her husband were separated, her family was falling apart and she didn't have a job. I encouraged her to go to Pima College and earn her Red Cross certification and then she became my school's health aide. She was so good at her job that we called her before we called an ambulance. The job changed the way she felt about herself and her view of the world.

We had a yardman who couldn't read and sometimes he asked me to decipher labels like the instructions on a box for killing aphids.

I wanted him to be our custodian, but some people didn't want him because he was illiterate. I told them that didn't make him unworthy of the job. He was good at his job and a good person. Sometimes I helped him out with a little money. Before long, he became custodian, and brought his two little boys to school so everybody could see them.

Needless to say, my building was always spotless.

44. Saying Goodbye

During the winters, I worked as a principal, but when summer came along I went back to the beer distribution business and kept the books.

Around 1955, after we'd been in Tucson about two years, we moved to Indian Ridge. By 1970, Harold wanted me to retire as principal of White and for us to buy a home in a better area. John was already through college and in medical school. I liked Indian Ridge and made him a deal. I'd teach a little longer and then we'd move to a fancy house in the '49ers, a country club in Tucson.

Although partial to little Thunderbird cars, Harold then bought his first big car, a Ford Lincoln Continental and we drove it to Omaha for John's graduation. Although he loved it, he wouldn't drive it to work. He drove an old car that he felt was more appropriate. He thought the big car would make employees think he was rich and flaunting it in their faces.

I thought Harold would never part with the Lincoln, but in 1973 gas rationing started and I came home one day and sitting in the driveway was a bitty thing I called the teacup. Harold had traded in his beautiful

Lincoln Continental for the most uncomfortable car I'd ever been in. We drove to California for vacation, and when we got back, Harold went down to the car lot, traded in the teacup and got another Lincoln.

I think he could have driven the Lincoln to work and nobody would have cared. The employees loved Harold. We had health insurance for them, long term disability, short term disability, life insurance, Workmen's Comp and eventually a dental plan. You name it, we had it.

Harold felt you had to look after your employees because they made us who we are. They did all the work. Why shouldn't we recognize them? This goes back to my ranch days when my father took care of the neighbors, anybody who worked for him and anybody who came to the door. That's the pioneer ethic: *you take care of people.*

Dennis Olson, who ran the day-to-day operations of the company, says that Harold "would sacrifice himself to make sure his employees were happy. I never saw an employer whose employees idolized a guy like his employees idolized him. They would do anything for Harold. Harold was the kind of person who could never conceive of gutting the money out of his company, hurting employees, raiding pension plans for his own gain. Protecting his business and his employees was his guiding principal."

That was Harold.

In 1980, after twenty years as a principal and administrator, I decided to retire. I was sixty years old and it was time to let the younger generation take over. It was hard to leave the school system after so much time. I knew I would miss the kids and the teachers.

The business was doing well and had been in the Butler building on 36th Street for quite a few years. Then suddenly, we were told to find a different warehouse. Miller said to keep their beer fresh the building had to be temperature controlled. Harold found the spot on South Euclid where the company is today and it took a couple of years to construct the building.

We moved in 1982 and it was around this time that Harold started not feeling well. He went back and forth to the doctor, but they didn't find anything wrong. Harold thought we should sell the business. I felt we had worked too hard and wanted to keep it.

"Then you go down there, I don't want to do it," he said. I always loved the business, and coming from a ranching family, we believed that you stayed in your business if it was possible to grow it. He called his sales manager and told him I was now president of Finley Distributing. And I took over running the company.

I hadn't been working as president of the company for long when one night in 1983 we were out at the '49ers and Harold fell ill. We were at the doctor's earlier that day and he gave Harold a clean bill of health. We went home and he had a cerebral hemorrhage because of an aneurism. Since the ambulance would take a long time to get there, I lifted Harold over my shoulder, carried him to the car and drove to the hospital.

As it turned out, whether I had called an ambulance or not didn't make a difference. He was alive when we got to the hospital, but he was not going to recover.

The doctor asked me to decide about unplugging him from life support, and I said that John was a doctor and should decide. The doctor said it was not John's job, it was mine.

Harold and I had had thirty-seven years together. He was only seventy years old. I was sixty-three, his child bride. It was time to let him go.

45. Giving Back

The best thing you can do when you have a trauma like Harold's death is get back to work and I did. By having my manager do the day-to-day at Finley Distributing, this allowed me the time to focus on promoting the company and giving back to the community.

The first time I tried to raise funds for a cause, my neighbor Rae Landeen and I went door-to-door in Indian Ridge asking for money for Tucson Medical Center. I had no idea what I was doing. One person gave $300 and I was ecstatic.

After Harold passed away, I served on a number of committees and over several years joined the board of directors for more than fifty nonprofit organizations, all the while continuing to work in the business.

One of the first organizations to invite me on the board was La Frontera Center. They wanted to build a child and family center where we could serve little kids who were not thriving. To create an annual fundraiser, we started the Mariachi Conference, a Tucson music festival. All its proceeds went to children's services. Now it is a world-renowned Mariachi Festival.[1]

I guess word got around that I was available. Unexpectedly, my friend Sally Drachman asked if I'd help with a major fundraiser for the Arizona Sonora Desert Museum. Why they chose me, I can't say. I'd never done fundraising on this scale. As it appears, I was not asked out of the blue.

Chris Helms, the former Development Director of the Desert Museum, had asked Sally to ask me if I would co-chair the campaign. "It has to be someone no one will say no to," he told her. Gracious, what a process just to pick up the phone and talk to me. I knew little about fundraising at the time and it was Chris who taught me everything.

"Thank God for Dorothy. Her personality lends itself to doing 'an ask' during the campaign," says Chris. "Plus her depth of knowledge about the community and the people in the community was enormous."

The dilemma for a wonderful place like the Desert Museum was that everybody thought everyone else gave money to the museum. Not only were we up against false perceptions, but the Desert Museum was asking for big money, more than in the past, and not many supporters had that kind of money.

Our biggest donor was Sue Small. Her husband Bill owned the Tucson Citizen, which was the major newspaper in town. I called up and made an appointment for lunch, and before we even had the first course, she said "I will give you $50,000 and Bill will give you $50,000 and the Stonewall Foundation will match you $100,000."

I thought that was pretty good.

Then I focused on Jack Greenway, son of Arizona's first congresswoman, Isabella Greenway, who owned the fashionable Arizona Inn. No one had ever asked him for money. Chris Helms had worked as a bartender at the Arizona Inn while he was in college and knew Jack. So Chris asked Sue Small to arrange for Bill Small to ask Jack. Seems like a complicated way to do things, but it works.

Bill brought Chris to a meeting with Jack at the Arizona Inn. You could tell it was serious because Bill wore a coat and tie, which he never did after he retired. Jack gave $10,000.

I was sure Jack would support the museum because my family had helped Isabella Greenway, Jack's mother, around 1909. Her first husband was sick with tuberculosis and the doctor said they had to go to Arizona. He suggested that they check out a place called the Animas in the Arizona-New Mexico area. Jack's mother was living in New York City and they moved near my family who befriended them. The Greenways have never forgotten their kindness.

When it comes to fundraising, connections help. The Arizona Sonora Desert Museum is the jewel in the crown for Tucson and Pima County, and we raised $3,500,000 in eighteen months. That may not sound like a lot of money for a big institution, but the campaign was at the end of the 1980s and early 1990s. The economy was bad and nonprofits were competing for scarce funds. All in all, it was a miracle we did so well.[2]

In 1983, a bunch of us founded the Education Enrichment Foundation (EEF) for TUSD. We raised money to get extra things for the schools and included the clothing bank in our efforts. In 2001, I was the honoree at the EEF fundraiser. I was pleased that a whole table was taken over by White and Schumaker teachers.[3]

Of all the nonprofits, I've supported the Tucson Children's Museum for many years. It provides children with fun and opportunities for learning about art and science.[4] I like their hands-on exhibits that kids can visit over and over. As we did not as a rule give beer money to children's organizations, I contributed my own money because it was all for children.

Along with many others, Cele Peterson, who had an upscale women's fashion store, and I helped rebuild the Children's Museum from the ground up financially. The previous administration incurred too much debt getting it ready, spending over $350,000 for office space instead of on projects, and the museum was faltering.

We raised money to hire Beth La Roche, former Vice-President of the Challenger Learning Center in Washington, D.C., as the new director of the center and found ways to retire the enormous debt without declaring bankruptcy.

The Children's Museum is important because it sparks a child's curiosity. When I was teaching at White, we didn't have much money for decorations, but hung prints of famous paintings around the school. A little boy came up to me and said, "Do you know why I come to school everyday?" I said I didn't know. He said "This is the only beautiful place that I have."

As well as pictures of famous paintings, we decorated the school building at White with the kids' art work. We framed them and the kids loved to come to school and go from picture to picture. That is why there's a Children's Museum, to give them a beautiful place and experiences they'd never had before.

Experiences like sitting on a police motorcycle or putting on firefighters' gear and jumping onto a fire engine. We put on an Indian powwow and Tucson Electric Power put up a display for kids to learn about electricity and magnetism. The museum had a puppet theater, art studio and exhibits that allowed children to interact with dinosaurs, the deep sea, and an enchanted rain forest.

For the first fundraiser, I was honored at the Doubletree Hotel by being thrown in a jail they'd built on stage. My granddaughter Jessica and a few others sat with me while we were served on trays like real inmates and my brother Tom roasted me. Before I arrived, they hadn't told me they were going to lock me behind bars.

It seems the Children's Museum also turned me into a matchmaker. I introduced the new director of the museum, Beth La Roche, to Tucson Mayor Bob Walkup. They got to know each other and got married at the Children's Museum.

Along with the Children's Museum, I have a big interest in the Challenger Learning Center of the Southwest.[5] When I first met Beth, she was working for the Challenger Learning Center in Washington, D.C., and I asked her, "How can we get one here?" That was the beginning.

The board knew it would cost about $2,500,000. Some people told me I couldn't raise the money because there were no big industries in Tucson willing to contribute. I went to the legislature and told Governor

Jane Hull what we were planning and asked for help. They gave us $600,000.

Then I knocked on the doors of a lot of corporations like Phelps Dodge where I knew people and they gave us money. We were still short, but we took a loan from the bank for the rest.

Today the Challenger Learning Center of the Southwest is one of 54 space shuttle simulators in the U.S., Canada and the UK. It was created as a living memorial by the families of the astronauts from Challenger Space Shuttle mission 51-L. As you may recall, the astronauts on board that 1986 mission were killed when the space shuttle blew up in the sky.

June Scobee Rodgers, wife of Dick Scobee, one of the astronauts who died, spoke at the dedication. She said, "Of all the centers, this would have been the closest to my husband's heart." And she cried. We had a huge crowd because her husband graduated from the University of Arizona. Nobody told me they were going to put my name on a plaque inside the building.

The Challenger Learning Center allows students in grades 4 through 8 to prepare for a mission and simulate a flight. The center provides special teachers and astronauts to teach kids math, science and communications. They learn to work together as a unit to achieve a goal. Our fundraising was essential for making it all happen.

I've received many honors for my work with children and I feel humbled by the attention. David Overstreet, principal of Duffy Elementary School, remembers the day I was invited to the Ray Davies Luncheon.

"They honored Dorothy in 2001 with the Ray Davies Humanitarian Award for outstanding service to children," says David, "and we all took Dorothy out for breakfast one morning to ask her to come to the luncheon and her line was, 'Well, no one will come to lunch for me.' We twisted her arm and people came out of the walls to make it a success."[6]

They didn't have to twist my arm that much. You know, people ask me, *Why do you give?* I give because I feel good when I give money. I give from my heart.

One of the ways it works: there is a group of people in Tucson and I give to their causes and they give to mine. Some of the big companies have a policy that they only give to certain causes. But if I call, they will give to me. I give to their causes so it works both ways. People don't tell me *No* because they know they will have to ask me for money one day and they don't want me to say *No.*

It's hard to decide which charities to give money to. First thing I ask is if it's for kids. Primarily, the project has to be for making a better world for children. Then I look at who the members are and who is on the board. If the people in charge have been generous to my causes, then I am generous to them. If they don't show real interest in the community, I don't bother.

I've always sought the betterment of children's lives. I learned that young girls who had babies out of wedlock were having trouble going to Pima Community College because they couldn't afford the tuition. I called Ana Valenzuela Estrada, then Special Assistant to the President at Pima College, and we met with those kids and got them into Pima by tapping into federal funds for kids who were unemployable. Then they were able to get an education and find jobs.

My parents were involved in helping kids and so I became involved. In the early years, my father and mother, a bunch of the other ranching families and the First Christian Church helped establish and support the Arizona Children's Home. Women made clothes and ranchers gave sides of beef. Somebody donated the property out in the middle of the country somewhere. With Tucson's growth, it is now in South Tucson.[7]

It was an orphanage but also had an adoption program. Transient groups often passed through Arizona and left babies behind. And there were kids whose families had abandoned them or the mother had died and the father couldn't take care of them. My mother continued to help the home after she moved to Tucson, and I was on the board a long time.

Helping children is my prime focus, but helping women succeed is another important goal. Flying back to Tucson one time, I got on the plane and sitting next to me was Dr. Marilyn Heins, a well-known Tucson pediatrician and women's issues advocate.[8] "Dorothy, do you think you could get some women together to support women's studies at the university?" she said. I said, "Oh yes."

We asked thirty people to breakfast in the faculty dining room. It rained so hard that morning, I thought, no one was going to show, but all thirty turned up. We named the organization WOSAC for Women's Studies Advisory Council.

I was the first president of WOSAC from 1988-1990. Of all the events, everybody loved the biannual Book Group where authors read from their works. That alone got us many new members and donations, and with the money we raised, we provided travel scholarships to graduate students presenting papers on women. Women's Studies has become a department at the University of Arizona and even offers a doctorate.[9]

I've tried to help so many groups. The League of Latin American Citizens or LULAC underscores my main objective: education for all children. I've sponsored the LULAC Youth Leadership Conference for the past fourteen years. More than 52,000 students have attended the conference and learned that "education is the key to success."[10]

I worked for the Tucson Urban League for a long time. It is in South Park, adjacent to South Tucson, and we have worked with the South Park Neighborhood Organization to find ways to deal with the poverty, crime and unemployment.

I helped with the credit union by putting money in and leaving it there so they would have capitalization. The Urban League started a Charter School and I assisted them in getting a grant from Angel Charity to build their school building. I didn't just do their fundraising, but taught the other people how to fundraise successfully.[11]

In the late 1960s and into the '70s, Tucson went ahead with plans for urban renewal and replaced or restored substandard buildings. In my opinion, it wasn't handled correctly. Without consulting the people who lived there, the city demolished old adobe barrio homes for a community center. Some of those people, and their parents and grandparents before them, had lived there for many years. They had paid rent and the city just went in and bulldozed the buildings. Even today people remember what happened and are still angry.

As a result, as the President of the Community Center for the Board of Trustees, we created the Tapestry Project.[12] The Tucson Convention Center Board of Trustees asked for exhibits representing the cultures of Blacks, Hispanics, Asians, Eastern Europeans, and Native Americans, which would demonstrate the role their culture played in forming Tucson. The Botanical Gardens was involved, too, and produced an exhibit of what the gardens looked like in the old barrio. We hoped through this exhibit that bureaucrats would become more sensitive to ethnic issues and learn to ask before destroying something irreplaceable.

A community event I supported for years was the Arizona Town Halls, a private nonprofit organization that holds three-day conferences twice a year to discuss topics of major concern to Arizona's future. I am still a member, but the thing that bothers me most about the Town Hall is that we gave our time, came up with great ideas that were published in a book, yet never saw them put into practice. We gave marvelous input and the ideas gathered dust.[13]

I believe the proposals were never implemented because the Town Hall organizers didn't involve the businesses, lawmakers or lobbyists enough. Action never flowed and I stopped going. The Town Halls are like holding a little bird. If you try to keep it under your wing, it will never fly. You lift your wing and the bird will fly. The Town Halls held the information way too tightly.

Making things work at the Town Halls was important to me because I had been exposed to political debate even as a child. It started with my family on the ranch. If there was a funeral or other gathering, old Governor

George W. P. Hunt, elected for seven terms from 1911 until 1932, would come to dinner.[14]

I sat in my chair like a chicken roosting while my father and the governor got into it. The man was bald with a handlebar mustache. At 300 pounds, he knew how to throw his weight around. My father got so mad he made sure everybody knew he was no relation to that old... Well, I won't tell you what he called him.

Governor Hunt had his picture taken with the leaders of the Industrial Workers of the World (IWW or Wobblies) and my family, especially Uncle Jim, couldn't tolerate a union man. The governor was accused of being a member of the IWW, which he was not, he just liked having his picture taken. Who it was with didn't much matter to him. He often had pictures taken with Arizona families when he came to Sunday dinner. He liked to give jars of jam and jelly as gifts from his wife, but word is that he had aides buy them by the case, wash off the labels and pretend they were a personal gift. I'm sure we ate some of those.

It never did matter to me what party the person belonged to. Governor Hunt was a Democrat, which should have pleased my dad, but the old governor was a little too Red for my father's taste. I am not a party partisan. I am more interested in who the person is. That was my father's philosophy and it is mine. I am a Republican but that doesn't matter. Lots of Democrats are my friends. I ask what a person will do for the state of Arizona if they are elected. Are they proposing good policy? Do they use good judgment? Do they ask the public for input?

I'll work with anybody for the public good, but not everybody thinks like me. In the late 1980s, I was appointed to the Blue Ribbon Committee to study the facilities at Kino Hospital, with the directive that it might need to be closed, and to see what we could do to provide health services to the people in the community.[15] We held many meetings; we went to the high schools and the neighborhood centers and listened to people say how they felt.

A couple of people who spoke at the meetings I will never forget. One was a woman who shook from nerves so badly I thought, *Oh my, I hope she doesn't pass out.* She described how Kino supplied her medications and because of that she was able to continue working. Another was a man who told us he'd be a homeless person if he couldn't go to Kino for his medications. And many others without insurance told us how Kino helped them stay healthy so they could go to work.

Since Kino was the only medical facility operating in the south part of Tucson, I voted to keep it open. It was a lifeline to many people. Afterwards, Ed Moore, the Pima County Supervisor, called me on the phone and said, "You are stupid." Then he went to the newspapers and told them he took me off the committee because I was too naïve.

The rest of the Board of Supervisors put me right back on. The issue was such a hot potato that they disbanded the Blue Ribbon Committee anyway. Eventually, regular medical patients were turned away and Kino was converted into a psychiatric hospital. I don't want to give you the impression that everything I touched turned into something wonderful.

Speaking of something wonderful... One Sunday in 1989, my son and daughter-in-law came over and we were sitting there all gussied up waiting to go out for brunch and the doorbell rang. It was a representative from the Chamber of Commerce with a big bouquet of flowers telling me I was *Woman of the Year.*[16]

It was a complete surprise, not to John and Audrey who were in on it. The chamber put my name and picture on billboards around town. I was chosen because several people nominated me. I don't know for sure who wrote the letters. I'm certain Ed Moore was not one of them.

For a long time, I've been involved with Davis-Monthan Air Force Base. They set up the Star Program that has one per state. In that program, we brought reservation kids to the base and taught them science, math and how to get along with each other. At Anna Lawrence Intermediate School, we picked out a bunch of the Yaquis at random. And for one day a week for five weeks those kids just ate it up.

Before the program, the kids were getting about 50 percent on math, science and reading in their tests. When they left they got 90 percent. When they gave the awards out at the Yaqui reservation, my goodness, I couldn't believe how pleased the parents were. On that success, I wrote to Senator Jon Kyl (R-Ariz.), and he put $2,000,000 in the budget for us to continue the program.

I became involved in Native Indian affairs and went to Chandler to the Salt River Pima-Maricopa Indians for a workshop on the direction for the American Indian Center. First, we decided that their services had to be better known to the Indian population.[17]

To that end, we decided that each person on the board had to have a chore. My chore was to see that the director met people who had lots of employees. That way the center's name could start getting out there.

As a member of the board, I was invited to the Indians sacred gatherings. They went out into the desert, pulled up plants and rolled them into something like a cigar. They lit it, pushed the smoke toward me with the palms of their hands and said something in their native tongue.

To that, I added *Amen.*

46. Our Front Line

I do a lot for our military, our front line against terrorists. It started with my husband who was always involved in some way with Davis-Monthan Air Force Base in Tucson because of the business. DM is home to the airmen and women of the 355th Wing and 12th Air Force. In 1986, a few years after Harold died, we created a booster group for the base called the DM-50. We started with 59 Tucson business and civic leaders, hence the name. Eventually we expanded it to 70.

Our purpose was to strengthen the relationship between DM's personnel and the civilian population and to improve the quality of life for the service people and their families. As well as funding an annual picnic for about 10,000 to 12,000 service people, a golf tournament, and hosting dinners and receptions to welcome new base commanders, we funded dozens of initiatives to assist in programs where government money was not available.

For example, we helped refurbish the Family Day Care lending library and the VIP quarters, provided funds for the Child Development Center, and new lighting for the new dorm basketball and volleyball courts, contributed greatly toward the DM Special Olympics and many more programs. The picnic alone cost around $30,000. In the first twenty years, we provided more than $500,000 of much needed funding.[1]

Our financial contribution and promotion of the base would have been enough if that was all that was required of us. But starting in 1987, the threat of base closures forced DM-50 to become a powerful lobby group overnight. So you realize how serious an issue this is, closing Davis-Monthan and other Arizona bases would devastate Tucson and the entire state.

More than 50,000 non-military Arizonans, including 23,000 in the Tucson area, owe their jobs and livelihoods to the bases. Across Arizona, the bases pump more than $9 billion dollars into the economy. DM, the biggest base in the state, contributes the largest share of that number. Can you imagine the economic impact on everything from automobile sales to jobs to grocery stores?[2]

When DM-50 was formed, Buck O'Reilly of O'Reilly Chevrolet was the president and I was chair. We'd been organized about a year when I got a call from Representative Jim Kolbe (R-Ariz.) and then from Senator John McCain (R-Ariz.). Senator McCain said, "Dorothy, don't panic, but when the afternoon paper comes out it's going to say we're closing Davis-Monthan."

I did panic, and immediately called Buck O'Reilly and he said, "Dorothy I'll be on the red-eye flight to Washington to find out what's going on. You get together a group."

After Buck returned, I asked the group, "How are we going to get off that list?" As part of the process, the Base Closure Committee had to hold a meeting in the affected community and tell us why we were on the list. We decided that after we heard what they had to say, we would go to Washington to plead our case.

I said to our group, "We're *not* going there to cry about why we need Davis-Monthan and how unkind it is for them to put us on the list. We are important and that's what we're going to keep in our minds."

We scheduled our meeting with the Fed at the Tucson Convention Center, put up *Save Davis-Monthan* billboards and called everybody we knew. The night of the meeting, they put out a few hundred chairs because that was the turnout other communities were getting. Four thousand people showed up and we didn't have enough seating. The overflow crowd went to the theater where the sound was piped in. Our numbers alone told the Fed how concerned we were.

After the meeting, we knew what the issues were and began planning a meeting in Washington. Senator McCain said, "Dorothy, we have to get the top brass at Pentagon over to a luncheon at the Senate Chambers, but we need somebody to sponsor it."

"No sweat," I said. "I'll pay for it."

As we prepared to go, I asked people at the Williams Air Force base to come with us because they were also on the list. "They'd never close Willie," they said. "We're too important."

Senators McCain and Dennis DeConcini (D-Ariz) sent out invitations to the top brass, and when we got to Washington and walked into the room, we found a huge group waiting for us. I made an introduction and said, "We're not here to beg you to do anything. But we want you to know how good we are and what you're going to lose if you close Davis-Monthan."

You know, they don't like whiners. I never put up with that, so why should they?

We had a lot of discussion, and asked what we could do to get out of this situation and prevent it from happening in the future. Foremost, they said to stop housing projects that would encroach on the base. With that knowledge, we went home immediately and met with the landowners near the base to stop development along the runway approaches. And we were successful.

On the day the Pentagon was going to tell us if we were off the list, we went to the Mayor's office to wait for the phone call. We sat there hoping our presentation had worked. They called and said we were *off* the list.

And Williams Air Force Base? They hadn't done anything to find out why they were on the list and they were closed. They weren't so important after all.

However, the base closures were not over. The Pentagon planned several more rounds that would go on for years and we had to make sure we stayed off the list for good. We kept working on the problem, doing everything the Pentagon suggested and set about becoming more responsive to the base.

We asked the CO what we could do for the whole base. He said a picnic would be nice. I was still the chair so a few of us from DM-50 set about organizing the event and before long we added an annual golf tournament. These were not frivolous little social meetings. They served to bring everybody together to share ideas over a common cause: *Save the base.*

From our gatherings, we found out that the military parents were concerned because their kids couldn't go to whatever TUSD school they desired. I talked to the district and now they can go to any school they want to. To further support the base, we sponsored a Special Olympics for the less-abled and went out to all the graduations and honors ceremonies. We were always there for the changing of the commands. If there was a tragedy, like a member of the military was killed, we were there to help.

The base closings continued. There are things Davis-Monthan has that nobody else has. It has access to the Goldwater Bombing Range and we have AMARC, the Aircraft Maintenance and Regeneration Center, also known as *the boneyard*. There is no place else the Air Force can put unused planes. If you closed DM, what would you do with the bombing range? Where would you store the planes?

The encroachment issue caused us continuous work. One of our big concerns was Keene Elementary School. It was at the end of one of the runways in the flight path. The children were in danger if something should happen. In 1994, we asked the school board to close it and they did. Instead of tearing down the building, *World Care*, which stores medical equipment for third world countries, was able to use it. After 9/11, they sent trucks of bedding, medical supplies and other goods to New York City. When Katrina hit, they sent supplies to New Orleans. So it's not just for other countries. World Care stores needed goods for America, as well.

The base closings threat is an on-going, never-ending problem. DM-50 is constantly on alert and promoting the base and I keep track of everything that goes on. You might say that I just love the military. I'd do anything for them and every chance I get to rub shoulders with military people, I take it.

One of those opportunities to hobnob with our armed forces was an astounding visit to the Nimitz aircraft carrier.

I was invited because I did the right thing for someone else. Here's what happened. In 1992, General Colin Powell, Chairman of the Joint Chiefs of Staff (he became Secretary of State in 2001), was coming to Phoenix to make a presentation.[3] Bob Turpin, USNR retired, who has served on dozens of nonprofit boards, called and asked if I was interested in attending.[4] I had always wanted to see Colin Powell and sent a check for the $10 ticket.

Then I went to a football game and bumped into Julius Parker, Jr., and his wife. He was a general and the highest ranking African-American Military Intelligence Officer in the history of the Army. Now he is one of the vice presidents at the University of Arizona.[5] He had served with Powell when they were in Germany, but he had not gotten an invitation to the talk. I said, "You have to be kidding me."

I went back to my office, called Bob Turpin and told him who Julius Parker was. Bob promised to scrounge up another ticket and put him at my table. I said, "Take my ticket, get another one and then let's have Julius and his wife go."

After the event, Bob phoned and told me what had happened. Everyone was in the anteroom, including Colin Powell, and in walked Julius Parker. "You should have seen them embracing each other," he said. Julius wrote me a letter and called to say how much he appreciated what I had done.

I always figured if you do something nice for somebody, then something nice will happen to you. A few days later, Bob Turpin called again and said, "How would you like to take a trip out to the USS Nimitz aircraft carrier when they're practicing war games in the Pacific?"

"I'd love it," I said, and asked Liz Alexander to accompany me. Liz had been very involved in DM-50 during the base closing episode and a year later became its president.

As we were to report to the naval base in San Diego early in the morning, we stayed overnight at the Hotel del Coronado overlooking the beach. At the base, we met the pilots of a little 4-seater prop plane that went out everyday to deliver mail and supplies. They asked my age, (I was 72) and became concerned about whether I could do all the climbing. Liz piped in, "She will do just fine."

We took off and flew quite a ways out into the Pacific. I wasn't scared one bit. After a while, one of them said, "There's our ship."

The Nimitz looked like a dot on the horizon, but as we got closer we saw what resembled a small city floating on the ocean. We screeched down onto the carrier's deck and the tail caught on the third arresting wire. The crews rushed out, pushed the plane back, and we pulled ourselves out.

After introductions, we had lunch with the captain and they showed us to our bunks. Then they took us way down below to see the shop area where they fixed anything that went wrong with the ship. The young men there said they didn't even know what the weather was like. They worked and were billeted down in the bowels of the ship.

Liz and I had the run of the ship. We were allowed to attend the ship's briefings and go up on the top deck whenever we wanted to. We watched the planes practice takeoffs and landings. Helicopters were in the air while the fighter jets fired off the deck in case a plane went over the side into the sea and they had to rescue somebody right away.

We were required to wear radiation detectors on our belts that would warn us in case of a leak. The Nimitz was one of the first ships powered by atomic energy. At that time, they hadn't put in new fuel for seventeen years and had never had a problem.[6]

After two days and nights on board, we prepared to return to San Diego, and that's when things got real exciting. We had to be catapulted off the deck of the carrier in a jet. The pilot asked if I had ever pulled a *g*? "Oh yeah," I said, "On the Concorde." He said this was not the Concorde.

We sunk ourselves down into the jet seats and pulled on our helmets. Then they restrained me with a harness. It had a big round apparatus over my belly, the straps came up between my legs, around my back and hooked over my shoulders. I was tied down like an astronaut during a space launch.

The deck hands pushed the plane into the catapult, jumped out of the way, and *Fooosh*... we were propelled off that thing at such a speed... I thought I was a goner.

The compression from the *g* force pressed me down into the chair and I couldn't breathe. The plane dipped a little, and then circled around and over the ship. A rescue helicopter was in the air nearby spinning its blades in case anything went wrong. We flew back to San Diego at breakneck speed.

Landing on the ship was nothing compared to being fired off the deck like a stone in a slingshot. I have a certificate to prove what we did. It says: *August 15, 1992. USS Nimitz, Arrested Landing and Catapult Assisted Take-Off Zero to 128 in 3 seconds.* How about that?

Before I headed off for this adventure, I told Bill Corcoran where I was going and he didn't believe me. He said women weren't allowed on the Nimitz. He'd been a captain in the Navy and thought he knew everything. After I left, he went down to San Diego to the naval base and asked if the Nimitz was in. They said it was out on maneuvers in the Pacific. "Is Dorothy Finley out there?" he said. "They took her out today," was the response. Bill said, "I was so damn mad." He had never heard of such things.

As it turned out, because of my interest in the military and willingness to help in whatever way I could, David Monthan named their Child Development Center after me. I am greatly honored. And I am deeply humbled in being awarded the 2003 Zachary and Elizabeth Fisher Distinguished Civilian Humanitarian Award for my work with the armed forces.[7] It was a labor of love.

47. Travels

When John was still a child, we took many car trips throughout the states and into Canada. For our 30th anniversary, Harold and I flew on the Concorde to Paris. Then we got on the boat in Amsterdam, went through the Keel Canal and out to Finland, into Russia and Sweden, flew to Ireland and then hired a driver to take us to Scotland.

We spent a lot of time in Cabo San Lucas, went to Japan, Kuala Lumpur, Korea, Hong Kong and Bangkok and spent many holidays in Hawaii. When I was a child reading books about other countries, I'd made myself a promise to visit exotic places when I grew up, and I did.

After Harold died, I continued seeing the world, but this time with Glenna who was a joy to travel with. We visited Russia, New Zealand, Australia, the Canary Islands, Switzerland, Spain and the Galapagos Islands.

The trip that I remember the most is the time I went to Kenya in 1988 with the University of Arizona to see Richard Leaky and *the digs*. He is the son of the famed fossil-hunters Louis and Mary Leakey, and he unearthed more than 200 fossils, his most famous being Turkana Boy, one of the most complete skeletons found anywhere.[1]

I wasn't with Glenna this time and didn't know anybody. We flew into Nairobi and Richard sent a plane to pick us up. There were only four of us on this little plane and I asked the pilot, "Where'd you learn how to fly?"

He laughed and said, "In Phoenix."

"Do you know where we're going?" I said.

"Not exactly, but we will look and we will find it."

That made me feel safe.

Soon he said, "Look down, "There is the lake. It is huge, you can't miss it. Now watch down there, you are going to see a couple of white spots. Those are 50-gallon drums painted white and that is where we are going to land. Just out where the lava is."

There was no wind sock to tell us which direction to bring the plane in, and all of a sudden we went *Wrrippp...* right down and landed. There was no knocking or banging. It was a perfect landing.

The landing strip was a dirt strip out in a cow pasture. This didn't bother me because we always landed in cow pastures when we went to Cabo San Lucas. I expected things to be primitive; it was a third world country.

We hopped out of the plane and there waiting for us were cars Richard had sent because we couldn't land on the shore where he was. The roads were awful. We bounced around over dirt ruts, just like at the ranch.

After we arrived at the camp, we met Richard. He was dressed casually wearing trousers. Everybody else wore shorts. He was the only Anglo and everyone else was Kenyan. We soon headed out to Lake Turkana and could see the valley where they were excavating animal fossils. He took us to the digs and lectured for about an hour. He was a captivating speaker, but, *Oh*, was I hungry.

We had eaten that morning, but hadn't had much of anything since. When dinner was finally served, I inhaled the food, a cooked meat with beans, rice and peas. I didn't dare ask what the meat was.

That night, before we went to sleep, we asked to go for a swim in the lake and went skinny-dipping. The water was cooler than sitting out in the desert. If I had known what I know now, I would not have gone near that lake. I didn't know the lake was home to poisonous snakes.

After our swim, we went back to camp and everyone was screaming. Apparently a viper had spooked them and somebody had chopped off its head with a shovel.

Everybody finally calmed down and we warmed ourselves by the fire. As the humidity and bugs were horrendous, we wore a lot of mosquito repellent. However, bugs don't bother me much. I'm used to them from the ranch. We sat around and Richard told wonderful stories well into the night of creatures that lived millions of years ago and grazed in a lush land that was now a desert.

Before we went to bed, one of the young gals and I decided we needed to go to the bathroom. We took our flashlights and headed for the bushes. All of a sudden an animal let out a hoot and she jumped on my back.

The girl was about forty years younger than me, for gosh sakes. She grabbed me around the neck like a drowning swimmer. She's lucky I didn't sock her one.

For lodging, they led me to something like a *yurt* that started off as brick for a few feet and then became a big tent. I slept on a thin mattress on a single bed. At the top of the tent was a large rubber ring resembling an old car tire that gathered the mosquito netting. We let that down to keep the insects out.

Next morning, we had pancakes and sausages and then set out for the dig site. Altogether, we were there two days and watched them excavate an enormous turtle. They had a fence around it to keep animals out so they wouldn't chew the bones. We were there to observe and didn't actually pick up a shovel and dig in the dirt.

After too short a time, we left and got back on a plane, a bigger one this time with about twenty seats, to go to Nairobi. On the way, we landed to refuel and boys wearing white starched jackets like doctors' smocks ran up to the plane and opened the gas caps. They put a chamois over the intake hole and poured the fuel through the fabric to get the dirt out.

We were told there was a nudist colony nearby, but they had a rule that nobody nude could meet the plane and we never saw anyone. At least nobody naked. An old man using a stick walked over and he had a wooden headrest over his arm. They sleep on them like pillows. I asked him if he wanted to sell it for $5 and that was okay. I haven't tried it out yet.

After we got to Nairobi, we decided to go exploring. We were with a bigger group of people and drove out into the desert in scout cars. One of the men said to the guide, "Where are the rest stops?"

"There aren't any," was the reply.

"Well, these ladies have to go to the restroom," said the man.

The guide pointed to bushes about a foot high and said we'd stop there.

One of the gals said, "Dorothy, I got to go." We walked over to the bushes and, all of a sudden, here is this big sentry carrying a gun standing over us. Mercifully, he turned his back while we took care of business.

Before long, our modesty in tatters, we asked them to stop anywhere and we went behind the car and peed. I mean, we were there three weeks. We wanted to see everything and bodily functions were not going to get in our way.

At one of the rivers, we saw hippos with their babies, but the guide warned us not to get too close. They can be quite vicious and we watched from the banks so they wouldn't charge us.

After that, we observed native boys watering their cattle in an area called the Singing Wells, so called because the boys sang while working. The cattle stood on a little hill while the boys took turns leading them down into a gully where the hand-dug wells were located.

How they watered their cattle is a marvel. The boys went down into the wells and stood on something like scaffolding. They dipped metal buckets into the water and then passed them up to the next boy who hooked the bucket onto a pulley. They moved the bucket along until it reached a trough where they poured the water in for the cattle to drink.

They chanted the whole time, lifting their buckets in time with the song. The songs call each cow and bull by name and tell the herdsman on the hill when to bring down the cows.[2] The whole process was very orderly with groups of cows coming and going.

A man in our group who had a ranch said, "This is an awful way to water cattle. What they need is a Briggs and Stratton. Why has no money been sent to put in a pump?"

It seems that it was. A philanthropic group had gotten them a pump and they had lots of fuel to run it. But the natives rejected the idea. Watering cattle is the job of the young boys. If they ran a pump, the kids wouldn't have a job and it would cut down on their socializing.

Their cattle were different than ours, very gentle. Using little sticks, the young boys from the time they were about six years old walked the cattle out to graze in the morning. Later, they milked the cows, put the milk in gourds and bled the cattle into the milk. That caused the milk and blood to curdle and the result was a nutritious drink. As you can imagine, the cattle were pretty scarred up from where the boys cut them on their necks.

Next morning around 5 AM before the sun came up, we drove to the Masai Mara animal reserve park on the Serengeti. We met up with people trained here in Marana, Arizona, to hot air balloon. I went to the other side of the world to meet people from my own neck of the woods.

We clambered into the balloon's basket and launched just before sunup while it was cooler. We sat on benches or stood on the plank floor and sailed over the animals below us as they grazed and ran. We couldn't hear a sound up there because we moved with the wind.

We were on safari, only with cameras, and I took lots of pictures of elephants, zebras, giraffes, warthogs, baboons and a carpet of wildebeest, but the area is most famous for its lions. We spotted many other animals, too, like antelope, hyenas, eagles and vultures.[3]

When we were ready to descend, they told us to put our heads between our knees and brace ourselves. It was at that moment I thought maybe this little sky ride was not the best of ideas. The balloon came down quickly and hard, and the basket was dragged over the rocks.

Despite the crash landing, we stepped out uninjured and headed over a hill where they had laid boards between butane tanks and set a table with red bougainvillea as the center piece. We then raised fluted glasses of champagne and began consuming a hearty breakfast of toast, sweet rolls, bacon and eggs and pancakes.

I didn't eat the pancakes, I was too full. Funny the things you remember.

48. What Matters

My life has always been filled with the laughter and melodrama of children. My grandchildren are grown up now, but they were such fun when they were kids.

After John and Audrey brought Jessica home from the hospital, I didn't go over right away. I didn't want to act like the intrusive mother-in-law before they had a chance to adjust to a new baby.

John called me at school and asked if something was wrong. Why hadn't I come to see my grandchild? I told him I thought I should wait to get invited and he told me to come right away. I dropped everything and rushed over. It was darn near impossible to get the smile off my face for weeks.

Just before Jessica was born, my teachers at Schumaker threw me a Grandmother Shower. They gave me gifts like diapers, bottles and wet wipes so I was prepared when I babysat her the first time. As soon as she was old enough, I took her to school so the teachers could tell me how gorgeous she was.

A few years later, I began taking her to school often to interact with the kids and the teachers. One time we were getting out of the car and a little wind was blowing and she said, "Oh, the wind is messing up my hair." The teachers heard her say this and one said, "Oh, Dorothy..." She meant: *prima donna.*

That was Jessica. If something went wrong, she put her head down on the table and cried out, "Oh, oh, oh..." After I picked her up at a friend's house one day, she threw herself on the table and said, "Ohhhhh... my house is so ugly." I asked her why and she said because her friend's house had a spiral staircase and hers didn't. At an early age, she was a full-fledged drama queen. It's hard to believe she's nothing like that now.

I loved having Jessica and her brother Alex come over after school. They always had something to gripe and carry on about. With Alex, it was his spelling. Why couldn't he get 100 on his tests? He soon became sorry he brought it up. I drilled him and drilled him until he came home proud as a peacock with a perfect paper.

Both kids learned how to do their homework from me. I was probably too hard on them about their lessons much like my Grandma Susan was hard on me. Jessica didn't want to do the work even though she loved getting good grades. Before long she did a turn-around, worked hard and then got mad at Alex because he liked to fool around.

Harold enjoyed reading to them when they were toddlers and they insisted that he read the story about the three little kittens who lost their mittens over and over again. It was in the Mother Goose Nursery Rhymes, a book Jessica still has in her attic in what she calls "my precious stuff box."

Next to the book, she has my grandmother's gloves and my grandmother's doll, which is made of kid leather with a china face and hands. I have a beautiful Indian squash blossom necklace made out of nickels from the Navajo reservation that the university says is one of the Native Americans' earliest pieces. I am leaving it to Jessica and she better wear it and not hide it in that box.

It's hard for me not to think of Jessica and Alex as kids. I remember taking them for rides in the golf cart at the '49ers up to the clubhouse and feeding bread to the ducks in the pond. I blew up a little plastic pool and let them play in it. Harold hung a tire from a tree and they pushed each other to see how high they could go. We had a big old hammock strung between two tall mesquite trees and they got in that thing and pushed each other until the hammock flipped over and they fell out on the ground. They laughed so hard. I had visions of broken bones and thought, *John will be on my case.*

Alex liked to sit on my lap when we were on the porch swing. One day we were swinging, the darn rope tore out of the board and we flopped down onto the ground. I held him out so he was safe and we laughed so hard.

Sitting on a swing with Alex seems like it was yesterday, but I know many years have passed and Alex is too big to sit in my lap now.

Other things have changed, too. In August 2008, I sold Finley Distributing to a group of investors and they intend to keep the name. I'm happy I didn't sell when Harold wanted to so many years ago. When I sold, it was worth twenty times more.

I suppose I'm retired now, but you'd never know it. I still attend a lot of meetings and participate in nonprofits to better the community.

But as far as memories are concerned, nothing compares to the joy I experienced teaching children and doing things for the community. Except, of course, watching my son John marry Audrey and the births of my two beautiful grandchildren.

I grew up in tough circumstances, but never let that hold me back. I was always taught to keep moving forward, to never give up, and to give back. Of all the lessons my mother and father taught me, it was to persevere and be positive, nurturing and compassionate to others. Look after family, your neighbor, and children everywhere.

My whole life has been dedicated to children, and I'd like to leave you with one more thought. It's something I said during an interview with *Inside Tucson Business* after being named in their 2006 Women of Influence issue:

> *"If you take care of kids, you don't have to worry about what the future's going to be like. A little help is all they need, but it makes all the difference.*
>
> *"Give them some hope and they'll transform themselves."*

Appendix 1

60 Rules for Success

Rebecca R. Montaño, Ed.D., former Associate Superintendent of Education for TUSD, outlined eight rules for success that she attributed to me during a talk at the Education Enrichment Foundation. That got me thinking... I've compiled a list that is by no means complete, but goes a long way toward making you a successful teacher or principal.

1. Never be late.
2. Never leave early.
3. Dress appropriately. Never wear jeans or shorts.
4. Submit your lesson plans weekly.
5. Teach on your feet, not on your seat.
6. Participate in every committee or activity happening in school.
7. Expect the principal in your class daily.
8. When something goes wrong, ask yourself why that happened? What were you thinking?
9. Treat everyone with respect.
10. Teachers have families, too. Support them and let them take care of family business.
11. Thou shalt not skip break time. It's important to socialize.

12. Show the children that the teachers are friends.
13. Create a pleasant environment where teachers feel supported and want to go to work to practice their trade.
14. Have high expectations for your teachers.
15. Expect teachers to work as hard as you.
16. Don't whine and complain. If you don't like something, change it.
17. Be demanding, but fair.
18. Sometimes you will want to smack a child for his bad behavior, but don't.
19. As a principal, be everywhere. In the classrooms, in the cafeteria, on the playground. Let everyone feel your presence.
20. Talk to everyone, the teachers, the parents and the kids every chance you get.
21. Immerse yourself in the community.
22. Be aware of the parents who are sick, the ones who don't have money, clothing or food and help out. School is not just about books but about acting like human beings.
23. Every child can learn if given the opportunity. Create those opportunities.
24. Don't ever say you can't do something. You can always find a way.
25. Never look down on kids. Every child or student in school should be treated equally.
26. Not every child has the same abilities, but recognize when the child is doing a wonderful job at his or her level.
27. Know the name of all your parents and kids.
28. If a child doesn't come to school, find out why.
29. Never lie to parents about anything.
30. Make the best of whatever happens.
31. Support the parents. Almost always take their side in an issue with their kids.

32. Make the parents feel part of the school. Meet them outside of school at the PTA, at school and social events. Create relationships.
33. Treat parents with respect and equality. Sit beside them, not behind your desk.
34. Work together with the parents for the benefit of their child.
35. Keep in touch with the people who worked for you.
36. Be a mentor. Tell everything straight. Encourage teachers to better themselves.
37. Don't necessarily tell people what to do, but model what you have done in the same situation if it was successful.
38. Carry yourself with confidence and dignity.
39. The child is the most important thing. That's why you're a teacher or principal.
40. Make a difference. You can.
41. Do a good job at whatever you do.
42. Be generous and supportive.
43. Listen.
44. Think, analyze, and speak up.
45. Tell teachers what it is like to be an administrator so they know why you do certain things.
46. Give teachers a voice in what happens at school. Create teacher councils for input and feedback.
47. Decide things jointly, even though the principal has the ultimate say.
48. Treat kids fairly. Treat them with respect.
49. Sometimes you have to be tough on kids. Many thrive on that.
50. Try to be cheerful no matter what happens.
51. There's no point in yelling.
52. Make things happen for the kids.
53. Protect the children.
54. Joke with teachers. Show you have a sense of humor.

55. Joke with kids, too. They love to laugh with you.
56. Give money if you can during a crisis, but it has to be earned. Make the children report back in a letter or essay on how they used your help and how they will pay back the community. Make them responsible.
57. Keep your school clean.
58. Be open-minded. Don't be prejudiced. Don't make distinctions between people.
59. Support your school politically.
60. If the issue is for the good of the community, then fight for it.

The rules were compiled with input from Rebecca R. Montaño, Ed.D., former Associate Superintendent of Education for TUSD and now educational consultant for The Education Trust; Glennalee Foulk; David Overstreet, principal of Duffy Elementary School; Norma Jean Don, a former student from Wakefield Junior High; Ray Clarke, former Director of the Tucson Urban League; Ana Valenzuela Estrada, former Special Assistant to the President at Pima College and now Arizona State Director of LULAC; and from Steve Jewett, former director of Governor Jane Hull's southern Arizona office.

Appendix 2

A Woman of Influence

Dorothy H. Finley has served in more than 50 organizations in some capacity. Among them are:

Arizona Aerospace Foundation
American Diabetes Association, honored on Nov 18, 1995
American Heart Association, supporter 1985
American/Israel Friendship League, board of directors
Arizona 4-H, Trustee 1988
Arizona Aerospace Foundation
Arizona Apprenticeship Advisory Committee
Arizona Bank, board of directors
Arizona CANAMEX Corridor Task Force, transportation subcommittee
Arizona Chamber of Commerce, board of directors, 1991-1993
Arizona Children's Home, board of directors, development committee chair
Arizona Elementary School Administrators, past president
Arizona Historical Society, board of directors, Southern AZ Division
Arizona Humanities Council, 1989-1991
Arizona Opera League
Arizona Sonora Desert Museum, fundraiser, foundation member

Arizona State Job Training Coordinating Council, Governor appointed
Arizona State Liquor Board, board member, Governor appointed
Arizona Theater Company
Arizona Town Hall, board of directors
Arizona Wholesale Beer & Liquor Association, AWBLA, member
Arizona-Mexico Commission
Arizona/Pima County Beer & Wine Wholesalers, treasurer, member 1986
Arthritis Foundation, Southern Arizona Chapter, 1999
Humanitarian Dinner Committee
B.E.S.T., (Better Education Serves Tucson,) member
Better Business Serves Tucson
Big Brothers/Big Sisters of Southern Arizona, board of advisors
Tucson Medical Center, board of directors
Catalina Foothills High School Grad Night 1999, 2000, supporter
Challenger Learning Center
CODAC Behavioral Health Services, Inc./Child & Family Resources, Inc, supporter, 2000
Communities United Against Abuse, honorary committee 1998
Community Food Bank, 1993
Cystic Fibrosis Foundation
Davis-Monthan Air Force Base, Star Program
Department of Corrections, Venture Team, 1998
DM-50, director for 2 years; president 1989-1990, vice-president 1988-1989, secretary 1987-1988
Eastern Star, member of Oasis chapter
Educational Enrichment Foundation
Encore International Holiday Classic, Tucson Unified School District Interscholastic Department, supporter 1990
Finley Distributing Co., Inc, President, 1983-2008
Friends of Kartchner Caverns
Girl Scouts of America, board of directors, 1986-1990
Golden Rule Award Panel for promoting volunteerism, Chairman

Goodwill Industries, fundraiser
Governor's Council on Workforce Policy
Greater Tucson Economic Council, 1997-1999, chair
Jewish Federation of Southern Arizona
Juvenile Diabetes Association
Key Group, women's networking organization, Secretary 1987
Kino Hospital, Blue Ribbon Committee
KUAT
La Frontera Center, Inc., supporter 1985
League of Mexican American Women
March of Dimes, fundraiser, 1988
Mariachi Conference
Metropolitan Education Commission, 1990-1993
Metropolitan Tucson Convention & Visitors Bureau, Chairman 1989-1990, Treasurer 1988-1989
National Association of Women Business Owners
One More Victory Ara! Celebrity Golf and Gala Weekend, supporter, The Ara Parseghian Medical Research Foundation
Pima & Santa Cruz School to Work Partnership
Pima Air and Space Museum
Pima Community College Foundation, Board of Directors, 1989-1991
Pima County Government Operations Committee, member
Pima County Juvenile Court System
Pima Health Care Commission
Pio Decimo Center for children and families, supporter
Resources for Women, advisor, member
Roots & Wings, honorary board member, fundraiser
Rotary, Catalina member
Sahuaro Girl Scout Council, Inc.
Santa Cruz Advisory Committee, member and supporter
SAWARA, Southern Arizona Water Resources Assoc., board member
South Park Avenue Improvement Project, 1998
Southern Arizona Leadership Council
Spare the Air Campaign, Blue Ribbon Committee member
Tapestry Project
The League of Latin American Citizens, LULAC
Tucson 30, member

Tucson Airport Authority, board member, Operations Council member, 1989
Tucson Boy's Choir, honorary chair
Tucson Children's Museum, board of directors, Chairman
Tucson Community Foundation, member
Tucson Convention Center Commission
Tucson Indian Center
Tucson Medical Center, board of directors
Tucson Metropolitan Chamber of Commerce, member, vice Chairperson
Tucson Museum of Art, member
Tucson School Administrators Inc., member
Tucson Sister Cities, Nouakchott, Mauritania, Chairman
Tucson Symphony Orchestra
Tucson Urban League, Inc., member 1991, 1992
TUSD Elementary School Administrators, president 1978-1979
TUSD Elementary School Principals, Chairman
United Cerebral Palsy of Southern Arizona
University of Arizona:
- Alumni Association, member
- Black Alumni Club
- Board of Regents Award, 2007
- Century II, Steering committee
- College of Business and Public Administration, Executive Committee
- Comadres, University Medical Center
- Comedy Connections, supporter
- Copper Bowl Platinum Club, member
- Delta Kappa Gamma, Education Society, Parliamentarian, past president
- Eller College Graduate School of Management
- Exercise & Sports Sciences, Chairman 1986-1988, Advisory committee
- Fiesta Bowl Winter Classic Basketball Tournament, partial underwriter
- Football banquet, 1985 underwriter
- Hispanic Alumni Club
- Ice Cats and Ice Cat banquet, underwriter, 1999
- John Button Solomon statue and mini-park, donation
- Letterwoman's Club, chairman

PHASE, board of directors
President's Club, member
Pi Lambda Theta, Honorary Education Society
Spring Fling, supporter
Stadium Club, member
Tucson Fiesta Bowl, supporter
Wildcat Club, member, 1985 Goal Getter fundraising committee
WOSAC, Women's Studies Advisory Council, founder, board member 1987-1989

Women on the Move Programs, YWCA of Tucson, 1987, 1998, 1999
Women's Foundation of Southern Arizona
Working Women 500, 1998, top women owned and run businesses
YMCA, fundraiser
YWCA, Bright Futures

Dorothy has received more than 30 major awards and honors. Among them are:

Air Force Association, Tucson Chapter, President's Award, 1996
Celebrating Exceptional Women Ceremony, winner October 1996, The RFW Network Connection, Vol 12, No 1
Challenger Learning Center, recipient of Take Up Space award, 1997
Child Welfare League of America, Western Region, Board Leadership Award, Oct. 21, 1996
Distinguished Citizen Award, University of Arizona, 1993
Doncaster Legacy Award
Dorothy H. Finley Child Development Center, Davis-Monthan Air Force Base
Dorothy H. Finley Space Exploratorium & Challenger Learning Center of the Southwest, 1999
Entrepreneur of the year, 1987
JC Penny Golden Rule Award, 1994
Jewish Federation of Southern Arizona, award April 30, 1998
Jimmy Hart Award, 1999, United Cerebral Palsy of Southern Arizona

La Doña de Tucson, 1998, Los Descendientes del Presidio
Metropolitan Commission, Lifetime Achievement in Education, Crystal Apple Award, 1998
National Spirit of Life Award, May 3, 1992, City of Hope
Pledge-A-Job Recognition Award, 1998, 1999
Ray Davies Humanitarian Award 2001 for outstanding service to children
Sidney S. Woods Service Award, University of Arizona College of Education, Alumni Association
Tucson Children's Museum, President's Award, 1997
Tucson's Most Influential People, 1994
Tucson Rape Crisis Center, 1992 Rosie Award Recipient
Tucson's Top Five Most Influential People, 1994
Tucson's Woman of the Year, 1989, Tucson Metropolitan Chamber of Commerce
University of Arizona, Board of Regents Award, 2007
University of Arizona, Women's Plaza of Honor, 2006
Venture Clubs of the Americas, The Mae Carvell Award, 1995-1996
Women Helping Women Award, Soroptimist International of the Americas, 1986
Women of Influence, 2006, Inside Tucson Business, April 10, 2006
Women On The Move, Lifetime Achievement Award, 1999
Women Who Helped Build Tucson, award Oct 2, 1998
Zachary and Elizabeth Fisher Distinguished Civilian Humanitarian Award, 2003

Notes

---

2. Roots and Cowboy Boots

1. Boleyn, Carey, Knollys, West, Dandridge, Ruffin, and Hunt. From Virginia to Arizona, Hunt Ancestors and Related Families, Vol I and Vol II by S. LeRoyce Paul and Betty Hunt Kaye. In particular, see Vol II, pages 155-156.

2. William Candler facts. From Virginia to Arizona, Hunt Ancestors and Related Families, Vol II by S. LeRoyce Paul and Betty Hunt Kaye. Pages 102-104, 108-111.

3. William Candler story. From Virginia to Arizona, Hunt Ancestors and Related Families, Vol II by S. LeRoyce Paul and Betty Hunt Kaye.108-111. Captain Sampson Leroy Harris. Ibid., pages 135-137, 175-176.

4. Susan Mary Harris. Ibid., pages 133, 175-176.

5. Huntts. From Virginia to Arizona, Hunt Ancestors and Related Families, Vol I by S. LeRoyce Paul and Betty Hunt Kaye. Pages 5-32.

6. Martha Dandridge Washington. Descendants of John Dandridge. Page 2. Genealogy prepared by Betty Hunt Kaye and Suan LeRoyce.

See also: From Virginia to Arizona, Hunt Ancestors and Related Families, Vol II by S. LeRoyce Paul and Betty Hunt Kaye. Page118-125.

7. CW owned plantation and slaves. From Virginia to Arizona, Hunt Ancestors and Related Families, Vol II by S. LeRoyce Paul and Betty Hunt Kaye. Page184-186.

8. Real estate $20,000. Personal estate $100,000. $120,000 converted from 1860 to 2007 dollars using

Inflation Calculator valued at: $2,738,612.44. www.west egg.com/inflation/infl.cgi. Accessed 10/28/2008.

9. Lucy Ruffin's grave desecrated. From Virginia to Arizona, Hunt Ancestors and Related Families, Vol I by S. LeRoyce Paul and Betty Hunt Kaye. Page 22-23.

10. CW's Loss of wealth. From Virginia to Arizona, Hunt Ancestors and Related Families, Vol II by S. LeRoyce Paul and Betty Hunt Kaye. Page 186. CW's personal wealth in 1870 Panola County Census as $500 and real estate as $3,000. $3,500 in 1865 converted to 2007 dollars using Inflation Calculator valued at: $46,897.95. www.westegg. com/inflation/infl.cgi. Accessed 10/28/2008.

11. Jim, Joe and Jack seek their fortunes. From Virginia to Arizona, Hunt Ancestors and Related Families, Vol I by S. LeRoyce Paul and Betty Hunt Kaye. Page 31-32.

12. Stewart Hunt. Hunt, Norman K. *The Killing of Chester Bartell.* Page 91-92. Phoenix, AZ: Cowboy Miner Productions, 2006.

See also: From Virginia to Arizona, Hunt Ancestors and Related Families, Vol I by S. LeRoyce Paul and Betty Hunt Kaye. Page 34-35.

13. How cows became wild. From Virginia to Arizona, Hunt Ancestors and Related Families, Vol I by S. LeRoyce Paul and Betty Hunt Kaye. Pages 12-13.

14. Description of Stewart Hunt. Bailey, Lynn R. and Chaput, Don. Cochise County Stalwarts, A Who's Who of the Territorial Years. Tucson, AZ: Westernlore Press, 2000. Pages 193-194.

See also: Hunt, Norman K. *The Killing of Chester Bartell.* Page 92. Phoenix, AZ: Cowboy Miner Productions, 2006.

15. Bisbee. http://www.ghosttowns.com/states/AZ/ Lowell.html. Accessed 10/28/2008.

16. Population of Bisbee and moneymakers. Varney, Philip. Bisbee, Arizona. Arizona Highways Books, 1994.

17. Stewart Hunt's ranches. Hunt, Norman K. *The Killing of Chester Bartell.* Page 91-92. Phoenix, AZ: Cowboy Miner Productions, 2006.

See also: From Virginia to Arizona, Hunt Ancestors and Related Families, Vol I by S. LeRoyce Paul and Betty Hunt Kaye. Page 34-35.

3. Rancho Sacatal

1. Homesteading. Layser, Earle F. Following the Lewis and Clark, The Last Homesteaders. New Holland News. www.newholand.com/na/News/nhn/JA04/V50No5_1.htm. Accessed 7/9/2007.

See also: Hargreaves, Mary M. Women Homesteaders on the Northern Plains. Agricultural History, 50 (1976): 179-189.

Soza, Edward. Hispanic Homesteaders in Arizona, 1994. www.elearn.arizona.edu/booksbyedwardsoze/hispan ichomesteaders. Accessed 9/30/2007.

The Stock Raising Homestead Act of 1916 and Mining Claims. http://64.233.167.104/www.earthworksaction.org /pubs/SHRA. Accessed 9/30/2007.

Homestead Act (1862). www.tiscali.co.uk/reference/ encyclopaedia/ hutchinson/m0022816.html Accessed 9/ 30/2007.

2. Rancho Sacatal weather. Strauss, Sarah and Orlove, Benjamin S. Weather, Climate, Culture. Oxford, UK: Berg Publishers, 2003. Pages 234-237.

3. 480 acres of deeded land/30 square miles of open. Hunt, Norman K. *The Killing of Chester Bartell.* Pages 15-16. Phoenix, AZ: Cowboy Miner Productions, 2006.

4. Wildlife. Sulphur Springs Valley draws record 36,708 sandhill cranes. The Daily Dispatch. www.douglasdispatch. com/articles/2008/ 01/25/news/doc479a43eaceda77044 37208.txt. Accessed 9/5/2008.

Sulphur Springs Valley, Bird Tour. www.skyisland tours.com/ Tours.aspx. Accessed 9/5/2008.

5. Homestead Act (1862). www.tiscali.co.uk/reference/ encyclopaedia/hutchinson/m0022816.html Accessed 9/ 30/2007.

6. Time to leave Rancho Sacatal. Hunt, Norman K. *The Killing of Chester Bartell.* Page 15-18. Phoenix, AZ: Cowboy Miner Productions, 2006.

7. Farming. From Virginia to Arizona, Hunt Ancestors and Related Families, Vol I by S. LeRoyce Paul and Betty Hunt Kaye. Page 43.

8. Tayopa Mine. Ibid., page 43. Also: back of book.

9. Inventory of riches in Tayopa Mine. Haydock, Tim. The Lost Jesuit Gold of the Sierra Madre. www.be-alter.net/dfriesen/tayopagold.html. Accessed 8/28/2007.

See also: Slowpokejoe (searched for Tayopa Mines). http://p073.ezboard.com/fancientlosttreasuresfrm72. Accessed 8/28/ 2007.

10. Gave up search for riches. From Virginia to Arizona, Hunt Ancestors and Related Families, Vol I by S. LeRoyce Paul and Betty Hunt Kaye. Page 43. Also: back of book.

4. War and Prosperity

1. Huge demand for beef during war. Litman, Simon. Prices and Price Control in Great Britain and the U.S. During the World War. New York: Oxford University Press, 1920. Page 249.

See also: Trimble, Marshall. Diamond in the Rough, An Illustrated History of Arizona. Norfolk, Virginia: The Donning Company, 1988. Page 206.

2. Price controls. Feed doubles in price. Litman, Simon. Prices and Price Control in Great Britain and the US During the World War. New York: Oxford University Press, 1920. Page 252-255.

See: Tinley, J.M. Behavior of prices of farm products during World Wars I and II. Journal of Farm Economics, Vol. 24, No. 1, Proceedings Number (Feb. 1942), pp. 157-167.

3. Move to Animas Valley. Hunt, Norman K. *The Killing of Chester Bartell.* Page 16. Phoenix, AZ: Cowboy Miner Productions, 2006.

4. Guadalupe Canyon ranch. Ibid., page 16.

5. Submarine warfare against neutral or Allied shipping. U.S. History II: The United States in World War I. www.cliffsnotes.com/WileyCDA/ CliffsReviewTopic/The-United-States-in-World-War-I. Accessed 10/29/2007.

See also: Feinstein, Stephen. The 1910s—From World War I to Ragtime Music, Decades of the 20th Century. Berkeley Heights, NJ: Enslow Publishers Inc., 2001. Pages 40-44.

6. The Zimmermann Telegram. http://encyclopedia.thefreedictionary.com/Zimmermann+Telegram. Accessed 11/02/2007.

7. Arizona contributed most troops. Trimble, Marshall. Diamond in the Rough, An Illustrated History of Arizona. Norfolk, Virginia: The Donning Company, 1988. Page 189.

8. US expansion of armed forces. U.S. History II: The United States in World War I. http://www.cliffsnotes.com/WileyCDA/CliffsReviewTopic/The-United-States-in-World-War-I. Accessed 10/29/2007.

9. Wobblies. Trimble, Marshall. Diamond in the Rough, An Illustrated History of Arizona. Norfolk, Virginia: The Donning Company, 1988. Page 206.

10. Wobblies and the Deportation. The Bisbee Deport ation of 1917. University of Arizona. www.library.arizona.edu/exhibits/bisbee/history/whoswho. Accessed 11/01/2007.

See also: Industrial Workers of the World (IWW or Wobblies).

Trimble, Marshall. Diamond in the Rough, An Illustrated History of Arizona. Norfolk, Virginia: The Donning Company, 1988. Page 206.

Varney, Philip. Bisbee, Arizona. Arizona Highways Books, 1994. Page 5.

5. The Shooting

1. Ben Roberstson; Gray Ranch. Hunt, Norman K. *The Killing of Chester Bartell.* Pages 93-94. 99-100. Phoenix, AZ: Cowboy Miner Productions, 2006.

See also: From Virginia to Arizona, Hunt Ancestors and Related Families, Vol I by S. LeRoyce Paul and Betty Hunt Kaye. Back of book, pages 7-9.

2. W.H. "Hut" Taylor. Hunt, Norman K. *The Killing of Chester Bartell.* Pages 19-21, 26, 32-33, 92-93. Phoenix, AZ: Cowboy Miner Productions, 2006.

3. Eldridge Place. Ibid., page 39.

4. Cowboys driving Hunt cattle. Ibid., page 22.

5. The shooting. Ibid., pages 23-26.

6. Alternative version of the shooting. From Virginia to Arizona, Hunt Ancestors and Related Families, Vol I by S. LeRoyce Paul and Betty Hunt Kaye. Back of book, page 8.

6. Mom Meets Dad

1. Guadalupe Canyon. Hunt, Norman K. *The Killing of Chester Bartell.* Page 91. Phoenix, AZ: Cowboy Miner Productions, 2006.

2. Sallie was born in Clayton, New Mexico, in 1885. Interview with Sallie Hunt. Taped on February 20, 1970, Douglas, Arizona. Interviewed by Anna Jane Eppinga. Assignment for Harwood Hinton Arizona History class, University of Arizona. Tapes are now archived at The Center for American History at the University of Texas, Austin.

3. John Partridge Hunt. Hunt, Norman K. *The Killing of Chester Bartell.* Pages 87-89. Phoenix, AZ: Cowboy Miner Productions, 2006.

Descendants of William Huntt. Pages 9, 12. Genealogy prepared by Betty Hunt Kaye and Suan LeRoyce Paul.

7. Trials and Tribulations

1. Uncle Jim threw a chair. Hunt, Norman K. *The Killing of Chester Bartell.* Page 89. Phoenix, AZ: Cowboy Miner Productions, 2006.

2. Bail set at $25,000. Inflation Calculator 1917 to 2007—$401,033.13. www.westegg.com/inflation/infl.cgi. Accessed 10/27/2008.

3. 10 percent bond at $2,500. Inflation Calculator 1917 to 2007—$40,103.31. www.westegg.com/inflation/infl.cgi. Accessed 10/27/2008.

4. Joe Hunt not allowed to go to war. Hunt, Norman K. *The Killing of Chester Bartell.* Page 28. Phoenix, AZ: Cowboy Miner Productions, 2006.

5. American killed by war and flu. Feinstein, Stephen. The 1910s, From World War 1 to Ragtime Music. Decades of the 20th Century. Pages 43-44, 58-59. Berkeley Heights, NJ: Enslow Publishers, Inc., 2001.

Price, R. G. Casualties of War—Putting American Casualties in Perspective, 11/3/2003. http://rational revolution.net/articles/ casualties_of_war.htm. Accessed 10/04/2007.

6. Agrarian Reform Act of January 6, 1915. Small Town Politics: Continuity and Change in Cuencamé, Durango, 1895-1930. Paper presented at annual meeting of Rocky

Mountain Council on Latin American Studies, Colorado Springs, Colorado, February 18-20, 1999. Agrarian decrees 1913, 1915. www.msu.edu/user/walerd/Small-Town-Politics.htm. Accessed 11/5/2007.

Mexican constitution denies fundamental property rights to foreigners. www.mnforsustain.org/immg_mexican_consti tution%20and %20illegals.htm. Accessed 11/5/2007.

The Mexican Constitution—History. http://vivasan carlos.com/ constitution.html. Accessed 11/5/2007.

Country Studies. Rural Society. Agrarian Reform Act of 1915 and the constitution of 1917 laid the groundwork for changes in Mexico's land tenure system. www.country-studies.com/mexico/rural-society.html. Accessed 10/2/ 2007.

Waller, J. Michael. Mexico's Glass House. How the Mexican constitution treats foreign residents, workers and naturalized citizens. Agrarian Reform. April 7, 2006/ www.heritage.org/Research/Latin America/bg753.cfm. Acc essed 11/5/2007.

7. Stewart Hunt's enterprises. Hunt, Norman K. *The Killing of Chester Bartell.* Page 91-92. Phoenix, AZ: Cowboy Miner Productions, 2006.

8. February 5, 1917, Mexican Constitution formalized seizing of property owned by foreigners. Mexican constitution denies fundamental property rights to foreigners. www.mnforsustain.org/immg_mexican_constitution%20and %20illegals.htm. Accessed 11/5/2007.

See also: The Mexican Constitution—History. http://vivasancarlos.com/constitution.html. Accessed 11/5/2007.

Country Studies. Rural Society. Agrarian Reform Act of 1915 and the constitution of 1917 laid the groundwork for changes in Mexico's land tenure system. www.country-studies.com/mexico/rural-society.html. Accessed 10/2/2007.

9. Going on the lam. Hunt, Norman K. *The Killing of Chester Bartell.* Page 56. Phoenix, AZ: Cowboy Miner Productions, 2006.

10. Dad warns Ben Robertson. Ibid., pages 21-22.

11. Dad to flee to Mexico. Ibid., pages 87-88.

12. Purchase of Miller Ranch. Ibid., page 88. Phoenix, AZ: Cowboy Miner Productions, 2006.

13. Prices collapsed into recession. Parry, Chris. Economic Trends (1920s). The Economy: From Boom to Recession.

www.investorguide.com/igu-article-939-economic-trends-the-economy-from-boom-to-recession. Accessed 10/26/ 2007.

See also: Perlman, Jacob. The Recent Recession of Farm Population and Farm Land. The Journal of Land & Public Utility Economics: Vol. 4, No. 1 (Feb. 1928), pp. 45-58. www.jstor.org/jstor/gifcvtdir/sp000388/5489000/sp04x0154x_1.1gif. Accessed 10/26/2007.

Post-World War I Recession. http://www.u-s-history.com/ pages/h1362.html. Accessed 10/26/2007.

14. Few government contracts for beef. Litman, Simon. Prices & Price Control in Great Britain and the US During the World War. Pp. 252-255. New York: Oxford University Press, 1920.

15. Mistrial on second-degree murder. Hunt, Norman K. *The Killing of Chester Bartell.* Page 62. Phoenix, AZ: Cowboy Miner Productions, 2006.

8. Having Babies

1. Found guilty of manslaughter Hunt, Norman K. *The Killing of Chester Bartell.* Pages 63-77. Phoenix, AZ: Cowboy Miner Productions, 2006.

2. Bail set at $5,000. Inflation Calculator 1917 to 2007—$57,499.24. www.westegg.com/inflation/infl.cgi. Accessed 10/27/2008.

9. My Childhood Ranch

1. Malpais, New Mexico. http://home.swbell.net/lwsummer/malpais.htm. Accessed 9/7/2006.

See also: Old Hachita, New Mexico. http:home.swbell.net/lwsummer/oldhachita.htm. Accessed 9/7/2006.

Skelton, Bart. A Visit to Cat Country. Guns & Ammo (Jan. 2006).

2. The Fresno Scrapper. Invented in 1883, a national historic mechanical engineering landmark. The American Society of Mechanical Engineers. Fresno, California: October 13, 1991.

3. Southeast Arizona Monsoon Progression. National Weather Service. http://www.wrh.noaa.gov/twc/monsoon/monsoon_progression.pdf. Accessed 10/27/2008.

See also: San Bernardino National Wildlife Refuge. www.arizona gudie.com/ whattodo/DisplayPark.aspx.

4. Buckin, Ray A. Cisterns to collect non-potable water for domestic use. http://edis.ifas.ufl.edu/AE029. Accessed 10/27/2008.

See also: Rainwater Cistern. http://www.rain-barrel.net/ rainwater-cistern.html. Accessed 10/27/2008.

The Homestead Cistern. Mother Earth News. www.mother earthnews.com/Modern-Homesteading/1978-05-01/The-Homestead-Cistern.aspx. Accessed 10/27/2008.

5. Self-Heating Iron. Coleman.www.jitterbuzz.com/indirn. html. Accessed 10/27/2008.

6. American Quarter Horse Association. http://www. aqha.com. American Quarter Horse Breed Description and Equine History. http://www.horses-and-horse-information. com/articles/american-quarter-horse.shtml. Accessed 7/3/ 2009.

Measure Horse Height. http://www.cowboyway.com/How To/ HorseHeight.htm. Accessed 3/29/2008. A hand is 4 inches, so Prince was about 44 inches or 3 feet, 8 inches tall. A typical ranch horse is about 14 to 16 hands, which is about 56 inches to 64 inches, or 4 feet 8 inches to 5 feet 4 inches.

7. Shetland Pony. Shetland Pony Society of North America. http://shetlandpony society.org. Accessed 10/27/2008.

8. Metal Tub Washing Machine. Domestic Technology, Part 3. http://www.sciencetech.technomuses.ca/english/school zone/ Domestic_Technology3.cfm. Accessed 10/27/2008.

See also: Maxwell, Lee. Saving Women's Lives. http:// www.oldie wash.com/articles/lives.htm. Accessed 10/27/ 2008.

9. Frijoles. Refried beans. A recipe for Mexican beans. http://southernfood.about.com/od/beansandblackeyedpea s/r/bl30103s.htm. Accessed 3/30/2008.

See also: Frijoles refritos. www.schools.ash.org.au/ths compst/Mexico/Frijoles.html. Accessed 3/30/2008.

Frijoles de Olla. Frijoles Refritos. http://myweb. cableone.net/howle/ page/frijolesolla.htm. Accessed 3/30/08.

10. Goodnights. Haley, J. Evetts. Charles Goodnight, Cowman and Plainsman. Norman and London: University of Oklahoma Press, 1936, 1949.

11. Beard, Dan. Mumbly Peg. www.inquiry.net/outdoor/games/beard/mumbly_peg.htm. Accessed 10/28/2008.

See also: Mumblety peg. How to Play Mumbly Peg. www.ehow.com/how_2243286_play-mumbly-peg.html. Accessed 10/28/2008.

10. Fleeing the Drought

1. Dry spell continues in Arizona. Los Angeles Times (Aug. 21, 1925). http://pqasb.pqarchiver.com/latimes/access/465260212.html. Accessed 11/16/2007.

See also: Arizona dry despite rains. Los Angeles Times (July 7, 1925). http://pqasb.pqarchiver.com/latimes/access/465086002.html. Accessed 11/16/2007.

NWS Tucson. National Weather Service. 3.63" May 1924 to April 1925. www.wrh.noaa.gov/twc/climate/monthly/may02.php. Accessed 11/16/2007.

Pacific Decadal Oscillation (PDO). Dry period in southwest 1890-1924 followed by wet period from 1925-1946. http://64.233.167.104/search?q=cache:HHZeXVs20VoJ:www.srnr.arizona.edu/nemo.

Monsoon facts and figures, 1896-1992. Earliest monsoon beginning on record: June 16, 1925. http://ag.arizona.edu/maricopa/garden/ html/weather/monsoon.htm. Accessed 11/16/2007.

Tropical storm. Sept. 20-25, 1926. Over 5 inches of rain fell in extreme southeast Arizona. http://arc-grandcanyon.axxiomportal.com/page.aspx?id=909. Accessed 11/18/2007.

2. Kelly, Bill. John Horton Slaughter. www.desertusa.com/mag00/jun/ papr/slath.html. Accessed 9/7/2006.

3. Ross, Catrien. Slaughter ranch house. Arizona Highways (Oct. 1986). John Slaughter. Half the house in United States, other half in Mexico. www.slaughterranch.com/slaughterranch/html/about_us.html. Accessed 9/7/2006.

See also: Outlaws and Lawmen of the Wild West, Part 2. Explorations. Broadcast Jan. 21, 2004. http://voanews.com/specialenglish/archive/2004-01/a-2004-01-20-3-1.cfm. Accessed 9/7/2006.

4. What is an Artesian Well? www.wisegeek.com/what-is-an-artesian-well.htm. Accessed 11/18/2007.

See also: Artesian well. The Columbia Encyclopedia, Sixth Edition, 2007. www.encyclopedia.com. Accessed 11/18/2007.

5. Kelly, Bill. John Horton Slaughter. www.desertusa.com/mag00/jun/ papr/slath.html. Accessed 9/7/2006

See also: Ross, Catrien. Slaughter ranch house. Arizona Highways (Oct. 1986). John Slaughter. Half the house in United States, other half in Mexico. www.slaughterranch.com/slaughterranch/html/about_us.html. Accessed 9/7/2006.

6. Interview with Sallie Hunt. Taped on February 20, 1970, Douglas Arizona. Interviewed by Anna Jane Eppinga. Assignment for Harwood Hinton Arizona History class, University of Arizona. Tapes are now archived at The Center for American History at the University of Texas, Austin.

7. Living with Javelina. Arizona Game & Fish. www.azgfd.gov/w_c/urban_javelina.shtml. Accessed 11/18/2007.

8. Roadrunner (genus Geococcyx). http://www.desertusa.com/mag98/sep/papr/road.html. Accessed 7/4/2009.

9. Uncle Joe Hunt. Hunt, Norman K. *The Killing of Chester Bartell*. Page 84. Phoenix, AZ: Cowboy Miner Productions, 2006.

10. Description of Uncle Joe. Ibid., page 86.

11. Acquittal. Hunt, Norman K. *The Killing of Chester Bartell*. Page 82. Phoenix, AZ: Cowboy Miner Productions, 2006.

12. End of the drought. Arizona Hurricanes and Tropical Storms, a History. http://arc-grandcanyon.axxiomportal.com. Accessed 11/18/2007.

11. School Days on the Malpais

1. The Little Red Hen by Joseph Jacobs. www.bres.boothbay.k12.me.us/wq/nnash/WebQuest/littl_red_hen.htm. Accessed 10/29/2008.

See also: This Little Chick at www.geocities.com/heartland/acres/7875/ chicken.html. Accessed 10/29/2008.

Three Little Pigs by James Orchard Halliwell-Philipps, Nursery Rhymes and Nursery Tales, 1843. Retold by Joseph Jacobs, 1898. www.shol.com/agita/pigs.htm. Accessed 3/26/2008.

2. Captain Sampson Leroy Harris, Antietam. From Virginia to Arizona, Hunt Ancestors and Related Families, Vol II by S. LeRoyce Paul and Betty Hunt Kaye. Pages 135-136.

3. Johnny Stride Pole. Rotary swing. www.toronto.ca/archives/rules/ spdsrotary.htm. Accessed 3/19/2008.

4. Charles Hunt shot. From Virginia to Arizona, Hunt Ancestors and Related Families, Vol II by S. LeRoyce Paul and Betty Hunt Kaye. Page 135.

5. Barber/doctors and butcher/doctors. Feldberg, Michael. An all but forgotten Colonial doctor. www.jewishworldreview.com/jewish/ history8.php3. Accessed 10/29/2008.

6. Dr. Charles Harris Hunt. From Virginia to Arizona, Hunt Ancestors and Related Families, Vol I by S. LeRoyce Paul and Betty Hunt Kaye. Pages 38-39.

7. Town of Apache. Geronimo Surrender Monument. http://www.bygonebyways.com/Arizona _80.htm. Accessed 3/19/2008.

8 Teacherages. Gardner, Brooks. The Teacherage. The Partial Observer, 9/30/2006. www.partialobserver.com. Accessed 3/19/2008.

See also: Carter, Patricia Anne. Everybody's Paid But the Teacher. Teachers College Press, 2002.

Maxcy, Spencer J. The Teacherage in American Rural Education. Journal of General Education, v30 n4 pp267-74. 1979.

9. Married teachers not allowed to teach. Mines, Kelly. Early Arizona Women Teachers. Page 2. www.ic.arizona.edu/ic/mcbride/ws200/mine-hist.htm. Accessed 7/9/2007.

See also: Cooper, James F. The First Hundred Years, The History of Tucson School District 1, Tucson, Arizona, 1867-1967. Editor: Fahr, John H. Page 105.

10. Poor salaries for female teachers. Mines, Kelly. Early Arizona Women Teachers. Page 2. www.ic.arizona.edu/ic/mcbride/ws200/mine-hist.htm. Accessed 7/9/2007.

11. Nasturtiums, colors. Gilbert, Linda. Nasturtiums. www. sallys-place.com/food/columns/gilbert/nasturtiums.htm. Accessed 3/27/2008.

12. Lice. Head Lice. KidsHealth, Nemours Foundation. http://kidshealth.org/PageManager.jsp?dn=KidsHealth&lice. Accessed 3/26/2008.

12. Recess

1. Dodgeball. www.gameskidsplay.net/GAMES/ball_games/dodge ball.html.

2. Crack the Whip. http://www.gameskidsplay.net/games/strength_games/crack_the_whip.htm. Accessed 10/29/2008.

See also: Children's Games. http://thelibrary.springfield.missouri.org/lochist/periodicals/bittersweet/fa731.htm. Accessed 3/19/2008. Page 4.

3. Hemp ropes for jumping. http://stanford.wellsphere.com/wellmix360/hemp-rope. Accessed 7/4/2009.

4. Reata cowhide rope. www.equibooks.com/reviews3.html.Page 2. Accessed 3/19/2008.

See also: Monaghan, Jay. The Book of the American West. New York: Bonanza Books, 1963. Page 345

5. Anti-Over. Children's Games. http://thelibrary.springfield.missouri.org/lochist/periodicals/bittersweet/fa731.htm. Accessed 3/19/2008. Page 4.

See also: Red Rover. Children's Games. http://thelibrary.springfield.missouri.org/lochist/periodicals/bittersweet/fa731.htm. Accessed 3/19/2008. Page 3.

6. Types of marbles. Ringer. LandOfMarbles.com/how-to-play.html. Accessed 3/19/2008.

7. Bull Durham tobacco bags for marbles. http://www.texasescapes.com/DelbertTrew/Bull-Durham-tobacco-cheapest-luxury.htm.

See also: http://ezinearticles.com/?Creek-on-Fire&id=251184. Both sites accessed 5/12/2008.

8. Urban legends about marbles. Agate Facts, Information and Description. www.bernardine.com/gemstones/agates. htm. Accessed 3/19/2008.

13. Readin', Writin', 'Rithmitic

1. Charles A. Lindbergh's book titled *We*. http://www.amazon.com/We-Charles-Lindbergh/dp/0899668321. Accessed 3/ 24/2008.

See also: Spirit of St. Louis touches down (Sept. 23, 1927). Arizona Daily Star, 9/09/2007. http://www.azstarnet.com/sn. Accessed 9/9/2007.

2. The Raven by Edgar Allan Poe. First published in 1845.
www.heise.de/ix/raven/Literature/Lore/TheRaven.html. Accessed 9/7/2008.

3. *Little Women* written by Louisa May Alcott. Published in 1868. The Literature Network. http://www.online-literature.com/alcott/littlewomen. Accessed 7/3/2009.

4. *Rebecca of Sunnybrook Farm* by Kate Douglas Wiggin, published in 1903. The Literature Network. http://www.online-literature.com/kate-wiggin/rebecca-of-sunnybrook-farm. Accessed 7/3/2009

See also: *House of the Seven Gables* by Nathaniel Hawthorne. Published in 1851. The Literature Network. http://www.online-literature.com/hawthorne/seven_gables Accessed 7/3/2009.

Daddy Longlegs by Jean Webster. A novel written in 1912. The Literature Network. http://www.online-literature.com/arthur-scott-bailey/daddy-longlegs. Accessed 7/3/2009.

14. The Great Depression Strikes

1. Subsidies for cattle. Goff, John S. Arizona, An Illustrated History of the Grand Canyon State. Windsor Publications Inc, 1988. Page. 112.

2. Dust Bowl. Feinstein, Stephen. 1930s, From the Great Depression to The Wizard of Oz. Decades of the 20th Century. Berkeley Heights, New Jersey: Enslow Publishers, 2001. pp 5-25.

3. Teenagers riding the rails. Feinstein, Stephen. 1930s, From the Great Depression to The Wizard of Oz. Decades of the 20th Century. Berkeley Heights, New Jersey: Enslow Publishers, 2001. pp 8-9.

See also: Riding the Rails: Teenagers on the Move During the Great Depression. New York: Routledge, 2003. www.erroluys.com/Ridingthe Rails.htm. Accessed 3/29/2008.

4. Kress traveling art show. The Kress Study Collection. http://is.uni-sb.de/projekte/sonstige/museum/kress_virtual_museum.html. Accessed 3/29/2008.

5. Bill Gidley family. www.mycochise.com/grooms1927fo2gom.php. Accessed 3/29/2008.

15. Food, Glorious Food

1. Jerky. Wasna/Pemmican Recipes. http://nappaw.tribe.net/thread/bda9334c-4799-4e97-b322-6724e98bcfa6. Accessed 4/1/2008.

2. Pemmican. www.physicalmind.com/pemmican.htm. Accessed 4/1/2008.

See also: www.encyclopedia.com. Accessed 4/1/2008.

3. Cracklins. www.wisegeek.com/what-are-cracklins.htm. Accessed 4/21/2008.

See also: Salt pork. Fatback. www.foodsubs.com/MeatcureBacon.html. Accessed 4/21/2008.

4. Plymouth Rock. http://www.ansi.okstate.edu./poultry/chicken/plymouthrock. Accessed 7/3/2009.

See also: Leghorn chicken. http://www.ansi.okstate.edu./poultry/chicken/leghorn. Accessed 7/3/2009.

5. Guinea hens. http://www.feathersite.com/Poultry/Guineas/BRKGuineas.html. Accessed 7/3/2009.

6. Empanadas. www.mexgrocer.com/665-empanadaas.html. Accessed 3/30/2008.

7. Tortilla making. www.cooking.com/advice/adgloss.asp. Accessed 4/21/2008.

8. Green corn tamales. www.azcentral.com/php-bin. Accessed 3/30/2008.

See also: Making and buying. http://emol.org/dining/greencorntamale.html. Accessed 3/30/2008.

9. Tamales Dulces. By Taylor Benson. www.peoplesguide.com/1pages/chapts/food/recipe/main/tamales-taylor. html. Accessed 3/31/2008.

See also: www.mexconnect.com/mex_/recipes/puebla/kgtamales3.html. Accessed 3/31/2008.

www.progressotamale.com/recipes/tamale/sweet.html. Accessed 3/31/2008.

www.theworldwidegourmet.com. Accessed 3/31/2008.

10. Ice cream making. http://answers.yahoo.com/question. Accessed 3/31/2008.

See also: www.girlinaweb.com/cooking-tips/15447.php. Accessed 3/31/2008.

16. Mom and Dad

1. Los Angeles and the water grab. The story of the Los Angeles aqueduct. http://wsoweb.ladwp.com/Aqueduct/historyoflaa. Accessed 4/8/2008.

See also: Archibold, Randal C. A Century Later, Los Angeles Atones for Water Sins. The New York Times, Jan. 1, 2007. www.nytimes.com/2007/01/01/us/01water.html. Accessed 4/8/2008.

2. Mark Twain, whiskey and water. The attribution has not been verified as a Mark Twain quote, although everybody thinks he said it and nobody has challenged it except this website. www.twainquotes.com/Water Whiskey.html. Accessed 10/30/2008.

17. Preachers, Salt Licks and Bugs

1. Aimee Semple McPherson. Los Angeles Almanac. www.laalmanac.com/religion/re10e.htm. Accessed 4/2/2008.

2. Arizona Bark Scorpion. Ditson, Mia. Bark Scorpions—Nothing to Mess With. www.dflt.org/aware ness/scorpions htm. Accessed 4/7/2008.

See also: Hedding, Judy. How to treat a scorpion sting. http://phoenix.about.com/cs/desert/ht/scorpionsting.htm Accessed 4/7/2008.

Arizona Bark Scorpion. www.geo-outdoors.info/scorp ions.htm. Accessed 4/7/2008.

3. Black Leaf 40 and tobacco. http://lists.ibiblio.org/pipermail/market-farming/2004-March/016417.html. Accessed 4/7/2008.

See also: Nicotine (Black Leaf 40) Chemical Profile 4/85. http://pmep.cce.cornell.edu/profiles/insect-mite/mevin phos-propargite/nicotine/insenct-prof-nicotine. Accessed 4/7/2008.

4. Pie safes. Build a pie safe. www.lowes.com/lowes. Accessed 4/7/2008.

See also: Vivian, John. An Old Fashioned Pie Safe. Mother Earth News. www.motherearthnews.com. Accessed 4/7/2008.

5. Yellow Jaundice. Jaundice—yellow skin (symptom). www.msha.com. Accessed 4/7/2008.

See also: www.nlm.nih.gov/medlineplus. Accessed 4/7/2008. Skin abnormalities due to Yellow Jaundice. www.after50health.com/skin-abnormalities. Accessed 4/7/2008.

Hepatitis C. http://www.cdc.gov/hepatitis. Accessed 7/3/2009.

Yellow Fever. www.cdc.gov. Accessed 4/7/2008.

Scarlet Fever. www.kidshealth.org. Accessed 4/7/2008.

6. Peeling Skin symptoms. Staph Infection. Sunburn. Blisters. http://www.home-remedies-for-you.com/remedy/Peeling-Skin.html. Accessed 4/7/2008.

See also: Strep infections, scarlet fever, toxic shock, eczema. http://www.askdrwarren.com/qa040405.htm. Accessed 4/7/2008.

Vitamin A Overdose. http://www.vitamins-supplements.org/ vitamin-A.php. Accessed 4/7/2008.

18. Roundups and Mountain Oysters

1. Winter temperatures on the Malpais. http://www.arizonaguide.com/whattodo/DisplayPark.aspx. Accessed 4/6/2008.

2. Booger Red Privett. http://www.tbartstables.com/Cowboy%20Mounted%20Shooting.htm. Accessed 4/6/2008.

3. Tapaderos or taps. www.equibooks.com/reviews3.html. Accessed 3/19/2008. Page 2.

See also: Tapadero documentary. www.equibooks.com/reviews3.html. Accessed 3/19/2008. Pages 1, 3.

4. Cattle Rustlers using running iron. http://www.linecamp.com/museums/americanwest/define_the-west/cattle_rustler/cattle_rustler.html. Accessed 4/6/2008.

See also: The Handbook of Texas Online. Cattle Rustling. www.tshaonline.org.handbook/online/articles/CC/jbc1.html. Accessed 4/6/2008.

Branding iron. http://www.cowboyshowcase.com/glossarycattle.htm. Accessed 4/6/2008.

5. Bull testicles. History of Rocky Mountain Oysters (and recipe). http://whatscookingamerica.net/History/Rocky Mtn Oyster.htm. Accessed 4/6/2008.

6. Cooking bull testicles on iron stove. History of Rocky Mountain Oysters (and recipe). http://whatscookingamerica.net/History/Rocky MtnOyster.htm. Accessed 4/6/ 2008.

7. Screw Worms. Mitchell, Ann P. All About Screw Worms. http://www.allaboutworms.com/screw-worms. Accessed 4/6/2008.

8. Laudanum. Victorians and Laudanum. http://drugs.uta.edu/laudanum.html. Accessed 4/8/2008.

See also: The Opium Poppy. What is Laudanum? www.poppies.org/faq/ advanced-usage/what-is-laudanum. Accessed 4/8/2008.

9. Turpentine. Oxydado, Rusty. Remember Mama's Recipes, Turpentine. http://waltonfeed.com/old/mama/turp.html. Accessed 4/8/2008.

See also: Folk Medicine. Turpentine. www.hort.purdue.edu/newcrop/duke_energy/Pinus_elliotti.html. Accessed 4/8/2008.

10. Castor Oil. http://ask.yahoo.com/20000519.html. Accessed 4/25/2008.

See also: Epsom Salt. Belander, Carol. The Wonders of Epson Salt. 10/15/2007. www.articlesbase.com/health-articles/the-wonders-of-epson-salt-236639.html. Accessed 4/25/2008. Note that Epsom is spelled Epson in this article.

Natural and/or Old-time Treatments for Worms. www.pfi.iastate.edu/OFR/Anthelmintics.htm. Accessed 4/25 /2008.

11. Petrified Wasp's Nest. http://chestofbooks.com/reference/The-New-Student-s-Reference-Work-VolI/pp0495.html. Accessed 4/8/2008.

12. Mexican folk medicines. Folk remedies common cause of lead poisoning. The Associated Press, Jan. 22, 2008. http://www.msnbc.msn.com/id/22782271. Accessed 4/22/2008.

See also: Lead Poisoning from Folk Home Remedies. Virginia Department of Health. www.vdh.virginia.gov/Epidemiology/DEE. Accessed 4/22/2008.

Lithium. http://www.drugs.com/lithium.html. Accessed 7/3/2009.

Zinc Sulfate. MedlinePlus. U.S. National Library of Medicine and the National Institutes of Health. http://www.nlm.nih.gov/medlineplus/druginfo/natural/patient-zinc.html. Accessed 4/22/2008.

Irish Potato. Blood Poisoning Cures. Earth Clinic, folk remedies and holistic cures. http://www.earthclinic.com/CURES/blood_poisoning.html. Accessed 4/22/2008.

13. Pinkeye. Oury, Marie-Pierre; Scharko, Patricia; and Johns, John. Pinkeye in Cattle, Infectious Bovine Keratoconjunctivitis. University of Kentucky, College of Agriculture. http://www.ca.uky.edu/agc/pubs/id/id135/id135.pdf. Accessed 10/31/2008.

14. Cottonseed cake. http://onlinedictionary.datasegment. com/word/cottonseed%20cake. Accessed 4/3/2008.

19. The Selling Business

1. Cockleburs. www2.ic.edu/prairie/cockle_burr.htm. Accessed 4/23/2008.

See also: Common cocklebur. Plants Poisonous to Livestock. http://extension.missouri.edu/explore/agguides/crops/g04970.htm. Accessed 4/25/2008.

2. Clabber. Bonny-Clabber. http://www.civilwarinteractive.com/recipeBONNY CLABBER.htm. Accessed 10/16/2008.

See also: Andrews, Eliza Frances. The War-Time Journal of a Georgia Girl, 1864-1865. Page 59. Note that clabber is spelled "crabber" here. http://docsouth.unc.edu/fpn/andrews.html. Accessed 4/24/2008.

Clabber. Backcountry Food Ways: North British Origins of Southern Highland Cooking. Crabber is spelled "crabber" here. http://xroads.virginia.edu/~ug97/albion/afood.html. Accessed 4/24/2008.

3. Johnson grass. http://extension.missouri.edu/explore/agguides/ crops/g04970.htm.

See also: Sacaton grass. http://www.highcountrygardens.com/catalog/product/ 91932. Accessed 4/23/2008.

Gamagrass. www.ppws.vt.edu/scott/weed_id/gama.htm. Accessed 4/23/2008.

Locoweed. Gates, Frank C. The Loco Weed and its Effect on Live Stock, Circular 115. August, 1925. Kansas State Agricultural College. See also: Plants that Poison. World Chelonian Trust, 2002. http://www.chelonia.org/articles/plantsthatpoison.htm. Accessed 4/24/2008.

4. Jimsonweed. Fishel, Fred. Department of Agronomy, Missouri MU Extension. Plants Poisonous to Livestock.

http://extension.missouri.edu/explore/agguides/crops/g0 4970.htm. Accessed 4/25/2008.

5. Poppies. Desert Wildflowers. Bladder Pod. http:// www.ci.twentnine-palms.ca.us/Desert_Wildflowers.94.0. html. Accessed 4/24/2008.

See also: Native American Ethnography and Ethnohistory. http://www.nps.gov/history/online_books/jotr/ history3.htm. Accessed 4/24/2008.

California poppies. http://www.gardenguides.com. Accessed 4/24/2008.

http://www.almaden.ibm.com/almaden/environs/wild flowers/poppy.html. Accessed 4/24/2008. www.desertusa. com. Accessed 4/24/2008.

Lupine. www.wildflowerinformation.org/Wildflower.asp. Accessed 4/24/2008. See also: Plants That Poison. World Chelonian Trust, 2002. www.chelonia.org/articles/plants thatpoison.htm. Accessed 4/24/2008.

6. Cows eat wild onions. Cow capers.http://sports. webshots.com/album/398168105hTBKwX. Accessed 4/ 24/2008.

See also: http://davesgarden.com/community/forums/t/ 812749. Accessed 4/24/2008. http://www.newton.dep.anl. gov/natbltn/100-199/nb184. htm. Accessed 4/24/2008.

http://www.turtletrack.org/Issues00/Co04082000/ CO_0408 2000_WildOnions.htm. Accessed 4/24/2008.

7. Snubbing post. *Western live-stock management*. Potter, E. L., et al. Macmillan Company, 1917. Pages 98-99.

20. My Dad Threatens to Shoot

1. Coatimundi. http://www.kostich.com/Coatimundi_ 001.jpg and _oo2.jpg.

See also: Coati. Physical Description. Feet. http://who zoo.org/AnlifeSS2002/bettsass/BS_Coati.htm. Accessed 4/4/2008.

2. Repeal of Prohibition. Feinstein, Stephen. Decades of the 20th Century: From the Great Depression to the Wizard of Oz. Enslow Publishers: Berkeley Heights, NJ, 2001. Page 13.

21. My Famous Cousin

1. Jack Williamson's story. Multiple sources for similar information.

See: The SF Site: A Conversation with Jack Williamson. http://www.sfsite.com/ 03b/jw77.htm. Accessed 7/5/2007.

Jack Williamson Obituary. http://books.guardian.co.uk/ obituaries/story/0,,1963945,00. html. Accessed 7/5/2007.

Fox, Margalit. Jack Williamson, 98, an Author Revered in Science Fiction Field, Dies. The New York Times, Nov. 14., 2006.

www.nytimes.com/2006/11/14/obituaries/14william son. html. Accessed 4/26/2008.

2. An Interview with Jack Williamson. McCaffery, Larry. www.depauw.edu/sfs/interviews/williamson54interview.ht m. Accessed 7/5/2007.

3. Aunt Lucy. Metal Man. Ibid.

4. Married Blanche Slaton Harp. http://www.depauw. edu/sfs/interviews/williamson54interview.htm. Accessed 7/5/2007.

5. Psychoanalysis. http://www.depauw.edu/sfs/inter views/williamson54interview.htm. Accessed 7/5/2007.

6. Weather forecaster. Fox, Margalit. Jack Williamson, 98, an Author Revered in Science Fiction Field, Dies. The New York Times, Nov. 14, 2006. http://www.nytimes.com/ 2006/11/14/obituaries/14williamson.html. Accessed 4/26/2008.

7. Felt undereducated. The Tribune. Williamson, 98, was sci-fi author, teacher in Portales. www.abqtrib.com/news/ 2006/nov/11/williamson-98-was-sci-fi-author-teacher-portales. Accessed 4/26/2008.

8. Isaac Asimov. Williamson, Jack. Wonder's Child: My Life in Science Fiction. Benbella Books, 2005.

9. Won most science fiction awards. Invented new words. http://books.guardian.co.uk/obituaries/story/0,,1963945, 00.html. Accessed 7/5/2007. The Tribune. Williamson, 98, was sci-fi author, teacher in Portales. www.abqtrib.com/ news/2006/nov/11/williamson-98-was-sci-fi-author-teacher-portales. Accessed 4/26/2008.

22. Time to Leave

1. Colorado Street Bridge. http://www.waymarking.com/waymarks/WM1P3E. Accessed 4/29/2008.

2. Suicide Bridge on Route 66. California Legends. www.legendsofamerica.com/ca-suicidebridge.html. Access ed 4/28/2008.

23. Alone and Scared

1. José Clemente Orozco. Old Master Artist. http://www.latifm.com/artists/Orozco_Jose_Clemente.html. Accessed 4/28/2008.

2. José Clemente Orozco. http://www.pomona.edu/museum/collections/prometheus/about.shtml.

See also: Orozco, Jose Clemente. An Autobiography with Leeper, John Palmer. Dover Publications, 2001.

3. Pomona College mural. Wall Man. Time Magazine, Oct. 13, 1930. http://www.time.com/time/0,8816,740519.00.html. Accessed 4/28/2008.

4. Powdered earthen paints. http://www.newschool.edu/infotech/fresco.del/howto3.html. Accessed 4/28/2008.

5. Fresco brushes. Ibid. Accessed 4/28/2008.

6. Charcoal. http://www.newschool.edu/infotech/fresco.del/glossary.html. Accessed 4/28/2008.

7. Making a paste. http://www.newschool.edu/infotech/fresco.del/howto4.html. Accessed 4/28/2008.

25. Getting Out the Hayseeds

1. Mason Opera House. http://www.ulwaf.com/LA-1900s/03. Accessed 5/12/2008.

2. Aida. http://www.broadwaymusicalhome.com/shows/aida.htm. Accessed 7/3/2009.

3. Pasadena Playhouse. http://www.pasadenaplay house. org. Accessed 7/3/2009.

4. Los Angeles Philharmonic Association. http://www.laphil.com. Accessed 7/3/2009.

5. Modern Dance. http://www.smithsonianeducation.org/spotlight/dance.html. Accessed 7/3/2009.

6. Viennese Waltz. Herbison-Evans, Don. History of Modern Ballrrom Dancing. Page 5. http://donhe.tripod.com/pubs/modern.html. Accessed 5/13/2008.

7. Simple Rules of Ballroom Dance Etiquette. Kim, Jean. http://www.hcs.harvard.edu/~hma-bdc/etiquette.html. Accessed 5/12/2008.

8. Clog Dancing. http://www.streetswing.com/histmain/z3clog1.htm. Accessed 7/3/2009.

9. Rogers and Astaire. Croce, Arlene. The Fred Astaire & Ginger Rogers Book. Duton, 1987.

26. The Honeymoon Ranch

1. White Mountains/Hannigan Meadow. www.cpluhna.nau.edu/Places/white_mountains.htm. Accessed 1/16/2007.

See also: http://hannaganmeadow.com. Accessed 3/11/2008.

2. Sugan. Pearce, T.M. Three Rocky Mountain Terms: Park, Sugan, and Plaza. American Speech, Vol 33, No 2 (May, 1958), pp. 99-107. Duke University Press. See also: MSN Encarta.

3. Graves Peeler. Cattlemen's Texas Longhorn Registry. http://www.ctlr.org/Resources/Legacy/index.html. Access ed 5/19/2008.

4. Jess Simpson. From Virginia to Arizona, Hunt Ancestors and Related Families, Vol I by S. LeRoyce Paul and Betty Hunt Kaye. Family stories near back of book, insert between pages 62 and 63. See pages 12-13.

5. Jess Simpson shootings. Ibid. Family stories near back of book, insert between pages 62 and 63. See pages 12-13.

6. Point of Pines Indian burial site. Robinson, William J. and Sprague, Roderick. American Antiquity, Vol. 30, No. 4 (April, 1965), pp. 442-452. Society for American Archaeology.

7. Dutch oven. State cooking pot, Utah. http://pioneer.utah.gov/utah_on_the_web/utah_symbols/pot.html. Accessed 3/30/2008.

28. Uncle Joe

1. After the Bartell shooting and trials. From Virginia to Arizona, Hunt Ancestors and Related Families, Vol I by S. LeRoyce Paul and Betty Hunt Kaye. Pages 45-49.

2. Obituary. Ibid., pages 46-47.

29. War Comes Again

1. Japanese attack Pearl Harbor. War declared. Feinstein, Stephen. The 1040s. From World War II to Jackie Robinson. Berkeley Heights, New Jersey: Enslow Publishers Inc., 2000. Pages 5-7.

2. Zeta Phi Eta. Only women until 1975. National Professional Fraternity for Communication Arts and Sciences. www.zetaphieta.org/ aboutzeta.htm. Accessed 5/27/2008.

3. Alpha chapter of Pi Lambda Theta. http://tiger.doane.edu/StudentHandbook/Organizations/Organizations&Activities.htm. Accessed 5/27/2008.

4. Delta Sigma Rho (Speech/Debate). http://cms.bsu.edu/CampusLife/StudentOrganizations/HonoraryandProfessionalFraternitiesandSororities/DeltaSigmaRho. Accessed 5/27/2008.

5. Delta Kappa Gamma. http://www.topix.com/student-societies/kappa-gamma. Accessed 11/4/2008.

See also: Delta Kappa Gamma Society International, State of Missouri, Papers, (WUNP4388). http://whmc.umsystem.edu/invent/dese-womsoc.html. Accessed 11/4/2008.

6. Ryan Airfield. http://www.tucsonairport.org/ga/html/ga_ryan.html. Accessed 7/4/2009.

See also: Avra Valley airport. http://www.marana.com. Accessed 5/26/2008.

Davis Monthan Air Force Base. http://www.dm.af.mil. Accessed 11/4/2008.

7. I. Miller Shoes. http://dlxs.lib.wayne.edu/d/dhhcc/bios/millershoes.html. Accessed 5/27/2008.

8. Jacome's Department Store. http://www.library/pima.gov/locations/main/jacome.cfm. Accessed 5/27/2008.

See also: http://www.kipnotes.com/RetailDepartmentStores.htm. Accessed 5/27/2008.

9. Monte Mansfeld. Brought DM home in his pocket. http://www.emat-tucson.org. Accessed 11/4/2008. See also: http://www.tucsonrodeoparade.org/Pages002/M_Mansfield. htm. (Spelling error of his name is part of URL). Accessed 11/4/2008.

10. Wire Recorder. http://www.recording-history.org/HTML/wire1.php. Accessed 7/3/2009.

11. Dr. Oliver Kelleam Garretson. Dean of the College of Education, 1950-1959. Reference: Executive Assistant to the Dean, College of Education. 10/26/2008.

12. Dr. Robert D. Morrow. The First Hundred Years: the history of Tucson School District 1, Tucson, Arizona, 1867-1967. Page 93.

13. Globe, Arizona. Goff, John S. Arizona, An Illustrated History of the Grand Canyon State. Northridge, CA: Windsor Publications, 1988. Pages 81-82.

30. My First School

1. Wakefield Junior High. Cooper, James F. The First Hundred Years, The History of Tucson School District 1, Tucson, Arizona, 1867-1967. Page 86. Wakefield was built in 1939 in Tucson's District 1 (Renamed the Tucson Unified School District in 1977) and was named after one of the first two women teachers in the district. Maria Wakefield traveled from California by railroad, boat and stage coach to teach, and became instrumental in founding the University of Arizona.

2. Noble Hiser. Cooper, James F. The First Hundred Years, The History of Tucson School District 1, Tucson, Arizona, 1867-1967. Page 133.

3. $1,700 would be around $20,000 in 2007. Inflation Calculator. http://www.westegg.com/inflation.

31. War Torn Sweethearts

1. B-24 Liberator tendency to catch fire. http://www.military-aircraft.org.uk/bombers/consolidated-b-24-liberator-bomber.htm. Accessed 7/3/2009.

2. Percy Jones Army Hospital. http://www.dlis.dla.mil/FederalCenter/Releases/story030110.asp. Accessed 5/27/2008.

3. End of World War II in Germany and atom bombs dropped on Japan. Feinstein, Stephen. The 1040s. From World War II to Jackie Robinson. Berkeley Heights, New Jersey: Enslow Publishers Inc., 2000. Page 46.

33. John Wayne Comes to Town

1. A real going jesse. "A going jesse." American Assoc iation of Rambunctious Persons. Issue of August 12, 2003. http://www.word-detective.com/081203.html. Accessed 6/ 10/2008.

2. Fairbank, Arizona. Death in the Desert. http://www. legendsofamerica.com/AZ-Fairbank.html. Accessed 1/22/ 2008.

3. Facilities in Fairbank. Kreutz, Doug. This is one classy town. Arizona Daily Star, 8/26, 2007. See also: Fairbank, Arizona. Death in the Desert. Http://www. legendsofamerica. com/AZ-Fairbank.html.

4. Red River starring John Wayne. http://www.10. epinions.com/mvie-review-7D3D-162741A1-390393B7- prod5. Accessed 12/3/2007.

See also: Dirks, Tim. http://www.filmsite.org/redr.html. Accessed 12/3/2007.

5. Quote from Red River aka The River is Red. 1948. www.dvdbeaver.com/film/DVDReviews8/red-river.htm. Acc essed 12/3/2007.

35. On the Move

1. Tombstone, Arizona. The Town Too Touch to Die. Legends of the High Desert. http://www.legendsofamerica. com/AZ-Tombstone.html. Accessed 9/7/2006.

2. Tombstone's Helldorado Days. http://www.tombstone web.com/events/ html. Accessed 6/14/2008.

3. Butler Building. http://www.butlermfg.com. Accessed 11/4/2008.

36. Pueblo Gardens

1. Pueblo Gardens Elementary School, 2210 E. 33rd Street, constructed in 1950. Six classrooms, administrative offices, and a nurse's room. Cooper, James F. The First Hundred Years, The History of Tucson School District 1, Tucson, Arizona, 1867-1967. Page 114.

2. Dr. Dorothy Talbert, who was the Intermediate Grades Supervisor. Ibid., page 141.

38. White Elementary

1. Irene Erickson, the Assistant Superintendent in charge of Elementary Education for TUSD. Cooper, James F. The First Hundred Years, The History of Tucson School District 1, Tucson, Arizona, 1867-1967. Page 170.

2. John E. White Elementary School, 2315 W. Canada, named after a former Tucson mayor and school board member. Ibid., page 150.

3. Pasqua Yaqui Indian Reservation. http://www.itcaonline.com/tribes_pascua.html. Accessed 6/30/2008.

See also: http://www.pascuayaqui-nsn.gov/history_and_culture/history/history4.shtml. Accessed 6/30/2008. www.fourdir.com/yaqui.htm. Accessed 6/30/2008.

39. Kids Make Me Laugh

1. Vietnamese kids and monsoons. The Climate of Vietnam. http://app.nea.gov/sg/cms/htdocs/article.asp. Accessed 7/1/2008.

40. Integration

1. Segregation since 1909. Cooper, James F. The First Hundred Years, The History of Tucson School District 1, Tucson, Arizona, 1867-1967. Page 51-53.

2. Dr. Robert Morrow tries to end segregation. Ibid., page 106.

3. Brodesky, Josh and Swedlund, Eric. TUSD desegregation order may end. Arizona Daily Star, 8/23/ 2007. http://www. azstarnet.com/sn/197796. Accessed 7/6/2008.

4. Bodfield, Rhonda and Sanchez, George B. TUSD free of desegregation order. Arizona Daily Star, April 25, 2008. http://azbilingualed.org/NEWS_2008/tusd_free_of_desegregation_order.htm. Accessed 7/6/2008.

42. Schumaker Elementary

1. Adaptive Education. www.stteresa. adl.catholic.edu. au/subjects/support.htm. Accessed 7/8/2008.

See also: Glaser, Robert. The New Aptitudes and Adaptive Education. CAE Newsletter, Vol. 4, No. 2, July 1973. http://eric.ed.gov/ERICWebPortal/custom/portlets/ record Details/detailmini.jsp. Accessed 7/8/2008.

43. After the Strike

1. Teacher's Strike of 1978. Tucson Unified School District. Bridging Three Centuries. The end of one era, the challenges of the next. 1960-1979, Part 4. http://www. tusd.k12.az.us/contents/distinfo/history93/ history9.html. Accessed 7/9/2008.

45. Giving Back

1. La Frontera. Mariachi Festival. www.lafrontera.org. Accessed 8/12/2008.

2. Arizona Sonora Desert Museum. http://www.desert museum. org. Accessed 11/3/2008.

3. Education Enrichment Foundation (EEF). http:// www.tusd.k12.az.us/eef. Accessed 11/4/2008.

4. Tucson Children's Museum. http://www.tucson childrensmuseum.org. Accessed 9/29/2008.

5. Challenger Learning Center of the Southwest. http:// www.pimaair.org. Accessed 8/12/2008.

See also: NASA Sites: Challenger STS 51-L Accident. http://history.nasa.gov/sts51l.html. Accessed 7/3/2009.

6. Ray Davies Humanitarian Award 2001 for outstanding service to children. http://www.tusd.k12.az.us. Accessed 11/4/2008.

7. Arizona Children's Home. http://www.arizonaschild ren.org. Accessed 11/4/2008.

See also: http://www.volunteersolutions.org/vctucson/ org/ 220382.html. Accessed 11/4/2008.

8. Dr. Marilyn Heins. SIROW Newsletter #61, Nov. 2000. http://72.14. 205.104/sirow.arizona.edu. Accessed 9/30/ 2008.

See also: Bolding, Betsy. Women Who Lead Reception. Women's Studies Advisory Council.

9. Women's Studies—department at the University of Arizona and even offers a doctorate. http://ws.web.arizona.edu/wosac. Accessed 11/4/2008.

10. LULAC. http://www.lulac.org. Accessed 11/4/2008.

11. Tucson Urban League. http://www.tucsonurbanleague.com. Accessed 11/4/2008.

12. Tapestry Project. http://www.emat-tucson.org/EMAT/TheTapestryProject. html. Accessed 8/12/2008.

13. Arizona Town Hall. http://www.aztownhall.org. Accessed 8/12/2008

14. Governor George W. P. Hunt. Goff, John S. Arizona, An Illustrated History of the Grand Canyon State. Northridge, CA: Windsor Publications. Page 96-98.

15. Kino Hospital cutbacks. Limberis, Chris. May 15, 2003. www.tucsonweekly.com. Accessed 9/29/2008.

16. Woman of the Year, 1989. See: Inside Tucson Business. Women of Influence, Jan. 17, 2008.

17. American Indian Center. http://www.ticenter.org. Accessed 8/12/2008.

See also: http://www.saltriver.pima-maricopa.nsn.us/community. Accessed 9/29/2008.

46. Our Front Line

1. DM-50. Activities. DM-50 Responses to MC3 Questions. Prepared by Bruce Dusenberry, Vice President, Jan. 2006. See also: Nett, Walt. Tucson Weekly, Media Watch. Published March 24, 2005. Accessed 8/9/2008.

2. What base closures would mean for Tucson and Arizona. Military spending has $4.5B impact in S. Knight Ridder/Tribune7/22/2008. http://investing.businessweek.com. Accessed 8/9/2008.

3. General Colin Powell, Chairman of the Joint Chiefs of Staff. http://www.afgen.com/colin_powell.html. Accessed 7/3/2009.

4. Bob Turpin, USNR retired. Joe Foss Institute. http://www.jfiweb.org/foss. Accessed 8/12/2008.

5. Julius Parker, Jr. http://www.pvamu.edu/pages/4298.asp. Accessed 8/12/2008.

6. Nimitz aircraft carrier powered by atomic energy. www.navy.mil/navydata/fact_display.Nimitiz. Accessed 11/4/2008.

7. 2003 Zachary and Elizabeth Fisher Distinguished Civilian Humanitarian Award. Tribute to Mrs. Dorothy Finley by Hon. Raul M. Grijalva of Arizona in the House of Representatives, Dec. 6, 2004. Congressional Record. E2166. "A crowning achievement presented to a person who demonstrates exceptional patriotism and humanitarian concern for members of the U.S. armed forces or their families."

47. Travels

1. Richard Leakey and the digs. The Leakey Foundation. www.leakeyfoundation.org. Accessed 9/5/2006.

2. Singing Wells. A proper walk in Kenya. http://64.233.169.104/www.makindu.org/news/2004_proper_walk_in_Kenya. Accessed 8/12/2008.

3. Animals seen on safari. Kenya's Great Escape Safari. www.zambezi.co.uk/safari/tours/kenya_great_escape_safari.html. Accessed 8/12/2008.

See also: AfricanMecca. http://www.africanmeccasafaris.com/kenya/safaris/parks/masaimarasafariballoon.asp. Accessed 8/12/2008.

Kenya Safaris. Hot Air Ballooning over the wildebeest migration. http://kenya.safari.co.za/Kenya_Travel_Articles-travel/ballooning-masai-mara.html. Accessed 8/12/2008.

Masai Mara. http://www.masaimara.org. Accessed 7/4/2009.

Appendix 1: 60 Rules for Success

1. The rules were compiled with input from Rebecca Montaño, former Associate Superintendent of Education for TUSD; Glennalee Foulk; David Overstreet, principal of Duffy Elementary School; Norma Jean Don, a former student from Wakefield Junior High; Ray Clarke, former President and CEO of the Tucson Urban League; Ana Valenzuela Estrada, Arizona State Director of LULAC; and from Steve Jewett, former director of Governor Jane Hull's southern Arizona office.

Bibliography

Adams, Ramon F. et al. Monaghan, Jay, Editor-In-Chief. *The Book of the American West.* New York: Bonanza Books, 1963.

American Experience: *FDR.* PBS Home Video, 1994.

Bailey, Lynn R. and Chaput, Don. *Cochise County Stalwarts, A Who's Who of the Territorial Years.* Tucson, Arizona: Westernlore Press, 2000.

Bailey, Lynn R. *Bisbee, Queen of the Copper Camps.* Tucson, Arizona: Westernlore Press, 2002.

Cooper, James F. *The First Hundred Years: The History of Tucson School District 1, Tucson, Arizona. 1867-1967.* Edited by John H. Fahr.

Dolan, Edward F. *The Spanish-American War.* Brookfield, Connecticut: The Millbrook Press, 2001.

Eppinga, Jane. *Images of America: Apache Junction and the Superstition Mountains.* Charleston, South Carolina: Acadia Publishing, 2006.

Eppinga, Jane. *Images of America: Tucson Arizona.* Chicago, Illinois: Acadia Publishing, 2000.

Feinstein, Stephen. *Decades of the 20th Century: The 1910s: From World War I to Ragtime Music.* Berkeley Heights, New Jersey: Enslow Publishers, Inc., 2001.

Feinstein, Stephen. *Decades of the 20th Century: The 1920s: From Prohibition to Charles Lindbergh.* Berkeley Heights, New Jersey: Enslow Publishers, Inc., 2001.

Feinstein, Stephen. *Decades of the 20th Century: The 1930s: From the Great Depression to the Wizard of Oz.* Berkeley Heights, New Jersey: Enslow Publishers, Inc., 2001.

Feinstein, Stephen. *Decades of the 20th Century: The 1940s: From World War II to Jackie Robinson.* Berkeley Heights, New Jersey: Enslow Publishers, Inc., 2000.

Feinstein, Stephen. *Decades of the 20th Century: The 1950s: From the Korean War to Elvis.* Berkeley Heights, New Jersey: Enslow Publishers, Inc., 2000.

Feinstein, Stephen. *Decades of the 20th Century: The 1960s: From the Vietnam War to Flower Power.* Berkeley Heights, New Jersey: Enslow Publishers, Inc., 2000.

Fitch, Edie. *The Heart and Hub of Eagle Creek.* Tucson: West Press Print Communications, 2006.

Goff, John S. *Arizona, An Illustrated History of the Grand Canyon State,* First Edition. Tucson, Arizona: Windsor Publications Inc., 1988.

Goff, John S. *George W. P. Hunt and his Arizona.* Pasadena, CA: Socio Technical Publications, 1973.

Haley, J. Evetts. *Charles Goodnight, Cowman and Plainsman.* Norman, Oklahoma: University of Oklahoma Press, 1936, 1949.

Horsley,Edith. *The 1950s.* New York, NY: Mallard Press, 1990.

How the West Was Won 1845-1893, Railroads. Episode 2. PBS.

US History: *The Roaring Twenties,* Volume 17.

Hunt, Norman K. *The Killing of Chester Bartell.* Phoenix, AZ: Cowboy Miner Productions, 2006.

Jones, Mary Ellen. *Daily Life On: The 19th Century American Frontier.* Westport, Connecticut: Greenwood Press, 1998.

Lauer, Charles D. *Arrows, Bullets and Saddle Sores, A Collection of True Tales of Arizona's Old West.* Phoenix, Arizona: Golden West Publications, 2003.

Mancini, Richard. *American Legends of the Wild West.* Philadelphia: Courage Books, 1992.

McCutcheon, Marc. *The Writer's Guide to: Everyday Life in the 1800s.* Cincinnati, Ohio: Writer's Digest Books, 1993.

McDaniel, Melissa. *Arizona.* Tarrytown, New York: Benchmark Books, 2000.

Pohl, Frederik and Williamson, Jack. *The Starchild Trilogy.* New York: Doubleday, 1963, 1965, 1969.

Rak, Mary Kidder. *A Cowman's Wife.* Boston and New York: Houghton Mifflin Company, 1934.

Shelton, Richard. *Going Back To Bisbee.* Tucson, Arizona: University of Arizona Press, 1992.

Sonnichsen, C. L. *Tucson, the Life and Times of an American City.* Norman, Oklahoma: University of Oklahoma Press, 1987.

Tanner, Ogden. *The Ranchers.* Alexandria, Virginia: Time-Life Books, 1977.

Trimble, Marshall. *Diamond in the Rough, An Illustrated History of Arizona.* Norfolk, Virginia: The Donning Company, 1988.

Trimble, Marshall. *Roadside History of Arizona.* Missoula, Montana: Mountain Press Publishing Co., 1986.

The Wild West. Foreword by Dee Brown. Companion volume to the television miniseries. Alexandria, Virginia: Time-Life Books, 1993.

Williams, Ben F., Jr. *More Tales of My Southwest.* Tucson, AZ: The Smokin Z Press, 2008.

Williams, Ben F., Jr. *Tales of My Southwest.* Tucson, AZ: The Smokin Z Press, 2007.

Williamson, Jack. *Brother to Demons, Brother to Gods.* New York: Bobbs-Merrill Company, 1976.

Williamson, Jack. *The Fortress of Utopia.* New York: Gryphon Books, 1998.

Williamson, Jack. Three From The Legion. New York: Doubleday, 1935, 1936, 1950.

Index

Acknowledgments

My granddaughter Jessica first suggested that I should write my memoirs, and when Jessica gets an idea in her head, there's no changing it. I hope this story is everything she wanted.

I'd like to thank my superb writer and editor, Allen R. Kates, MFAW, who helped me sort through many years of memories and events and turn them into what I hope is a good story that everybody wants to read.

I thank Cousin Betty Hunt Kaye, her daughter Susan LeRoyce Paul, a professional genealogist, and Cousin Norman (Ken) Hunt for their input and hand-holding. As a writer about the Old West, Ken knows the pitfalls and rewards for putting yourself out there.

For manuscript analysis, suggestions and encouragement, I thank Bruce J. Dinges, Ph.D., Director, Publications Division, Arizona Historical Society.

For their kind thoughts and support, I also thank Ray Clarke, Bill Corcoran, Norma Jean Don, my son John Finley, Glennalee Foulk, Jim and Loma Griffith, Chris Helms, my brother Tom Hunt, Katherine Jacobson for conducting the initial interviews, Steve Jewett, Rebecca Montaño, Dennis Olson, David Overstreet, Gordon Overstreet, Beth Walkup, and the Honorable Mayor Robert E. Walkup, City of Tucson, AZ, Ana Estrada Valenzuela, and Bill Valenzuela.

Lastly, a big thank you to the rest of my family for their good-natured support and laughter during this long writing process.

Dorothy Hunt, Circa 1940